Your Small
Business Computer

Your Small Business Computer

Evaluating, Selecting, Financing, Installing
and Operating the Hardware and Software that Fits

Donald R. Shaw

Business Counselors, Inc.
Parsippany, New Jersey

VNR VAN NOSTRAND REINHOLD COMPANY
NEW YORK   CINCINNATI   TORONTO   LONDON   MELBOURNE

Copyright © 1981 by Van Nostrand Reinhold Company Inc.

Library of Congress Catalog Card Number: 80-15810
ISBN: 0-442-27540-4
ISBN: 0-442-28137-4 pbk.

Manufactured in the United States of America

Published by Van Nostrand Reinhold Company Inc.
135 West 50th Street, New York, N.Y. 10020

Van Nostrand Reinhold Limited
1410 Birchmount Road
Scarborough, Ontario M1P 2E7, Canada

Van Nostrand Reinhold Australia Pty. Ltd.
17 Queen Street
Mitcham, Victoria 3132, Australia

Van Nostrand Reinhold Company Limited
Molly Millars Lane
Wokingham, Berkshire, England

15 14 13 12 11 10 9 8 7 6 5 4 3

Library of Congress Cataloging in Publication Data

Shaw, Donald R.
  Your small business computer.
  Includes index.
  1. Small business—Data processing. 1. Title.
HF5548.2.S4413   658'.022'02854   80-15810
ISBN 0-422-27540-4
ISBN 0-422-28137-4 pbk.

To Evelyn

Preface

As I write these words, hundreds of small businesses are getting themselves into trouble, some so deep that it may threaten their very existence, all in the interest of embracing the latest and best "improvement" that modern technology has to offer: automation.

As this book will show, automation has the potential for dramatically enhancing your business, providing better response to customer demands, improving allocation of people, facilities, inventory and the other assets of your trade, reducing clerical and other costs, and improving the tempo, uniformity and management control of your business activities—if, that is, the method is wisely chosen and the introduction properly managed.

I doubt you'll argue with my assertion in Chapter 8 that "you probably don't need an automated system that reduces cash flow by getting out late and inaccurate billing, loses track of inventory and receivables, promotes tardy and inappropriate buying and scheduling decisions, alienates customers and employees and takes up all of your time, desperately trying to patch up the damage"—if, that is, you've read that far.

But that's just the problem. The reason many small business owners and department heads in larger ones get into trouble with computers is simply that they don't know enough about them. The temptation to avoid the learning process is just too great: pick up the phone, call a computer company or two, and, presto, they'll come in, study my requirements and tell me what I need! So what do I have to know about computers?

Plenty! Probably no other single innovation has so much potential for good or ill in your business. None is more intimidating to the average layman. None is more typically oversold and underprepared for. Nowhere else except in the realm of computers does the head man readily relinquish control over so vital a determinant of the future success of the enterprise, unwarily relegating it into the hands of technicians and vendors.

You need to know the facts about what can go right and wrong, how to select the correct path and protect yourself against the pitfalls and how to deal effectively in the world of computer types, costs, programs, forms, procedures, terminology, proposals, contracts and so on. But first, you have to understand what computers are, how they work and the basic principles of their "care and feeding."

Take the time and have the patience to study the early chapters of this book covering fundamentals. You may not immediately perceive how useful the ABC's of computing are going to be to you, but you'll handle the strategic, legal and managerial issues which come later with much greater skill and confidence if you can rely on a knowledge of the basics.

With a solid background, you should be ready to take advantage of the potential offered by some of the most significant advances in technology today.

Donald R. Shaw

Contents

Your Small Business Computer

1
Computer Costs and Performance

A top executive of IBM observed recently that had the air transportation industry made as much progress as the computer industry in the last 25 years, it would now cost $1 to fly from New York to California and take about 10 minutes. Exaggeration?

Not really. The typical computer in 1953 cost around $3,000,000; occupied a whole wing of a building; required elaborate air conditioning (in some cases, chilled water for cooling) and special power sources measured in thousands of kilowatts; was extremely difficult to program and use; and had far less speed and capacity than today's typical minicomputer, which costs only one-hundredth as much.

Table 1-1 illustrates the incredible downward plunge in cost taken by computers in the past two and a half decades, because of, first, the introduction of the transistor and, later, employment of "integrated circuits," which have circuit elements equivalent to transistors by the thousands deposited on a flat silicon surface using photochemical etching. One result has been an incredible increase in performance per dollar of costs, depicted in Table 1-2. The relative improvement is on the order of 600 to 1!

Along with improved performance and lower costs has come dramatically reduced size. Table 1-3 gives some idea of the magnitude of the change. The central processing unit (CPU), the "heart" or "brain," of a Univac II of 1958 vintage, recently replaced at Computer Data Corporation in Gardena, California, measured 9 x 10 x 14 feet![1] It contained fewer circuit elements than one of today's most common microprocessors, the Zilog Z-80, which contains 8,500 circuits on a silicon chip approximately 0.1 by 0.1 inch square.

Forecasts for circuit densities of the 1980's are so implausible that one hesitates to quote them: 1 million circuits per chip, 100 million

[1]*Datamation* (June 1978): 145–149.

Table 1-1. Typical Computer Costs.

1953		$3,000,000
1964		750,000
1979	mini	20,000–50,000
	micro	5,000–20,000
1983 projection	mini	10,000–20,000
	micro	2,000–10,000

memory "bits" in 1 cubic centimeter. Yet, the improvements that have occurred in just a few months during the preparation of this book leave no doubt that such magnitudes will be achieved.

IMPLICATIONS

Dr. Lewis M. Branscombe, chief scientist at IBM, observed at the 1978 fall Comp Con, a prestigious computer conference, that data processing capability has been improving steadily at 15–25% per year, communications technology at about 11% per year, while personnel costs have been rising at the rate of about 6% per year (much faster recently). The implications are pretty clear: whenever and wherever computers can be employed in place of labor, it is economical to do so, and a particular use that is uneconomical at one point in time will probably become economical at a later point in time.

This is certainly what has happened in the case of small business. A few years ago the typical distribution, manufacturing or service company with $1–5 million in sales couldn't have dreamed of owning a computer. A bookkeeping machine, even an elaborate electronic bookkeeping machine, yes, or shared use of a data processing service

Table 1-2. Cost Per 100,000 Computations.

1952	$1.26
1958	0.26
1964	0.12
1975	0.01
1979	0.005

SOURCE: James Grout, "The Computer Revolution Has Just Begun," *Barron's* (25 August 1975): 11–20 and material supplied to the author by IBM Corporation.

Table 1-3. Storage Space Per 1 Million Characters in Memory.

1954	400 cubic feet
1977	0.06 cubic feet
1980 projection:	1 million in 1 cubic centimeter

SOURCE: Information supplied to the author by IBM Corporation and product information from Texas Instruments Inc. and Intel Corporation appearing in *Computer Decisions* (June 1979): 10 and *Datamation* (February 1979): 215–216.

bureau's facilities, yes; but a computer, costing several thousand dollars per month, surrounded by an entourage of operators and programmers, situated on a raised floor with special power and air conditioning? Not likely.

Yet today, with a fully equipped business-oriented computer system the size of an office desk available for as little as $15,000–20,000, fully programmed, and operable by clerical people rather than computer specialists, why not? Indeed, today's low costs and relative simplicity have brought computers and computing within the reach of perhaps 500,000 newly targeted candidate, small business users and that many or more individual departments of larger organizations.

Venture Development Corporation of Wellesley, Massachusetts, a market research firm, says the use of desktop computers (under $10,000 in cost and usable by people without extensive computer training) will grow 46% a year from the present level of 17,600 units valued at $243 million to 276,000 units valued at $1.8 billion by 1983.

And how can we ignore the boom in "hobby" computers being sold in stores all over America, many to small businesses for commercial use? One source estimates that about 8,000 hobby machines, costing as little as $500 apiece, were shipped in 1977, many to businessmen. *Datamation* (June, 1978, pp. 273–275) forecasts that the business-oriented segment of the personal computing market will reach $700 million in 1980. Such machines will be deployed as "business information appliances" like "chess pieces" within companies.

Let's, however, refrain from overemphasizing the $500 computer at this point. The facts show that the hobby computer physically equipped to do business work costs more like $5,000 than $500, lacks the programs needed to function effectively and requires "care and feeding" by a dedicated, do-it-yourself engineer/businessman willing to devote an extraordinary amount of his or her time. More on this later.

Nyborg, McCarter and Erickson, in an extensive study of the industry showed that the dollar volume of computer shipments has been doubling every 5 years, while minicomputer shipments have almost quadrupled between 1971 and 1976 and are in the process of doing so again by 1981. The installed population, worldwide, of such systems is expected to reach nearly 400,000 by 1981. The authors also conclude that by 1985, 90% of the cost of data processing will be people costs, not hardware, making it the most labor-intensive industry in the world, with the possible exception of agriculture.[2]

In another important study of the industry, T. A. Dolotta and associates project that performance divided by cost has improved by a factor of 100 every 10 years since 1955 (actually it's even better than that, taking into account more recent advances), but programmer productivity has only improved by a factor of 2.7 in the same period and will go to 3.6 by 1985, at which time computers will be a million times more cost-effective than they were in 1955.[3] The disparity is clear.

Warren Nuessle of Fox Morris Personnel Consultants is reported in *Computerworld* (January 8, 1979, p. 7) as finding, based on a survey of 17,000 companies, that computer specialists are soon to surpass engineers as the nation's most sought-after professionals. Nuessle says demand is increasing 15% per year, and employers are offering 9.75% higher average earnings packages for computer professionals, with programmers topping the list at 12–13% more wages and fringe benefits.

THE SECOND REVOLUTION

Today's office is already the most labor-intensive segment of society. A 1968 *Fortune* magazine supplement called "Information Processing and the Office of Tomorrow" points out that industrial produc-

[2]W. Erickson, P. M. McCarter, and P. S. Nyborg, *Information Processing in the United States: A Quantitative Summary* (Montvale, N.J.: American Federation of Information Processing Societies, 1977), p. 55.
[3]T. A. Dolotta et al., *Data Processing in 1980–1985: A Study of Potential Limitations to Progress* (New York: John Wiley & Sons, Inc., 1976), p. 191.

tivity has increased 90% since 1968, while office productivity has gone up a scant 4%. As we introduce inexpensive computing and data processing equipment into the office, do we stand on the threshold of a second industrial revolution, multiplying the administrative and decision-making effectiveness of business and government in the same way mechanization revolutionized the productivity of manpower and capital in the production and transportation of goods? Or are we about to substitute a new kind of bottleneck, an expensive and in-chronically-short-supply computer analyst and programmer, for the old one?

One of the main purposes of this book is to help make sure that doesn't happen—at least in *your* office—by preparing you to make the kind of sensible decisions that will employ computing where it fits, provide the right combination of facilities and avoid the technical traps and dependencies that derive from shortages of experience, competent people and sensible practices in the industry.

CAVEAT EMPTOR

The dramatic improvements in computer technology, together with better systems analysis and programming techniques, leading to solidly crafted, flexible business "packages" are bringing the computer within practical reach of hundreds of thousands of new end-users: small firms doing as little as $250,000 a year in business, and tiny branches and departments of larger institutions employing only a few people. And the trend continues to march inexorably forward as the cost per unit of computing continues to decline, while competing administrative labor costs escalate.

For many, this "second industrial revolution" means:

Smoother operation
Better control
Reduced inventory
Better customer service
Higher productivity
Greater profits (or cost-effectiveness)

But in all too many cases, because of the inexperience of the buyers and the slipshod and sometimes deceitful practices of vendors, small computers are poorly selected, misapplied and misunderstood, so they become liabilities instead of assets.

Your best protection is to thoroughly understand the principles involved, how to deal with them pragmatically and how to make right decisions and drive hard bargains, to insure that you buy what you need and get what you pay for. That's what this book is all about.

2
What Computers Do and How

WHAT COMPUTERS DO

Computers employed in business do a few simple things.

· Accept information (Input)
· Act on it (Compute, Compare, Sort, Substitute)
· File the result (Store)
· Print or display the result (Output)
· Operate under predetermined step-by-step control (Program)

These functions are quite analogous to what we humans do in similar situations. A clerk, for example, accepts and records a customer order over the telephone (Input). He or she acts on it by looking up customer and stockkeeping information for things like customer address, item prices, warehouse location and inventory on-hand balance (Compare); determines whether the order can be filled; and then extends and totals it (Compute). The clerk produces, manually or by typewriter, shipping documents such as picking tickets, packing slips, shipping labels and, perhaps, an invoice (Output), while carefully posting the effects of the transaction to Accounts Receivable, Inventory, and Sales Commission accounting records (Substitute and Store).

All the while, the clerk in this example is functioning in accordance with a procedure (Program) which may not be written or formalized, but is nonetheless carefully worked out and well remembered. If this weren't so, the results would be unpredictable, inaccurate and, should the clerk be interrupted during the process by a phone call, question or flight of absentminded fancy, vital information could go astray.

One of the greatest attributes of a computer is its inherent consistency. Like all machines, it does break down now and then, but when it's working it doesn't drift. It follows *its* procedure or program with absolute fidelity, performing computations and postings with flawless accuracy—unless, of course, it meets with inaccurate input data or unanticipated conditions that weren't properly analyzed, incorporated and tested when the program was developed.

Therein lies the other side of the equation: since the computer is a machine, it does not exercise independent judgment. Except in very special cases, far afield from business data processing, it doesn't learn from experience, interpret what things "probably" mean as opposed to what came in from a document, or "wonder" why a particular customer who normally orders 144 widgets (one case) at a time is suddenly ordering 144 *cases* this time.

One of the prices we pay for employing a computer is that somebody must program every minute nuance of its operation. And if that somebody knows a lot about computers but little about our business, we have to think of all the possible needs and conditions arising from a particular procedure (like order processing) and *communicate* them to the programmer in advance, so he can design and prepare the program.

This is precisely the area where most computer failures occur: either in the original analysis of the job to be done or in fully and accurately communicating that solution, first to the programmer, and then through him to the machine. In other words, you may tell the programmer, "Look, I want you to build a routine into the order entry system to flag and set aside orders for more than nine cases of any item where the extended value exceeds $1,000. Chances are that's a mistake that we'll want to check out and verify with the customer or the salesman." If you don't, then don't blame either the programmer or the machine if a truckload of expensive widgets leaves the warehouse destined for a customer who only wanted a few of them, because somebody confused cases for units.

The net result of a properly applied computer is that it can:

Accept, compare, combine, compute, replace, store, print or display information
　At superhuman speeds
　　With virtually flawless accuracy
　　　According to rigid, unvarying procedures

Yes, but how?

HOW COMPUTERS WORK

Why You Should Understand Computers

As you will be reminded, again and again, the most important ingredient in successful implementation of a computer or computing service to your business is *you*. You have to make the hard and final decisions, shoulder the risks, bear the "birth pangs" and live with the results. Well, you say, since computers employ all this exotic technology you've been ranting about for the past chapter and a half, why not just leave the whole thing to the experts?

First, you can't afford to leave such a powerful influence upon your success or failure exclusively in the hands of others, and, second, you *can* understand computers. They're basically very simple in concept and easy to understand. Once you master the simple principles governing computers, all computers, and pick your way carefully through the terminology (jargon is a better word for it), then you'll feel comfortable discussing computers with anyone: salesmen, technicians, consultants, your staff; and you can begin making solid, sensible decisions backed by clearly understood facts.

Thousands of businessmen have already achieved this comfortable familiarity with computing; some even to the extent of doing their own computer programming, though I don't recommend that except in a few special cases. And why shouldn't they? Have you ever met the president of a printing company who didn't understand how presses work and who didn't enjoy discussing the characteristics and merits of various types and brands of printing equipment? The computer is every bit as important a production tool in many businesses as the machinery, facilities or rolling stock—even more so in some companies. So why shouldn't top management have complete command over the computer? Indeed, can they afford not to?

The Lightning Fast Electronic "Whiz"

Perhaps you'll be surprised to learn that all the much vaunted "intelligence" of computers consists of is the ability to count up to one. Yes, that's right. The ability to count from zero to one. All the logical and arithmetic circuits of a computer do is detect the absence or presence of an electronic impulse, defined as "zero" in the first case and "one" in the second. These impulses can be moved by transmitting them through wires, or the equivalent of wires, and stored either temporarily or permanently by using the impulses to trip switches which can be checked later to see if they remain in an on (one) or off (zero) condition. These banks of switches are called "memory" and can re-create the stream of impulses originally sent when called upon to do so. We speak of this process as "reading" memory.

The trick is that patterns of impulses are assigned universal meanings by us humans, and we are able to design other circuits which *interpret* these patterns into human-sensible language (numbers, letters and punctuation) and are able to display them in that form on documents or on the face of a TV-like screen.

The Decimal System

Consider first the decimal system, which is based on a device that can register ten conditions, our complement of fingers. In the decimal system, the digit positions, starting with the "units" position can count from zero up to nine (ten "conditions" or "states" in all) and then, if another digit is added, reset to zero and carry one to the next position to the left. That position is the "tens" position, and when it's filled, the number carries to the next leftmost position, which is the "hundreds" position. Look at it pictorially in Table 2-1.

Table 2-1. The Decimal System.

Each position registers zero through nine and then carries to the left.

POSITION:	CALLED:	DERIVED BY MULTIPLYING VALUE IN POSITION BY:	INDICATED POWER OF 10:
X	100,000's position	100,000	10^5
X	10,000's "	10,000	10^4
X	1,000's "	1,000	10^3
X	100's "	100	10^2
X	10's "	10	10^1
X	units "	1	10^0

Although we aren't conscious of it because we've done it so often, what we do when we see a number like 1,984 is mentally register 4 x 1, 8 x 10, 9 x 100 and 1 x 1,000 to interpret or evaluate that number.

The Binary System

Because electrical devices can only register two states of being, on or off (one and zero), we have to employ the "binary" numbering system with them rather than the decimal.

The principles are the same, except that each position, instead of counting up from zero to nine and then carrying to the left, counts from zero to *one* and then carries. Correspondingly, the positions are evaluated by powers of *2* instead of powers of *10*. (Look at Table 2-2.) Now we have a numbering system which can be safely manipulated by something as limited as an electronic computer that can't count past one.

A computer can easily add, subtract, multiply, divide, compare, move and store strings of ones and zeros in accordance with the rules of binary representation. The only problem may be when we humans have to get involved with putting information into the computer and getting it back out again, in a form we can understand.

This is accomplished by special circuits so elaborate that they can not only register the numbers zero through nine, but all the upper and lower case alphabetic characters and common punctuation marks as well—at least 64 in all and on some computers, as many as

Table 2-2. The Binary System.

Each position registers zero through one and then carries to the left.

POSITION:	CALLED:	DERIVED BY MULTIPLYING VALUE IN POSITION BY:	INDICATED POWER OF 2:
X	32's position	32	2^5
X	16's "	16	2^4
X	8's "	8	2^3
X	4's "	4	2^2
X	2's "	2	2^1
X '	units "	1	2^0

128 "states." That special circuitry, which can be at least 100 times more costly than the regular binary circuits of the machine, is reserved for only those few "windows" into and out of the computer through which we humans intervene, typically in conjunction with keyboards, display tubes and printers.

Bits

If you're shopping for a computer and haven't heard about "bits" yet, you soon will. The term "bit" is a contraction of Binary Digit. A bit is a binary digit position, capable of registering off and on, or zero and one. A typical binary number consisting of 6 bits might look like this:

101011

This one happens to have the same value, reading from right to left, as the decimal number 43, which you can check against Table 2–1 by multiplying each position by the appropriate power of 2 as follows:

BINARY NUMBER	POSITION	MULTIPLY BY	EQUALS
1	32's	32	32
0	16's	16	0
1	8's	8	8
0	4's	4	0
1	2's	2	2
1	units	1	1
		Total	43

Binary Arithmetic

Having come this far, if the reader's spirit remains sufficiently undaunted, let's take a brief excursion into binary arithmetic before putting all the pieces back together into a representational system for business data processing.

Table 2–3 shows two simple examples of binary additions, the first without carry-overs, the second with carry-overs. Remember, the rule is that when a bit position is "zero," adding a bit to it sets it to a "one"; if it's already a "one," adding another bit resets it to "zero" and carries "one" to the next position (which is the next higher power of 2).

Table 2-3. Simple Examples of Binary Arithmetic.

A.

POSITION	BINARY NO.		BINARY NO.		RESULT
8's	0		0		0
4's	0	+	0	=	0
2's	1		0		1
1's	0		1		1
Decimal equivalent:	2	+	1	=	3

B.

POSITION	BINARY NO.		BINARY NO.		RESULT
8's	0		0		0
4's	0	+	0	=	1
2's	1		0		0
1's	1		1		0
Decimal equivalent:	3	+	1	=	4

The reader can see now how simple the basic, inner workings of a computer, any computer, really are. But how does it all relate to accounts payable or mailing list maintenance or relieving inventory based on the movement of goods? To understand that we have to look at how data of all kinds is coded and stored by a computer.

DATA REPRESENTATION

The Memory Cell

The most common memory devices used in computers are tiny magnetic donutlike cores or semiconductor equivalents. In the case of core memory, the tiny cores, only about 0.1 inch in diameter, are strung on intersecting wires which, depending on the direction that current passes through them, have the ability to (1) magnetize the core in one direction, (2) magnetize the core in the other direction and (3) later sense in which direction the core is magnetized. Figure 2-1 shows schematically how this works.

Memory Organization

Long ago, most of the computer industry settled on a way of representing decimal numbers, alphabetic characters, punctuation marks and other special characters as "strings" or patterns of bits. The

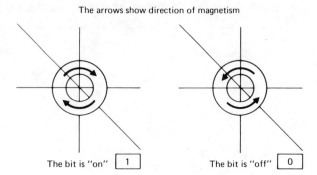

Figure 2-1. Core Memory.

system is actually partly derived from the old punched card method. It's called BCD, or Binary-Coded Decimal, and it works, in most computers, in the following way. Memory is organized into strings or blocks of bit positions called "words," usually 16 bits long in small business computers. Each word, or block of 16 bits, has a distinct "address," which is its beginning position in the grid of thousands of similar memory positions in the entire memory of the machine.

If you know what you are looking for and where, you can "access" a word at a specified address and "read it out" of memory to some other device, where, if you could examine it, you would find a block of 16 bits organized into two 8-bit characters called "bytes," each of which is set up to store one numeric, alphabetic or special character. Figures 2-2 and 2-3 show this progression.

Thus, beginning with individual memory positions capable of storing 1 bit, we can organize them in such a way that data (numbers, letters and characters) can be "written" (stored) into specific 8-bit bytes, usually grouped into 2-byte words, and then later recalled or "read out" for further manipulation.

File Structure

All this is important to the computer user for two reasons: (1) it explains the basic elemental blocks out of which he will build his computerized data files, and (2) it is the denominator by which we match the storage capacity of the machine to a particular user's memory requirements.

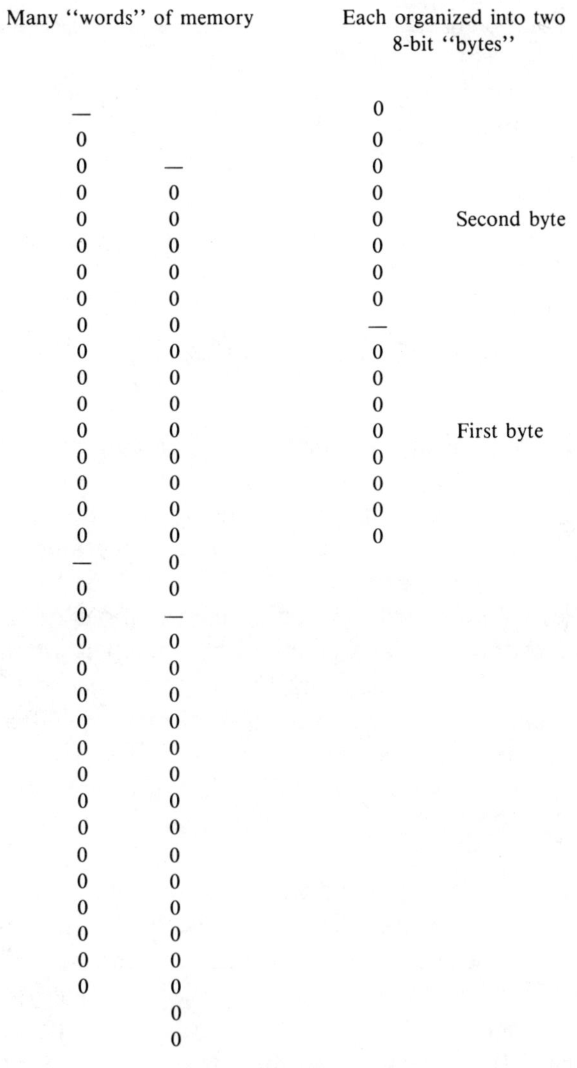

Many "words" of memory   Each organized into two
                                        8-bit "bytes"

```
        —                         0
   0                              0
   0         —                    0
   0         0                    0
   0         0                    0        Second byte
   0         0                    0
   0         0                    0
   0         0                    0
   0         0                    —
   0         0                    0
   0         0                    0
   0         0                    0        First byte
   0         0                    0
   0         0                    0
   0         0                    0
   0         0                    0
   0         0                    0
        —    0
   0         0
   0         —
   0         0
   0         0
   0         0
   0         0
   0         0
   0         0
   0         0
   0         0
   0         0
   0         0
   0         0
   0         0
   0         0
   0         0
             0
             0
```

Figure 2-2. Word Structure of the Typical Small Business Computer.

To make it clearer, consider automating an accounts receivable (A/R) file consisting of 500 customer accounts. How much space do we need to store this information? First, let's analyze what is needed. We organize the intended receivables record into "fields" of data, each one of a specific maximum size. For example, we might define customer account number, a maximum of 6 numeric digits, as the

Each byte is set up to store one character of data: a numeric digit, an alphabetic character or a special character. Examples:

0	1	1
0	1	1
0	0	0
0	0	0
= "1"	= "a"	= "b"
0	0	0
0	0	0
0	0	1
1	1	0

Figure 2-3. Byte and Data Representation.

first field in the A/R record. Next might be company name, maximum 22 alphabetic characters, then street address, city and state, zip code, amount owed, date of last payment, and so on.

After making sure we have covered all the necessary fields of information, we define the result as the "format" or "layout" of the accounts receivable record, consisting of a number of fields of various lengths. Adding the character counts together, we might derive a record length of 190 characters for the A/R record. That means that, in this example, if we intend to work on a specific receivables record in computer memory we must reserve 190 bytes of memory space to hold it, and that the entire A/R file will consist of 500 records, each 190 bytes long, or a total of at least 95,000 bytes of file storage.

So, storage requirements begin with bits, organized into bytes which are grouped into specific data fields. In the A/R example, all the fields of data concerning one specific customer are defined as a "record." All the customer records considered together constitute the accounts receivable "file," and all the files in the business (receivables, payables, payroll, inventory, and so on) are referred to as the "data base."

The sum total byte count of the data base, with some allowances for overhead, inefficiency and room for expansion, determines the storage size requirement for the appropriate components of the computer. Just to put it in perspective, the small business data bases typically encountered fall in the 2-10 million-byte range. There are many exceptions, and, even within this range, many users do not require that all of the data be accessible at all times.

Data Flow within the System

Fundamentally, all computers are organized alike. Figure 2–4 shows a schematic layout of the major components. The main arena for action is "memory" which contains the program and data being worked on at a given moment. To that are attached a storage device which holds the programs and data not required at that particular instant in time, input devices through which to get data into the machine and output devices through which to obtain results. The CPU or Central Processing Unit is what performs the actual arithmetic and logical "work" on the data under control of the program. Data flows (in the form of streams of bits) to and from each of these components of the machine, as indicated by the arrows, along circuit paths called "channels" or "buses" under the control and coordination of the CPU.

The CPU physically initiates and directs the flow of data bits throughout the system and performs the logical comparisons and arithmetic on that data which constitutes "processing." It does this in step-by-step conformance with a predetermined procedure called a "program."

Programming

A special form of data. The program, like all information in the computer, is stored and manipulated as strings of bits and is, therefore, another kind of data. The format or layout of a program word

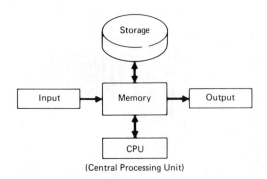

Figure 2–4. Functional Diagram of the Computer.

is quite different, however, from that of an accounts receivable data field, for example, and its purpose is quite different.

To understand programming, think of an old-fashioned player piano. The program is analogous to the piano roll which is coded with "instructions" in the form of perforations that cause the hammers to strike the strings in predetermined sequence and timing to produce the right song (output). See Figure 2–5.

The computer as player piano. The program in a computer is similar to a player piano in many respects. It is stored in a coded form: coded holes in a paper in the piano, coded strings of bits in a portion of memory. It provides instructions at the minute detail level: just as there's no single hole in the piano roll that instructs the instrument to play Beethoven's Sonata no. 5, there is not a single or even small group of codes that means "post accounts receivable" to a computer.

Instead, there are instructions that when decoded into specific actions by the machine (we call that "execution" of the program) result in things like comparing the contents of one 16–bit word to another specific word and then setting a switch to "on" if the first is equal to or greater than the second. Other examples would be the addition or subtraction of two strings of bits in specific memory locations and storing the result in a reserved area called a "register," and then, as another instruction step, moving the contents of that register to a third area of memory.

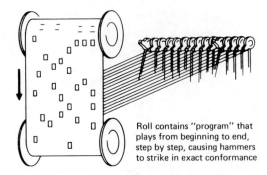

Roll contains "program" that plays from beginning to end, step by step, causing hammers to strike in exact conformance

Figure 2–5. The "Program" in a Player Piano.

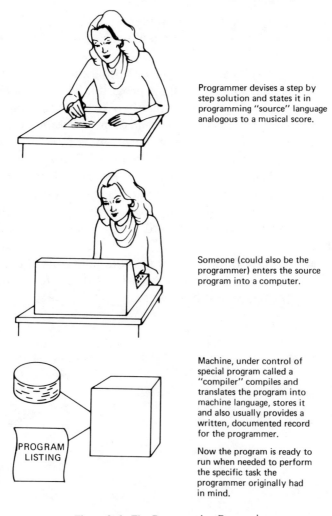

Programmer devises a step by step solution and states it in programming "source" language analogous to a musical score.

Someone (could also be the programmer) enters the source program into a computer.

Machine, under control of special program called a "compiler" compiles and translates the program into machine language, stores it and also usually provides a written, documented record for the programmer.

Now the program is ready to run when needed to perform the specific task the programmer originally had in mind.

PROGRAM LISTING

Figure 2-6. The Programming Progression.

Going back to the player piano analogy, the musician's original notation, or language, is in a form he and other musicians comprehend easily, namely, the treble and bass clef staff notation common to all written music. However, that human-sensible language had to be translated at some point into machine language (the patterns of holes in the piano roll) in order to be "executed" on a player piano. Programs are written originally in a kind of semi-English shorthand notation like music called "source language" and then, too, are translated, mechanically by a computer program called a "compiler," into an executable "machine-language" program. See Figure 2-6.

The executable machine-coded form of programs bears no resemblance to the original source-language program. Most programmers cannot read strings of bits any better than Beethoven could, if he were with us today, make any sense out of perforations in a piano roll, even if those perforations represent his most familiar composition. Beethoven could, however, easily read his original (source) music and, if need be, make changes to it for subsequent retranslation to coded machine-language (piano roll) form. Mark this point well. It bears on the subjects of documentation and program maintenance, which will be considered many times in the course of our discussion.

For now, let us turn to the parts of the computer, one at a time, in the next three chapters, to see how each is used and to learn more about their performance and cost characteristics.

3
Storage

MAIN AND SECONDARY STORAGE

In the preceding chapter we observed that computers are subdivided into memory and storage, with data frequently flowing between the two. Actually, this distinction is misleading. *All* electrically or magnetically recorded data is in storage. Computer memory is just a special case where a limited amount of very high-speed, relatively costly components are used for "working" storage, while dormant, unused data and programs reside on slower, less costly auxiliary or secondary storage. The division is a purely economic one. Many large-scale machines in the "supercomputer" class come equipped with millions of bytes of main memory—enough to store a whole data base for a small business without resorting to "storage." That class of machine, however, once the data were input, could process the whole day's work in a few minutes, but it would cost hundreds of thousands of dollars.

The more practical approach is to keep the computer and its memory rather small—big enough to do the job, but not too much bigger—and then "swap" data and programs to and from slower, less costly storage as needed.

TYPES AND SIZES OF MEMORY

In the mini- or microcomputer realm, people talk about 16K, 32K, 64K, and sometimes 128K. What does that mean? First of all, memory is denominated in sizes based on a power of 2, because the "address" of a particular memory location is expressed in binary terms.

A binary address 4 bits long can identify precisely 16 locations, or 2^4. Try it on paper by marking down all the different combinations of ons and offs or ones and zeros possible in quartets of four positions. Counting the 0000 condition, there are precisely 16. As you go on up the scale, assuming you had set aside a 1-byte (8-bit) field to represent memory address, you'd be limited to 2^8, or 256, individually addressable memory locations. But since most minicomputers use a 16-bit word, the most common choice is a 2-byte or 16-bit address, which gets you precisely 65,536 addressable locations. (See Table 3–1.) If each were a word, 16 bits long, then the machine could be said to contain 64K words or 128K bytes of addressable memory.

Wait a minute! How does 65,536 get to be 64K? The answer is to be found in a little computer "in" talk. Among computer people "K" doesn't mean 1,000, as it does to bankers and personnel administrators, it means 1,024 or 2^{10}, which has come to be handy shortcut indication for memory sizes.

The only thing you have to remember is that when somebody says 64K, they're talking about approximately 64,000—but 64,000 *what*? Bits, bytes or words? Better find out, because there's a difference of 8:1 between bytes and bits, and 16:1 between words and bits. And some of the newer top-of-the-line minicomputers use 32-bit words so they can address very large memories, running into the thousands of K. As a matter of common usage, a memory of 1,024K or 1,048,567 bytes is often referred to as one "megabyte." It's close to a million bytes and can be thought of in those terms, but it's actually 1,024 x 1,024 bytes and takes 20 bits (2.5 bytes) to address.

The Typical Minicomputer Memory

The business owner or department head implementing a mini- or microcomputer-based system will most likely encounter machines with 16K, 32K, or 64K of memory, part of which will be used up by

Table 3–1. Memory Sizes.

The number of directly addressable memory locations is a function of the number of bits in the address field, hence powers of 2.

$2^2 =$ 4	$2^{10} =$	1,024[a]
$2^3 =$ 8	$2^{11} =$	2,048
$2^4 =$ 16	$2^{12} =$	4,096
$2^5 =$ 32	$2^{13} =$	8,192
$2^6 =$ 64	$2^{14} =$	16,384
$2^7 =$ 128	$2^{15} =$	32,768
$2^8 =$ 256	$2^{16} =$	65,536
$2^9 =$ 512	$2^{17} =$	131,072

[a]Referred to as a "K."

the machine itself in doing its own "housekeeping," as described in Chapter 6. How much is enough? That depends on the nature of the job(s) to be done and on the architecture of the particular machine and its associated housekeeping programs.

A technically astute analyst can usually come up with a reasonable estimate of how much memory is required to perform the various functions needed, to see if they'll all "fit" in a given sized machine. The trouble is that the only technically astute analyst around is usually employed by the vendor and is strongly motivated, perhaps subconsciously, to believe he can "shoehorn" everything into a given sized machine to keep the price down in hopes of getting the order.

Throughput

A complicating factor is the trade-off between throughput and memory size. Work usually runs faster on machines with larger memory than with smaller. We say the total system has greater throughput in the first case, where "throughput" means the sum total of useful work into, around, and out of the machine. The reasons for this are two. If a program is larger than the available memory space in which it has to run, it is usually broken up into segments or modules, only the active ones of which are in memory at one time. Each time the job needs a segment of the program that isn't in memory, it has to wait for the machine to go get it from storage, which, if it happens often, as it usually does, slows the machine down, reducing its throughput.

The other reason is related to the fact that some machines in the small business computer class allow more than one program to be active at the same time. This is called "multiprogramming" and can improve total throughput by doing other work while a particular program is stalled, waiting for completion of an input or output operation. But this is only worthwhile if the memory is big enough to accommodate the additional program or programs. Hence, this can be another trade-off between memory size and potential throughput.

Memory Type and Speed

Typical mini- and microcomputer memories are constructed either of magnetic cores or blocks of tiny photochemically etched cells on silicon chips. The advantage of the latter type, referred to as semiconductor or MOS (Metal-Oxide Semiconductor) memory, is that it's cheaper and more compact. The disadvantage is that if the power goes off, the contents of memory are lost unless the machine is equipped with a temporary battery-backup system that keeps the memory intact for an hour or two until power is restored.

Both types of memory are very fast, usually in the range of a microsecond (one-millionth of a second), to access the contents of a particular location. Along with the other components of the machine, this frequently supports average instruction-execution speeds in the range of 10 to 100 microseconds, or at least 10,000 program steps per second, which is very fast in comparison to the operator at a keyboard who can only key in about 6 characters of data in the same 1-second space of time running at his or her peak speed.

Generally speaking, memory speed and memory size are not going to be significant limitations for you in today's small business computers. But lots of other things, tangible and intangible, are, so it's wise to test the whole system in your shop using your data, or using a situation as similar as possible, before becoming irrevocably committed. Later if it turns out that a faster machine or larger memory than the one proposed and agreed upon *is* required, it's valuable to have the vendor contractually responsible for making up the difference.

STORAGE

Backing up the relatively expensive, limited-size, high-speed memory is storage. It's usually much cheaper than the memory component, at least on a per-byte basis, much slower and very much larger. Unlike memory, some kinds of storage can be physically removed from the machine and held elsewhere for later use, and, unlike memory, some forms of storage are not addressable at random, but must be read sequentially, from beginning to end, one record at a time.

Sequential versus Random Storage

The earliest form of computer storage, dating back to the 1950's, was punched cards. A deck of cards representing the customer accounts receivable file, for example, was introduced into the machine in a sequenced stack and read one card at a time from customer

number one through customer number x. Transactions—charges, receipts and adjustments—were also punched into cards, sorted in the
same sequence and read by a different card reader (or on the same
one in interfiled or collated fashion).

Prior balance and status information was updated by the amounts
of the new transactions, and, as each customer was completely processed, a *new* customer accounts receivable card was punched out of
the machine. The new file was just like the old one, and in the same
sequence, but was updated with the entire batch of transactions just
processed.

Even when this process moved to magnetic tape storage, which in
concept is like a deck of punched cards recorded magnetically and
strung out along the length of a ferrous oxide–coated ribbon, it was
still relatively slow. It isn't unusual for a computer to spend from 5
to 30 minutes or more reading one reel of magnetic tape from beginning to end. That really isn't much time when you consider that
the tape could have contained thousands of records; and, had we
batched a whole period's transactions, for example, a day, a week or
a month's worth, it would have been a small investment in time to
pass the whole file.

Figure 3-1 illustrates the principle of sequential batch processing.

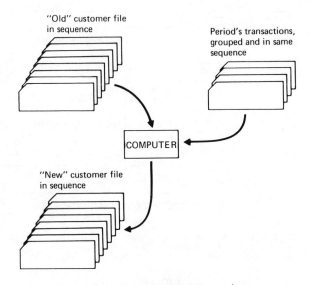

"Old" customer file
in sequence

Period's transactions,
grouped and in same
sequence

COMPUTER

"New" customer file
in sequence

Figure 3-1. Sequential Batch Processing.

In today's computers, the files would most likely be on magnetic tape, but the idea is easier to grasp using cards. Figure 3–2 makes the matching and updating process even clearer. Here, as you can see, we have an "old" or current customer master file on magnetic tape in customer number sequence. We've saved up a batch of transactions to be processed against that file on punched cards and sorted them into customer number sequence. Where a match or "hit" occurs, we perform the appropriate updating of information and write out the new information on a different tape.

In order to keep from fragmenting the customer file or getting it out of sequence, either of which would render it useless, we carry forward all the unaffected customer records exactly as they were on the old tape, yielding one new customer file, complete and in proper sequence.

This is a very efficient process where we have a great many transactions and a high "hit" ratio against the file, but extremely inefficient where the opposite is true. The most extreme instance would be

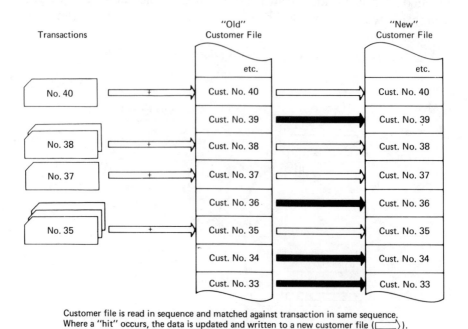

Customer file is read in sequence and matched against transaction in same sequence. Where a "hit" occurs, the data is updated and written to a new customer file (⟹). Otherwise, the customer record is written onto the new file unaltered (■▶).

Figure 3–2. Sequential Updating.

a case where we had only one transaction to process and had to read and rewrite the entire several hundred or several thousand customer records to do so.

Yet, isn't that exactly what we'd like to be able to do in most businesses? Process each transaction as it arrives, in person, on the phone or in the mail, and respond to it without waiting for a large batch of work to accumulate.

Transaction Processing

To process work, as it comes, a transaction at a time, requires access to data at random. Data already in memory *is* accessible at random. But if stored data is organized on a sequential medium like magnetic tape, then transaction processing is virtually impossible. Is that bad or good?

If the application is payroll, for instance, it may be perfectly adequate, perhaps even preferable, to keep files on sequential media because:

· Sequential files are easily removable and stored elsewhere for safekeeping.
· They don't "clutter" the computer data base with information that is only required at certain infrequent intervals.
· Privacy and security are easier to maintain.
· File storage is less expensive.
· Processing is inherently more efficient, at least with respect to the computer time and resources it consumes for a given amount of work.

Small Businesses Are Transaction-Oriented

With the exception of certain applications (like payroll) in which the data doesn't change from one periodic processing to the next, most businesses benefit from transaction processing. The improvements are usually manifested in better customer service and quicker reaction to changing conditions. For example, if an employee stops in with a question about last week's paycheck, one can refer to the gross pay, check and deduction registers that were output at the time of the last payroll processing. Nothing can alter what was done at that time and no adjustment can be made until next payday.

But exactly the opposite may be true with respect to a customer who drops in to inquire or phones about the availability of a specific quantity of a needed commodity. The inventory listing dating from last week shows what the available on-hand balance *was* at that time, but it doesn't reflect orders received to which merchandise has been consigned, recent over-the-counter sales and vendor shipments that have been received into inventory since then. If it's impossible to give the customer an honest on-the-spot answer, it may cost a sale, or weaken the relationship with that particular client, particularly if the competition *can* make such commitments and live up to them.

Likewise, the business that knows it is out of stock or reaching a dangerously low inventory level on a particularly fast-moving item as soon as the demand materializes, rather than waiting for a weekly or monthly inventory analysis report, obviously has the upper hand. It can take action by reordering, expediting previously ordered shipments not yet received, locating stock from other sources, or developing a temporary substitution.

The same thing can be said about other controlling and accounting functions that are time- and attention-critical like credit and collections, manufacturing control, drug prescription fulfillment, insurance policy issuance, real estate listing, transportation routing, travel reservations, laboratory testing, industrial quality control and many others.

Random-Access Storage

To minimize the requirement for expensive, high-speed random-access memory, yet retain the ability to process transactions in "real time," as events actually occur in the business, IBM engineers in the late 1950's developed the first random-access magnetic disk storage devices. These were expensive, slow and primitive by today's standards, but they accomplished the feat of storing a large data base outside the main memory of the computer, ready for instant (or almost instant) recall when needed.

Thus began the whole in-line or on-line processing era that today supports instantaneous processing of transactions; remote data communications via telephone, microwave and satellite facilities; word processing; electronic mail and a host of other extant and emerging techniques.

How Magnetic Disks Work

Most magnetic disks operate like a kind of magnetic phonograph, with a sensitive magnetic read-write "head" on an access arm which moves under command of the CPU to a specific recording track on a rotating platter coated with ferrous oxide material. Once positioned, the device waits for the particular sector of the track containing the desired data to spin around under the head. Then the data is read magnetically at very high speeds, into the computer memory.

Once in memory, the data is usually acted upon in some way and very often is *updated* with new information based on the transaction that gave rise to its access in the first place. The new updated version of the record is then delivered, under CPU control, back to the read-write head whereupon it is rewritten on the magnetic disk over the now erased sector that originally contained it. This process is called "updating in place."

Contrasts between Random and Sequential Processing

Contrast random updating in place with sequential processing described earlier. In sequential processing we read the "old" file and rewrote an entirely new one, without in any way destroying or disturbing the old file. One of the important benefits of sequential processing is that, if we subsequently discover a mistake resulting from human error or machine malfunction, we can always revert to the old file and reprocess the transactions.

Such is clearly not the case with random storage, unless we happen to have enough of it to use it sequentially like magnetic tape, in which case we've given up both its economic and transaction-processing advantages.

File Backup and Reconstruction

In the case of sequential file storage, as a regular procedure, users always "save" a generation or two of the file, under lock and key, off-premises, if possible, and in as damage- and fireproof an environment as possible. This is to provide "backup", something to fall back on if the current tape is lost, damaged, or turns out to have been processed erroneously. To rely on luck and hope nothing goes wrong is the height of folly and not just courts, but almost guarantees, disaster.

The same thing applies in a more complicated fashion to random-access storage. The usual method of protecting oneself against catastrophic loss of information is to periodically copy files to a removable medium such as a magnetic tape (or another disk, if one of the removable variety is available) and treat it in the same way as the backup tape discussed in the previous paragraph.

Disk Failures

If records stored on disks have been erroneously updated, because of human error, "bugs" in the program or machine failure, it is sometimes possible to selectively correct only those records which were misposted. Frequently, however, when the mispostings are very numerous and/or difficult to pinpoint, or when the disk has "crashed," rendering the information on it totally useless, it will be necessary to *reconstruct* the affected files.

If you have been copying the files at the close of business each night, then the worst that can happen is that you must restore the data base to where it was at the close of business yesterday and re-process all of today's transactions up to the point of the failure.

Disk crashes *do* occur. One can absolutely and unconditionally guarantee the following:

1. If you are a tape user, you will on occasion inadvertently erase the current master tape.
2. If you are a disk user, you, the program or the machine will occasionally destroy the contents of the current disk file.

So if you want to stay in business after the crash, *some form of file save-and-reconstruction procedure is absolutely essential.* It should be a part of the vendor-supplied systems software discussed in Chapter 6. If not, you or your applications programmer will have to create it.

STORAGE DEVICES

Tape

Because disk storage was the better medium, but considerably more expensive than magnetic tape, it gained ascendancy slowly. We are now at the point, however, where random-access disk storage costs little if any more than tape. Actually, in terms of the number of bytes of information that can be contained at one time on a single device, on big computers it is already cheaper than tape. The "threshold" cost, that is, the lowest price for the minimum system, until very recently was much higher than tape. That's why a number of small computer systems like the IBM 5100 and the Datapoint 2200 were originally available with cassette tape devices only. Now, because of technical and economic breakthroughs in the realm of "floppy" disks, the threshold cost of a minimum disk system is less than the least expensive commerical-grade tape unit.

All this is by way of suggesting that, except in special cases, and where tape is used in conjunction with disk as a removable file "copy-and-save" medium, you probably will not, and should not, consider a sequential magnetic tape as your main data base storage medium. Therefore, rather than spend your time and attention on an approach you're unlikely to use, let us turn our attention to the various types of disk files.

Types of Disks

There are two fundamental types of disks: platter or "hard" disks, and flexible or "floppy" disks. The platter disks vary, starting with a single platter about the size of an LP record, coated on one side with magnetic material, with a single read-write head on a plunger that moves from track to track. Others are coated on both sides. Some have multiple platters in a kind of "layer cake" arrangement with a common set of structurally connected read-write arms that move in unison across all platter surfaces, top and bottom, simultaneously.

The multiple read-write heads provided a significant speed improvment over earlier models of the 1960's, in which a single access arm had to travel up and down from platter to platter and then move to the correct track. Some disks now have multiple heads per disk surface to reduce travel time still further.

As a result, we are now past the point where platter-disk access speed is likely to be any kind of limiting factor in the throughput of your installation, assuming you are not an "information utility" serving dozens or hundreds of users simultaneously.

Typical Platter Disk

To prove the point, let's analyze the most prevalent hard platter system of today. It has one fixed platter and one removable one, each with two recording surfaces, capable of storing a total of either 5 or 10 megabytes (million characters of data). Why the difference? Recording density. The 10-megabyte disks record twice as many characters per inch of surface because of a higher resolution recording and reading technique. Twenty- and 40-megabyte and even larger disk drives employ a combination of higher densities and a larger number of platters to achieve the increased storage capacity. The gains in size and speed provided by the larger disks reduces the cost per byte as one goes up the scale, but this does not justify buying more than is needed beyond a reasonable allowance for overhead and growth.

The typical platter disk, as shown in Figure 3–3, takes an average of 40 milliseconds (40 one-thousandths of a second) to position the heads over the desired recording track. Once in position, the mech-

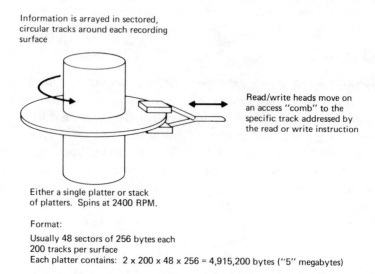

Information is arrayed in sectored, circular tracks around each recording surface

Read/write heads move on an access "comb" to the specific track addressed by the read or write instruction

Either a single platter or stack of platters. Spins at 2400 RPM.

Format:
Usually 48 sectors of 256 bytes each
200 tracks per surface
Each platter contains: 2 x 200 x 48 x 256 = 4,915,200 bytes ("5" megabytes)

Figure 3–3. Typical Arrangement of Platter or Hard Disk Storage.

anism must wait until the desired information spins around under the head. That comes to half a revolution, on average, which is another 12.5 milliseconds, at 2,400 revolutions per minute. Then, depending on the length of the sector to be read or written, it takes another millisecond or so to carry out that final step.

Summing up, we're talking about less than 60 milliseconds (0.06 second) per access. To put it in perspective, a typical order-entry application might consume 15 disk accesses to process a 5-line order, including retrieval and updating of customer and stockkeeping records. Remember, the data has to be located and read once, and then updated and rewritten back to the data base. That takes at least two disk accesses.

So our hypothetical 5-line order takes 15 x 0.06 seconds, or less than *1 second* of disk time. The fastest order-entry clerk in the world at a computer keyboard could flex his or her fingers only about six times in the space of a second, only a small part of the total keystroking required to enter a 5-line customer order. So, even if several clerks were entering ordering data simultaneously at breakneck speed, it's improbable that disk access will be a limiting factor.

Removable and Nonremovable Platters

Platters or hard disks come in both fixed and removable forms. The fixed, or nonremovable, disk drives have the advantage of being somewhat faster, more reliable and less expensive than comparable removable disks. Removable disks, usually in the form of "packs" of one or more platters encased in a protective plastic cover, have some advantages of their own. First of all, the file "copy-and-save" problem is solved by duplicating important files periodically to a second pack, removing it and storing it in a safe place. Secondly, the size of the computer data base is made infinitely extensible by virtue of the removability feature.

The Off-Line Data Base

As was the case with magnetic tape, portions of the data base containing information of no use at the moment can be removed and stored in a file cabinet. We then refer to these files as "off-line."

That part of the data base which is still physically "mounted" on a disk drive and immediately accessible to the machine without human intervention is "on-line." Going back to the payroll example, there's probably no urgency requiring payroll files to be on-line. It's probably also true that payroll processing can be scheduled at a time when some other process, like accounts receivable, can be deactivated. If so, then the disk pack containing A/R can be demounted from the machine and replaced with the payroll pack.

That means that a disk complement of a given capacity (5 megabytes fixed and 5 megabytes removable is typical and many small business computers come with a combination of the two) can be used for a data base well beyond 10 megabytes. If we had three 5-megabyte packs on the sidelines, the total file capacity of the system could be thought of as 25 megabytes, despite the fact that we are paying for only 10 megabytes of disk drive capacity.

The rub is that the 15 megabytes of disk information stored off-line aren't accessible except on a rigidly scheduled, periodic basis or at the expense of interrupting the present process. The interruption might mean not only a reduction in efficiency but also a delay in getting the present job done and, perhaps more to the point, a significant delay in getting at the desired information.

For example, a customer is on the phone disputing his account balance, as shown on a dunning notice. You need a rundown of transactions, particularly payments received, since the last statement was prepared. If the information you're looking for is available only from the A/R disk pack stashed in a filing cabinet, or alternatively from scanning each day's cash receipts journals printed since last month's close, then you're going to have to do some research and call the customer back later. Is that a problem in your business? Maybe, or maybe not, but it's certainly a disadvantage compared with that hopelessly antique, ledger-card posting system you used to have before you modernized with a computer. Under that system you merely reached into the ledger tray, retrieved the customer's card, and were prepared instantly to talk intelligently with him about his problem.

Having computerized files on-line all or most of the time can get you back electronically to the convenience of those old visible records, combined with the many real advantages of data processing.

The Floppy Disk

A good all-around compromise for many small businesses and departmental units is the flexible or floppy disk approach. "Floppies," more properly known as "diskettes," look like and are about the size of 45 rpm phonograph records and come encased in a cardboard jacket, which is never removed (reading and writing is accomplished though a narrow "window" in the jacket).

The advantage of floppies is that they're cheap. Both the mechanical drive and the medium, the flexible platter itself, are a fraction of the cost of hard disk. (Table 3-2 portrays typical cost, capacity and performance characteristics of the types of disks likely to be encountered.) Also, a diskette is very quick and easy to mount and demount in the drive, usually requiring only a few seconds to come to the full "ready" status. And it is almost indestructible and impervious to dust and other environmental threats, so much so that floppies are often sent with impunity by courier or regular mail between companies and organizational units in simple containers.

However, the bad news is that floppies are much smaller in capacity than hard disks and much slower. The typical diskette drive, with one disk mounted, has an on-line capacity equal to the storage capacity of the particular flexible platter employed. As of only a short time ago, that meant a maximum of 0.25 megabyte or about 250,000 bytes. Recently, computer manufacturers have begun producing "double-density" diskettes with approximately 500,000-byte capacities and, still more recently, "two-sided, double-density" diskettes with approximately 1 megabyte of storage. A disadvantage of

Table 3-2. Typical Disk File Characteristics.

Type of Disk	Capacity Increments in Megabytes	Total Capacity of Typical System in Megabytes	Total Access Time in Milliseconds	Time to Read 200-Byte Record in Milliseconds	Approximate Price per Megabyte
Fixed	2.5–40	10–20	60	1	$1,000
Removable	2.5, 5.0	10	75	2	1,000–2,000
"Floppy"	0.25, 0.5, 1.0	1.5–3.0	400	4	3,000–4,000

Threshold Price:
Minimal hard disk system: 5-megabyte drive (2.5 removable): under $8,000.
Minimal floppy disk system: two 0.25-megabyte drives: under $2,500.

the larger capacity diskettes is that they are more apt to malfunction because of contamination and mishandling than the simpler ones.

As is the case throughout computerdom, there are still more trade-offs. In return for the extra convenience and lower costs of floppies, one finds himself limited to a smaller on-line data base, for example, a maximum of six 0.5-megabyte diskette drives, or 3 megabytes in all. And, with access speeds in the range of 400 milliseconds instead of 60, as was the case with hard disk, perhaps something on the order of one-seventh the theoretical throughput capacity. Yet, if disk speed is not a limiting factor, and if the total data base is small, or if it's large but only a fraction of it is needed on-line at one time, then floppies can be extremely effective.

SUMMARY

To sum up the storage situation, you might think of storage as an economical extension of high-priced computer memory, and removability as an even lower cost extension of storage. Tape is, in the minicomputer realm, outmoded, except to add removability in an otherwise fixed-disk situation. Disks are either of the rigid, fixed platter or of the flexible diskette (floppy) variety. Both are accessible at random and hold large amounts of data relative to main memory, but there are numerous capacity, speed and convenience trade-offs to consider between them.

It's wise to get some expert help in determining what file storage medium to use, how, and how much, in any particular situation. The best test is a demonstration of an application identical or nearly identical to your own under realistic conditions.

4
Other Peripheral Devices

IMPORTANCE AND FUNCTION

The devices attached to computers that transport data into and out of the machine and/or store it external to the main memory and CPU are called "peripheral devices," or, simply, "peripherals." They are so designated because they remain on the periphery of the computer, yet their role is anything but peripheral. Almost all modern business-oriented mini- and microcomputers are fast and reliable, and capable of performing business data processing functions commensurate with their size and cost. They begin to diverge, however, in the variety, quality and cost of available peripherals. The differences between systems become even more apparent in the realm of vendor-supplied software and systems support, discussed in later chapters.

Peripherals are of crucial importance, because they supply our "windows" into and out of the system and take care of all staging and storage of data while it's not in use. Peripherals can also become a big expense, a serious bottleneck and an aggravating source of service problems. Because peripherals are relatively expensive compared to the rest of the system, frequently accounting for two-thirds or more of the total cost of the hardware complement, a delicate trade-off is called for between buying a comfortable margin of overcapacity and keeping the price of the system within reason.

For example, a 300-line-per-minute printer in the Digital Equipment Corporation (DEC) line costs $11,800. A comparable 600-line-per-minute printer costs $22,000 and a heavy duty 1,250-line-per minute unit costs $38,470. The lesson is clear: one had better know how much printing capacity he needs before making that kind of a selection. If he buys too much, he's overspent by more than the entire cost of the CPU and memory (the computer itself); if he buys too little, he will hold back the entire system—like making a runner wear weighted boots.

Because peripheral devices are mainly mechanical rather than electronic, they generally account for the lion's share of downtime and maintenance headaches. It sometimes pays to buy more or more expensive peripherals to minimize such problems.

INPUT DEVICES

Key-to-Disk Machines

One of the simplest computer input methods is to use a machine independent of the computer that records data on a diskette which can later be physically or electronically transported to the computer for processing. Sometimes this technique proves advantageous where the data-input function cannot be conveniently coordinated with processing because of timing or geography. In some respects it's more expensive because the key-to-disk machine is itself a limited-purpose microcomputer, and some of the advantages of on-line data entry discussed in Chapter 7 are lost. Nevertheless, tens of thousands of such machines are in use, the most numerous of which are IBM 3741's and 3742's. The 3741 has one keyboard station, the 3742 has two. Representative prices are:

	PURCHASE	MONTHLY MAINTENANCE FEE
3741 Model 1	$4,680	$42
3742 Model 1	$5,420	$52

Both machines offer numerous optional editing and operator convenience features that can significantly upgrade the cost, and both record data on standard 0.25-megabyte diskettes which can be read by a majority of business minicomputers.

Typewriter Input Devices

Another fairly common device for computer input is the teletypelike keyboard on what is equivalent to an electronically attached electric typewriter. The usual printing or typing features of these devices are also employed as part of the input process to help guide the operator in the keying process, and, sometimes, to provide a record of what was put into the system. These machines are discussed in more detail in the section Input/Output Devices.

Punched Cards

An almost vanished form of input, at least in the small computer realm, is the punched card. It can still be found where the new system shares data with an existing system that employs punched cards. It would be extremely rare to find punched cards as the medium of choice for input in an entirely new installation, because both on-line (direct into the computer) and key-to-diskette methods are faster, cheaper and, in many situations, less subject to error. If punched cards are in the picture, however, a reader can be attached to most business-oriented small computers for around $5,000 and an increase in maintenance costs of around $70 per month.

Paper Tape

Paper tape is another vanishing form of input for computers of all types. Compared to punched cards, paper tape is more compact; the devices that create it and the peripherals that read it are cheaper; and the data, once punched, cannot easily be lost or taken out of sequence. The same points, however, can be made even more strongly with respect to diskettes. Nevertheless, there are still numerous bookkeeping and posting machines and a host of teletype installations that use paper tape as the basic medium of data exchange. If a modern mini- or microcomputer has to work with such existing equipment, it may require a paper tape reader. Fortunately such are available. A slow (30 characters per second) paper tape reader costs about $750 and adds about $8 per month to the maintenance bill.

INPUT/OUTPUT DEVICES

Peripheral input/output devices combine input and output capabilities in one unit. Magnetic tape and disk units are actually input/output devices; that is, they transport data into the computer from outside and receive and record processed data (output). But since their main function is storage, we'll reserve discussion until we reach that category.

The remaining input/output devices are either keyboard printers or keyboard CRT's. The CRT, which stands for Cathode Ray Tube, simply substitutes a TV-like video tube for the printer, so instead of producing printed "hard copy" in its output role, it flashes images on the screen instead.

The CRT-type machines are much faster than comparable printers and somewhat more reliable. The are noiseless and display a whole page of information on the screen in a compact and easily comprehensible way.

The disadvantage, of course, is that the device itself leaves no permanent hard-copy record of either the data that was entered or of the computer-initiated responses: each successive image washes away the data previously displayed in the same location on the screen. (There are some CRT's that have local memory of their own which can retain a few pages of data for subsequent recall, but these are expensive and the fact remains that no written record is produced.)

Solution: where necessary and cost-justified, combine both a CRT and a printer serving the same operator workstation. Many users elect this approach, but be cautious about using it unless the hardcopy record is required *at the workstation* and *at the time of entry*. Why? Because:

- Document preparation (printing) can be done more efficiently on a high-speed line printer attached to the computer and dedicated to that purpose only.
- A combination CRT and print station costs considerably more than either by itself.
- A printer of the type associated with CRT's is usually much slower than the CRT itself and can, therefore, slow it down considerably, depending on how it's used.

For example, it's unusual to see a CRT running at less than 120 characters per second, and many operate at nearly 1,000 characters per second. It's equally unusual to see an attached printer faster than 30 characters per second. Therefore it could take 30 times as long to print out the contents of the screen as it did to receive and display the data originally, making it a technique to be used sparingly, if at all.

Keyboard Printers

There are still a few old teletypes in use as computer input/output stations, but because these devices are noisy, slow and produce poor-quality print, they have been supplanted by more modern character printers of three types.

Impact matrix printers. These rather bulky electric typewriter-like machines make character impressions on paper through a typewriter ribbon as patterns of tiny needlelike dots. Seen by the naked eye, from a reasonable distance, the result looks like slightly "funny" typewritten material, certainly adequate for internal documents and reports and for many kinds of external commercial communications such as invoices and vouchers.

The ones used in conjunction with keyboards as input/output devices generally run at 30 characters per second, cost around $2,400 and are maintained under contract for about $25 per month. They are quite reliable, fast becoming the industry's "workhorse," but are incapable of producing what most people would term "correspondence-quality" printed output.

Daisy-wheel printers. Beginning with the 15-characters-per-second, "dancing ball" print head of the IBM Selectric and graduating upward to the faster daisy-wheel printers pioneered by Diablo are a progression of high-quality electric typewriters capable of producing top-quality documents at, most typically, 45 characters per second. Some of the newer machines pick up additional speed by printing bidirectionally; that is, at the end of a line, they print the next one backward, from right to left, to avoid a carriage return. Prices run about 30–50% higher than comparable matrix printing varieties. Reliability has not been quite as good but is improving with the introduction of more durable print heads.

Nonimpact printers. There are a number of low-speed, low-cost, nonimpact character printers on the market, the most notable of which emanate from Texas Instruments Incorporated. The technique used is generally of the dot-matrix variety described earlier, but instead of striking the paper, these nonimpact printers leave a pattern of electrically charged spots which are instantly "developed" electrochemically.

These printers are inexpensive, silent, compact and portable, but even though the device itself costs less than an impact printer, the paper doesn't (it is chemically coated and costs several times what plain paper does). Also, the print quality and contrast is noticeably inferior, and no carbons can be produced. If multiple copies are required, the user must either resort to a copying machine or repeat-print the original as many times as needed.

Because nonimpact character printers are usually about half the cost of the impact variety, they often fit into such light-duty applications as an auxiliary page-printing attachment to a CRT or for field use as a lightweight portable terminal.

CRT's

The ranking champion input/output device for computers, large and small, is the keyboard–CRT combination. There are perhaps one million such units in use in the United States as of this writing, and the number is growing at better than 25% per year. The reasons are simple: nothing works as reliably and well, costs as little and is as acceptable to an operator for carrying on a dialog with a computer.

Most CRT's can be programmed to highlight portions of the displayed message with special bright or blinking characters; ask questions and leave spaces for answers, as in a questionnaire; retain the format of the questionnaire while erasing the previous answers in preparation for the next transaction; tab, skip or return to areas of the screen; allow correction of errors before the message is transmitted to the computer; and perform many other functions adaptable to specific uses.

The typical unit has a typewriter keyboard, a separate 10-key "pad" similar to an adding machine for fast input of numeric-only data, a set of "function keys" for instructing the machine what to do and a 12-inch CRT screen designed to display up to 24 lines of information, 80 spaces in width, or a total of 1,920 character positions. The 24 x 80–character format corresponds to a 1,920-byte memory, called a "buffer," inside the CRT, each position of which contains either a number, character or blank which is used to refresh the displayed images on the screen several times per second.

The typical keyboard CRT, as described, costs around $2,200 to purchase and $25 per month to service under a maintenance agreement. The most popular minicomputer-CRT with an integrated low-speed printer attached costs about $4,000 and $60 per month maintenance. Costs of these devices have been coming down rather rapidly because they are more electronically than mechanically endowed. Thus, it seems a safe bet that ones similar to today's standard units will be available as regular components from major computer manufacturers for between $500 and $1,000 by 1985.

OUTPUT DEVICES

Printers

The most ubiquitous computer peripheral, other than the CRT, is the printer, which comes in a variety of types and speeds to suit the nature of the printed output called for. Almost all computer applications result in some kind of permanent output product such as a check, voucher, statement, inventory status report, balance sheet, or name and address label. Sometimes these are preprinted forms in which the computer fills in blanks, like a payroll check, and sometimes they are blank paper on which the computer imprints both headings and data. The latter is cheaper, requires fewer form changes, hence less handling, and is suitable for most internally circulated documents; the former is more expensive, more presentable and generally used where matters of legality, formality and company "image" are concerned.

In either case, computers tend to put forth a lot of printed paper, so much so that form costs, even of the unprinted stock variety, are a factor, and so is storage space for both the raw material and the finished results, many of which are kept for future reference.

If this sounds like a suggestion to hold down the quantity of printed output from your computer or computer-based service by employing a bit of judicious management-by-exception, it is. Despite this consideration, you will undoubtedly succumb to the urge to spew out tons of paper from your computer, because it's so fast and easy to do and because it is "better to err on the side of too much information than too little." One possible middle-ground solution may be found in micrographics, described in a following section.

Character Printers

The first two categories of keyboard printers, previously discussed under input/output devices, comprise the most common small computer output method. The impact matrix printer and the daisy-wheel printer, minus the keyboard, of course, both make excellent low-volume line printers for "production" type output such as invoices, statements, reports, and listings.

Obviously, if letter- or correspondence-quality output is required, then the daisy-wheel has the edge, although at a sacrifice in output speed. For about the same money, with a somewhat diminished print quality, one can purchase a high-speed matrix printer. These cost in the range of $2,800 to $3,500 and print at 120 or 180 characters per second, whereas the fastest daisy-wheel printers run at 45 to 55 characters per second.

For the moment one can dismiss the nonimpact printers as being too slow, of poorest print quality and too expensive to run in production mode because of the high costs of coated paper. However, within 5 years of this writing, xerographic imaging techniques will be perfected, technically and economically, that far surpass impact printing in every respect, including lower cost, higher speed and better quality. These will eventually supplant impact character printers in most applications.

Besides printing one character at a time, including blanks, character printers space up one line at a time, like a typewriter. Some have primitive "skipping" features, but the movement of paper through blank lines is very slow compared to line printers. Some printers have the ability to compress the time it takes to print long strings of blanks, but, basically, white space takes almost as much time to print as actual data.

Line Printers

As the name implies, line printers print one entire line of data at a time, instead of forming each character and blank separately. This is accomplished by having as many character-imaging units as there are print positions in the line. Almost universally, this means 132. At 10 pitch, or 10-characters-to-the-inch width, this yields a printing field 13.2 inches wide on a form 14 7/8 inches wide, including sprocket holes. To realize the extent to which these computer forms have taken over our lives, one has only to witness a so-called ticker-tape parade in New York City. After the celebrants pass, the street is generally a foot deep, not in ticker tape or confetti, but perforated, fan-folded standard-width computer forms—literally by the hundred of tons.

Line printers are designed for continuous, heavy-duty production printing, starting at 150 lines per minute at the low end, and graduating up to about 1,200 lines per minute in the most expensive models. In addition, all have high-speed "carriage-control" features that permit much faster than normal passage of blank lines.

For example, in printing an invoice on a 300 line-per-minute (lpm) printer, the heading, ribbon and body-line timing could be calculated by dividing the average number by 300. If the average is 18, including scattered blank lines, then it should take 18/300 or 0.06 minutes to print that portion. If the next portion is a variable number of blanks, culminating in a total line at the bottom of the form, we handle this with a "skip" command in the program that causes the printer to move paper at, in some cases, five times the regular rate, reach the desired next line, stop and resume printing at the normal rate. If the average number of blank line spaces in our invoicing example were also 18 (3 inches at the usual 6-lines-to-the-inch vertical print spacing), then these lines would pass at the equivalent of 1,500 lpm: 18/1,500, or 0.012 minute.

What's the point? The point is that line printers have production-oriented features in addition to their inherently faster print speeds that make them more suitable for heavy-duty applications. And, it is not easy to calculate exactly what the gain in output will be in going from one kind of printer to another. To be accurate, one must match the print speeds, tabbing and skipping speeds and forms-handling features to the actual workload, extend the estimated timings by the projected volume of each type of form and report to be printed and then make allowance for time lost because of scheduling, changing forms and maintenance.

I wish it were possible to lay down a simple rule of thumb for you to use in predicting printer throughput, such as a 70–70–70 formula, which "guesstimates" that the average printed line width will be 70 characters; that an average 70% of the potential print lines will be used, the rest skipped, and that the printer will be busy a maximum of 70% of the business day. I wish that were possible, but it isn't. Every situation, every computer operating schedule, every workload, in terms of form layout and volume, is different. On the other hand, you might use something like that as a very rough first approximation.

A fast line printer costs more than a whole minicomputer system minus the printer, so the selection must be made very carefully. The typical 300–lpm printer costs around $13,000 and adds $100 to the monthly maintenance bill. A 600–lpm model costs more than $20,000 and $110 per month maintenance, and one manufacturer offers a 1,250–lpm model for $38,470 and $185 per month.

Two final thoughts on printers. One of the most common bottlenecks in small business computers is limited printing capacity, because printers are expensive and because our appetite for data seems to grow in slightly greater proportion than our capacity to print it out. Second, you don't have to do all your printing the same way. Some companies successfully employ two or more lower-speed printers, each dedicated to a specific type of form, in order to minimize cost and reduce paper handling (changing forms). It's something to at least consider in a given situation.

Punched Cards and Paper Tape

Input in the form of punched cards or punched paper tape is rare these days, but rare indeed is the minicomputer called upon to *output* these media. Nevertheless, it can be done, but it's slower than any other form of output and quite expensive. For example, in the DEC line, a punched tape reader costs $750 and $8 per month for maintenance, whereas a reader with a punch attachment costs $5,060 and $41 per month, and the punch operates at only 50 characters per second. Card punches are in the same general arena, except somewhat faster and more expensive. Some manufacturers simply don't offer card or tape punches anymore.

Micrographics

Something you have a greater likelihood of encountering as a specialized form of output is microfilm, either in reel form or as individual multi-image sheets called "fiche." Microfilm and microfiche make excellent archival storage media for large volumes of computer output, yet they can be read, and if necessary photocopied, by inexpensive viewing equipment.

Micrographics and the principles of forms management are far outside the scope of this book. However, you need to be aware that computer printouts, in their full 14 7/8-by-11-inch, fan-folded printed form can be taken to a micrographics service bureau and converted automatically to microfilm or microfiche.

Furthermore, if you have the volume to support it, additional economies can be obtained by delivering a magnetic tape, disk or diskette to the service bureau instead of the bulky printouts and, in the unlikely event you have need for enormous quantities of microfilm, you can attach something called "COM" directly to your computer. A COM, or Computer Output on Microfilm device, is faster than a line printer but costs about the same and produces microfilm or fiche directly, without any intermediate steps.

It's not likely you'll need your own COM device, but you should certainly consider microfilming bulky, infrequently referenced historical information and, perhaps, widely distributed current data like catalogs, parts lists, indexes, or credit authorization lists. Many organizations have cut printing, reproduction, distribution and storage costs in this manner.

FILE STORAGE DEVICES

When viewed from the point of view of the CPU and memory, file storage components are really input/output devices, and that's exactly how the computer and its software treats them. Also, in a very real and practical sense, removable storage *is* a common input/output (I/O) medium. Many companies exchange tapes, disks and diskettes among computers and between separate keyboard devices and computers. In other cases the data never leaves the physical environment of the computer, but once written to storage, technically it has been "output" (verb) to the storage device. When we need it again it has to be "input" (verb) from the device.

From Chapter 3 we already know about the various types of storage devices and some of their characteristics. It will only be necessary to summarize them, adding representative price ranges.

Magnetic Tape

Relatively expensive and rare for small computers, magnetic computer tape is sometimes used as a file copy-and-save medium, but even then, it is outnumbered by tape cassettes and removable disks. The minimum magnetic tape drive with its associated controller (attaching circuitry) costs about $7,700 and $75 a month to maintain. A faster, more or less industry-standard model costs around $13,000 and $100 per month. At that price you'd be getting a device that reads at 36,000 characters per second and can store more than 10 million characters of data on one reel (2,400 feet) of tape. Remember, however, that to get to a given data item, you must read the tape from beginning to end, one record at a time. In the example just given, to read 10,000 records, each one 400 characters long, would take approximately 5 minutes. That's just to read them; processing and rewriting, if any, would take additional time. The physical medium, the blank reel of tape itself, costs around $8.00, an inexpensive way to store millions of characters of data.

Cassette Tape

One way of escaping the high cost of industry-standard, magnetic tape equipment is to scale down to cassette tapes, which are smaller, slower and cheaper. The time it takes to pass a given number of records is even greater, by a factor of at least 5, and the total capacity of a cassette is usually less than 0.25 megabyte. Yet for some applications, magnetic tape cassettes work well and are quite a bit easier on the pocketbook. For example, in the Burroughs line, the least expensive standard magnetic tape unit is $8,600, whereas their standard cassette drive costs $1,940. Maintenance rates are $21 and $6, respectively.

Fixed Disks

The major exponent of fixed disks on minicomputers at the moment is IBM, with fixed-only hard disks on both its System 32 and Series 1 product lines. On the Series 1, hard disk units require an attachment feature for $815 and $8 per month maintenance, plus the disk itself. A 9-megabyte disk costs $6,895 and $44 per month, a 13.9-megabyte disk is priced at $8,595 and $69 per month.

In the DEC product line, by contrast, a 5-megabyte, nonremovable disk unit is $5,100 plus $54 per month, but that's after the first drive and controller, which costs $9,900 and $81 per month.

The disadvantage of these otherwise attractive options is that some other device is required to remove information from the system for safekeeping and to extend the size of the data base by "swapping" files off-line to on-line.

Removable Disks

The common form of removable hard disk is a single platter "pack" with either 2.5- or 5-megabyte capacities. Expansion drives beyond the first offered by DEC, comparable to the 5-megabyte fixed model mentioned above, are the same price but only 2.5 megabytes in size. Honeywell sells a combination 2.5-megabyte-fixed and 2.5-mega-byte-removable drive for $7,400 and $60 maintenance. Interestingly, that drive is available in double density (5-megabyte-fixed and 5-megabyte-removable) for only $600 more, $8,000 plus $80 maintenance.

Several manufacturers offer even larger removable disk drives at commensurately reduced per-megabyte costs. Most small businesses won't need the extra capacity, but there's no reason to shy away from them if the requirement exists. One consideration with these larger drives is the cost of the medium, the blank pack itself. Some are as much as $400 apiece. The smaller 2.5- or 5.0-megabyte, single-platter packs cost between $85 and $150 apiece. Even at that price, a large library of off-line files, file-save copies and history data on disk packs could run into a considerable amount of money and require a significant amount of space for storage.

Diskettes

Diskettes, or floppy disks, have become extremely popular on small systems because of their low cost, easy handling and durability. The medium itself costs around $4. Drive and associated controller prices vary a great deal from system to system, but many are in the range of $1,500–2,000 plus $15 per month maintenance for a single drive and $2,500–3,000 and $30 per month for a dual (two-drive) combination.

There is not a great deal of difference in price between the 0.25-megabyte and 0.5-megabyte versions, nor for that matter, the 1-megabyte variety. Not all manufacturers offer a choice, and some users, given a choice, stay with the 0.25-megabyte version to retain compatibility with existing equipment such as key-to-disk data-entry machines and other computers. Other than that, if the manufacturer offers greater density, there appears to be no compelling reason not to avail oneself of it.

Lately, some of the new microcomputers have been appearing with "minidiskettes." These are still less expensive, slower, smaller versions of the standard floppy. Whereas the smallest-capacity standard diskette is 7.5 inches in diameter and stores approximately 250,000 bytes, the minidiskettes are only 5 inches in diameter and store 90,000 characters. Prices tend to run about $1,000 per drive, less in some instances.

Just to complicate things, some of the manufacturers are in the early phases of development and introduction of double-sided and double-density minidiskettes, following in the path of the standard product. One recent announcement boasts a megabyte-per-drive capacity comparable to the largest standard floppy.

It's probably safe to predict that 7.5- and 5-inch floppies will overlap considerably in price and capability and the choice will eventually be one of compactness versus compatability with older equipment.

SUMMARY

Tapes are useful for off-line storage of data that will be processed in batches, for safekeeping of backup file copies and for archival storage.

Fixed disks are good for active files to be updated on-line, on a transaction-by-transaction basis, but they require a removable medium for backup.

Removable hard disks have the same characteristics as fixed disks but can themselves be used in place of tape for the copy-and-save function, as well as permitting the user to "swap" on-line and off-line files as a way of extending the useful (but not always instantly available) data base.

Floppy diskettes represent an interesting middle ground. They are as inexpensive and easy to handle as cassette tapes, yet, when on-line are accessible at random. Drawbacks are, of course, the size limits imposed on the on-line portion of the data base and somewhat slower accessing and reading speeds.

Printers are a problem to choose because the high-capacity, line-at-a-time varieties are so expensive. Users who can, get by with lower-cost character printers, but printing-capacity bottlenecks often appear as their appetite for more data and analytical reports grows.

CRT–keyboard combinations are the standard input medium for small computers and account for a good deal of the output requirement as well, particularly when a hard-copy document is not required.

Keyboard printers of the teletype and electric typewriter type also appear as I/O devices with the advantage of a permanent, hard-copy output capability, but many users prefer the extra speed and more comfortable man-machine interaction of the CRT.

Other options, usually reserved for special cases, include punched card, punched tape and computer output on microfilm.

5
Data Communications

DETACHED PERIPHERALS

Almost all modern business computers (the exceptions include electronic bookkeeping machines and the smallest microcomputers) permit various peripheral devices to be operated at a considerable distance from the computer itself. It's not unusual to find CRT's and/or printers scattered throughout a building or complex of buildings (for example, in the sales order department, accounting department and plant or warehouse of the same company), each serving a specific purpose for a specific group of users.

There are limits of course, typically a maximum of 2,000–5,000 feet of cabling, but within those bounds the peripherals perform exactly as if they were installed in the same room as the central system. The only limitations imposed by this kind of operation are those of convenient human communications; that is, an operator may not be able to look up from the screen and say, "The machine is down," or "I got a funny message on the screen; what do I do about it?" and expect an immediate response from the person in charge. Thus, coordination and training have to be more thoroughly planned and carried out.

The other obvious limitation of such a setup involves sacrificing some degree of flexibility. If the accounting department is experiencing heavy month-end processing, it may be very difficult for them to "borrow" a CRT in the warehouse for a few hours to help "dig out" from under the peak load. Considerations like this may give rise to a "semi-batch" approach, in which a sizeable accumulation of transactions of a particular type are saved up and then, perhaps after regular processing hours, put into the machine in assembly-line fashion. This might be the optimal way to get certain jobs done anyway. Inventory adjustments following a semiannual physical count, period-end adjusting journal entries, weekly payroll entries and the like do not require instantaneous processing and might better be handled as a batch, especially if they interfere with important operational functions like order processing and production control.

BEYOND THE PALE

However, once beyond the 2,000-, 3,000- or 5,000-foot limit, whatever it is for a particular machine, detachment of peripherals brings in a whole host of new considerations under the heading of "data communications."

For the moment, at least until the telephone company introduces a new service that, at this writing, has only been described conceptually, the standard approach to remote computing is via attachment to the regular telephone network through something called "modems."

Modems

The problem would be far simpler if the telephone system spoke binary like computers, but, as of now and for the immediate future, it doesn't. It speaks as you do, with variations in current strength (amplitude) in almost exact correspondence to the sound of your voice. Engineers call that an "analog" network because the signal—electric current variations—are analogous to your voice, or whatever other original sound is picked up.

To make it possible to transfer bits (hence bytes, fields, records and files) across the telephone line, they must first be converted to signals which "modulate" the telephone-line current in analog mode, and then be "demodulated" back into binary on/off code for the computer or computer terminal at the other end. We call the translation device at each end of the line a "modem," which stands for modulator-demodulator. It synchronizes and translates signals to make the exchange of data across phone lines possible. This is presented pictorially in Figure 5–1.

Terminals

In the preceding paragraph the word "terminal" referred to one component in a two-way conversation with the computer. As a matter of industry practice, *any* device on the *remote* end of a telephone

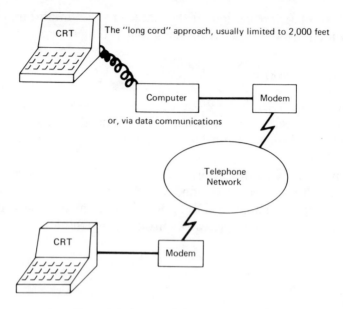

Figure 5-1. Remote Peripheral Operations.

wire, transmitting data to or from a computer is referred to as a "terminal." You can think of terminals as computer devices on a very long cord, one that could stretch for hundreds or thousands of miles, if necessary.

However, there is a difference. A peripheral device within standard cabling distance of the computer is generally connected via an elaborate multiwire cable that carries control and synchronizing impulses separately from data. This is faster and more efficient than mixing the two. But the telephone network consists, basically, of 2-wire pairs, so the "housekeeping" information that enables terminals and computers to talk to each other in an orderly, intelligible way has to be *intermixed* with data on the same pair of telephone wires. This has the effect of reducing the potential speed of data exchange and drastically complicating it, at least from the computer's point of view.

Communications Software

The special programs required to get terminals talking to computers is called "communications software" and is described in more detail in the next chapter. For the moment, let us simply say that once telephone, satellite, microwave or other forms of remote data communications are introduced, the complexity of computer software required to support it goes up drastically. The good news, however, is that most of this software and its complex "protocol" (housekeeping and control procedures) are mercifully screened from, and opaque to, you, the user. Most, if not all, the systems software needed to accomplish this is usually supplied by the manufacturer.

Aside from the supporting systems software from the computer vendor, there are typically some differences in the way one designs applications programs to work in a remote communications environment. Often, the program needs to identify the source of the transaction, treat it differently from "home office" business and direct the responses back to the correct point of origin. Once again, in order to simplify and organize remote processing and reduce interference with other work, it *may* be advisable to transmit and process in batches. Many computer applications require instantaneous processing and/or response. For example, a hotel reservations network wouldn't be very effective if today's room requests had to be saved until tonight's or tomorrow's batch-processing run. By that time, weary travelers would surely have made other arrangements.

Incidentally, you will hear batch processing via a telephone hookup referred to as, not surprisingly, "Remote Batch" processing. You may also encounter this operation referred to as RJE or Remote Job Entry. That term has a different and specialized technical meaning, but when it crops up in a small business computer context, the speaker generally is using the term carelessly and really means Remote Batch, not RJE.

Maintainability

One other complexity worth mentioning to a prospective data communications user has to do with serviceability of the arrangement. Because the terminal is a long distance away from the people who have responsibility for keeping the central system running and operational, and because three new variables have entered the trouble-causing and trouble-shooting picture, maintaining a communications-based system is more difficult.

There are more things to go wrong in the chain: the terminal, its modem, the telephone line, the modem on your end and the additional computer components and software involved. It is a more difficult and technically taxing job to recognize if something has gone wrong, where, and what to do about it. Sometimes there's finger pointing among the responsible parties, each one blaming the malfunctions on someone else.

Usually, coordination and performance problems do get ironed out over time; it does get easier to identify problems and to get them fixed. It's fair to say, however, that start-up difficulties in a communications environment are more perplexing, last longer and can on occasion "kick up" again when least expected, for the simple reason that human frailties are magnified by distance. Added to this is the phone company's constant modification and expansion of its networks to meet growing needs.

Communication Costs

The greatest single deterrent to the use of remote data communications is cost—cost of the remote terminal, cost of a modem to attach it to the telephone line, cost of the line itself, cost of the modem on the computer end, and cost of upgrading the computer hardware and software so it can deal with the added demands and complexities of communications.

Speed, Volume, and Cost Trade-offs

Most peripherals, when directly cable-connected to the computer, transfer data at a rate of at least 9,600 bits per second. As pointed out in Chapter 4 the typical CRT screen contains 1,920 character spaces. At 10 bits per character (8 bits plus "overhead") it takes 2 seconds to fill the screen at 9,600 bits per second. That's not bad. But the conditions for transmitting at 9,600 bits per second (or 9,600 "baud," after the Frenchman, Baudot, who invented the original teletype code) are much more expensive than transmission at slow speeds.

The modems for both ends, if rented from the telephone company, cost more than $100 per month each. Slower modems with speeds of 300 bits per second (bps), for example, cost only about $25 per month. There is a range of costs for intermediate speed capacities. You may be able to save some money by purchasing the modems outright instead of renting them from the phone company, but the speed-cost relationship remains the same—greater speed, greater cost.

You also have to consider the phone line. The regular "switched" network which handles all the intra- and intercity dial calls can't reliably support speeds over 2,400 bps without some special "conditioning." But to perform that conditioning, the phone company has to identify the precise path through which the signals will pass; that is, they have to connect through a permanent path called a "dedicated" line. The dedicated line, then, after permanent routing and conditioning, becomes yours to use exclusively, full time, at a commensurate monthly cost. As a very rough approximation, figure about $1 per mile per month, but a lot depends on the distance involved, and whether it's intra- or interstate and the kind of conditioning required.

So unless you have the volume to (1) demand more than low-speed communications and (2) keep the dedicated line busy several hours a day, you might be better off using the slower, regular switched-network approach. Might be, but not necessarily, because tolls mount up, too. A 5-minute "session" between a terminal in Des Moines and a computer in San Francisco costs the same as a regular direct-dial call of the same duration between the same two points. Five minutes a day is one thing; 5 hours is something else (and probably something to be avoided, either by going with a dedicated hookup or by forsaking remote data communications altogether).

Somebody—you, your vendor, computer analyst, or a consultant—is going to have to examine these time, volume and cost trade-offs very carefully in order to decide the best way to go. And cheapest isn't necessarily best. At 300 bps, it takes 64 seconds to read or write the entire contents of a CRT screen. Can your operator or customer afford to wait that long? Perhaps yes, perhaps no. It depends on the nature of the job to be done.

ALTERNATIVES

There are alternatives to data communications. If the nature of the data to be communicated isn't time-critical, doesn't need to be reflected immediately in company records and doesn't demand an instant response, perhaps the best answer can be found among the following alternatives:

- Send the source documents (orders, bills, time cards, and so on) via mail, UPS or courier to the computer site and have them entered into the system at a time convenient for all concerned.
- If the delay is tolerable, but the source documents don't travel well (perhaps because the people that understand them best are not at the computer site), then consider a remote key-to-disk set up. A $100–200-per-month machine can be rented (or purchased) that looks and acts pretty much like a computer terminal to the operator, but that produces a magnetically encoded medium such as a diskette instead of communicating directly with the computer.
- At this juncture, you have the option of sending the diskette via mail, UPS or courier, *or*
- You can, using a standard feature of most remote data-entry machines, dial up the computer site through the regular phone network and transmit the contents of the diskette all at once in a batch either to the computer, or more likely to another key-to-diskette machine similarly equipped. At this point the data is either in the computer or only a few footsteps away on an easily inserted medium.

SUMMARY

The field of data communications is much richer in substance and subtleties than can possibly be addressed here. The things to remember are:

- After cost considerations have been evaluated, a data communications system can be easily and routinely installed.
- It does introduce complexities, but these have proved to be manageable by many organizations, at least some of which are like your own.
- There are some compromises and alternatives that need to be considered in balancing the level of service and speed of response against economic realities.
- You will certainly want to analyze cost, volume and speed trade-offs very carefully before making a decision.

6
Systems Software

DEFINITION

In its broadest sense, "software" refers to all programs and those materials directly associated with programming, such as flowcharts, file layouts, program listings and other documentation. For our purposes, the programs themselves will be called "software," and the other items will be referred to as "documentation and training materials."

Not all software is alike. The programs that specify step-by-step processing procedures for your jobs (payroll, order entry, accounts payable and the like) are called "applications software." Applications software is analogous to a musical score: it may represent a wonderful piece of music, but it has no sound or substance until somebody *plays* it. The notes, as written, represent *instructions* to an *interpreter,* the musician who will read the notes and translate them into physical action—finger movements on a piano, for instance.

The act of interpreting the musical creator's intentions, as written in musical notation—let's call that "source language"—into actual, physical music is what systems software is all about. Systems software interprets and/or translates programming source language into physical activity in the computer, and times and coordinates that physical activity so it comes out the way the applications programmer planned it.

In a musical analogy, the score is the applications software, the pianist the systems software, and the piano the computer. The pianist *interprets* the source language into finger and pedal actions, but he does so in a smoothly *coordinated* fashion, with proper timing and phrasing, so the music comes out as the composer conceived it. We always have all the systems software we need as long as a skilled pianist is sitting at the keyboard. But suppose we want to speed things up a bit and play the Minute Waltz in 30 thousandths of a second? Impossible! The pianist simply can't think and act that fast.

We could resort to a player piano and "compile" the keyboard actions of the pianist into holes in a piano roll. Now the "source language" has been translated into directly executable "machine language," and we can play the roll as fast as the mechanism can go.

LANGUAGE PROCESSING

Interpretation

We've defined one of the major functions of systems software as the process of changing the source code into machine code. If that is done, as it is in the case of a live pianist, each time the program is played (executed), we call that "interpretation" and the element of systems software that does it, an "interpreter."

Compilation and Assembly

If, to gain speed and efficiency, we decide to translate the source code permanently, in advance, into machine code, we can "assemble" or "compile" the source program into machine language using an "assembler" or "compiler." These are two very common elements of systems software which differ in an important way.

Assemblers. An assembler takes a step-by-step, human-sensible program and translates it point for point into a machine-language program. For all practical purposes, it's a note-for-note translation, although some assemblers allow us to precode commonly used routines and call for them by name. Think of the composer's calling for certain chords by name, rather than spelling out each note in detail.

Compilers. Compilers do the same things assemblers do, except they work from a notation scheme that is a step or two further removed from machine language. A compiler is analogous to the simplified "learn-to-play-at-home-in-your-spare-time" method using symbols and color codes to shortcut the laborious and time-consuming process of learning music and spelling everything out note for note.

Since creators of compilers have the freedom to use any kind of shorthand notation they please, an extremely chaotic condition could arise unless they agree on standards. Fortunately, with the help of certain industry trade groups, the American National Standards Institute and the U.S. Department of Defense, they have.

We say that a particular compiler, its language notation and rules of language usage (syntax), is "standard" if it conforms closely to the agreed-upon industry-wide specifications. The payoff is supposed to be compatibility, that is, the ability to transport a source program written for one machine to a different machine and, after recompilation, have it work without modification. Common languages which various manufacturers have implemented include:

- COBOL. *CO*mmon *B*usiness *O*riented *L*anguage. A very popular but fairly complex language. Flexible and powerful.
- BASIC. *B*eginners *A*ll *P*urpose *S*ymbolic *I*nterpretive *C*ode. Originally a highly simplified mathemetics language but lately extended for business use. Simpler than COBOL but somewhat less efficient and less flexible.
- RPG-II. Second go-round of *R*eport *P*rogram *G*enerator, a highly simplified, limited, somewhat inefficient but very useful and popular language. Easy to learn.
- Fortran. *For*mula *Tran*slation language originally designed, as the name implies, for mathematical problem solving, but now extended for business use. Quite flexible and efficient but, like COBOL, not the easiest language to learn and use.
- APL. Another math-oriented language that has grown into a powerful business language that is as easy to use as BASIC. Efficiency of some implementations has been questioned. The title stands for *A Programming Language*.
- PL-I. IBM's *P*rogram *L*anguage *I* was intended to replace both COBOL and Fortran with one superpowerful, flexible language. Acceptance has been poor because of complexity. Not likely to be a bigseller on small business computers.

Limitations of Language Implementations

Assemblers. Assemblers are typically very powerful and efficient. The problem is that good programs are written by very skillful, thoroughly trained programmers. It's impossible to write good assembler programs unless you're a qualified programmer. Also, assembler programs don't travel well from machine to machine. Assembler languages are too close to machine language, and machine languages tend to vary radically from product line to product line.

Compilers. Compilers and their associated language standards are meant to accomplish two things: (1) make programs easier to write and modify and (2) make programs executed on one machine compatible on other machines. Compared with machine- and assembly-language programming, all the compiler languages have succeeded in the first aim. Also, because programming is easier (especially in APL, BASIC and RPG-II), productivity of competent programmers is increased, and adequate programs can be written by less competent programmers.

With respect to the second goal, transportability or compatability, there are problems. No matter how abstract, music written for piano is hard to play on the tuba. To some extent, basic architectural differences between machines preclude direct transliteration of programs. Furthermore, each compiler implementation is different. Vendors do this to adapt the languages slightly to take better advantage of the differences among the various machines.

As a general statement, no program written for one manufacturer's equipment will run unmodified on a second manufacturer's machine, unless the second machine is an exact imitation of the first. As a second general statement, less modification will be needed if a relatively standard compiler language is involved than would be the case with a unique assembler or a nonstandard compiler or assembler. This is important because some number of years from now, you may wish to transport your programs to a new and different machine. Use of a standard compiler language will make that task materially easier because (1) the new machine will likely support the same language with a compiler only modestly different from the one you're using, and (2) if you do reprogram from scratch, the logic of your present programs will be easier to follow, read and understand, because compiler languages are more human-oriented and less machine-oriented than other alternatives.

Which Language is the Best?

If you use one of the standard compiler languages mentioned, and the vendor has done a good job of implementing it on his machine, and good training and support are available, it really doesn't make much difference which language you choose. Your choice should be the language you're familiar with and feel comfortable using. However, if *you* (entrepreneur or department manager) are going to do all or part of the programming yourself, then it's probably wise to avoid COBOL, Fortran and PL-I. They're for the pros.

SYSTEM CONTROL

Another important function of systems software is *control.* We can use a musical analogy again, but this time we will consider a whole orchestra, which is more like a computer than a single instrument is. The *conductor* performs the coordinating and control function; he monitors the various components of the orchestra and makes sure each is doing its part exactly in tempo and in exact conformance with the score (program). He issues the commands to each of the components to start, stop, maintain tempo, phrasing and other subtle nuances that make for a successful and harmonious execution of the composer's work.

Without a conductor the orchestra would generate only noise. The same thing is true for a computer. Without an "operating system," which performs the coordinating and control functions, passes out the parts, so to speak, to each of the components, monitors their performance and, through electrical signals rather than a baton, adjusts the performance to conform to the program, only unintelligible electronic noise would ensue. However, here the analogy ends. Conducting an orchestra, even a big one, is *easy* compared to what a computer operating system has to do. It has to react to novel situations as they develop while execution is in process, and the piece is never played the same way twice! Let's see why.

Functions of an Operating System

Interaction with an operator. Although the programs are already written, the operating system never "knows" which of them are going to be executed, when or in what sequence. That depends on an operator *instructing* the machine what to do. And that depends on the operating system's ability to carry on a dialog with the operator, to interpret commands according to a prearranged language, and to execute them.

Maintaining the systems library. The foregoing means that the operating system must "know" where the programs are and which ones are available, and it must be able to "go get" them. To do this, it has to perform a "librarian" function, cataloging and storing new programs, and retrieving them as needed. It also has to have the ability to get rid of old programs as "new editions" are published or as they fall into disuse.

Initialization. After retrieving the desired programs from the systems library, the operating system must then "initialize" them, that is, set them up to run. That often involves placing them in memory (analogous to rearranging the orchestra seating to make room); instructing them which incoming data to use, where it will be, and what to do with results; and resetting certain counters and signal "flags" to their initial zero or beginning posture.

File Management. Once the programs are started, they will need data, and that requires still more librarian functions. Perhaps the best way to visualize this is to imagine a program that needs a particular accounts receivable record to which it will post a transaction. The program notifies the operating system that it needs the A/R record for customer number 13796. It doesn't "know" where that record resides, and, furthermore, it lacks the power and privilege of going out after it—that's the job of the operating system. If it weren't so, chaos would result. Individual programs would be accessing, updating and rearranging each other's files in an uncontrolled and unpredictable fashion. The data base would soon be useless as a bow and arrow in a dense fog.

To prevent this, the operating system catalogs files, maintains them, and delivers desired records to the executing programs as they're called for, all in a controlled and coordinated fashion. Only the operating system "knows" where files are physically stored in the attached magnetic storage devices. It's not only a necessity for coordination purposes, it's a big benefit with respect to the individual programs. There might be 100 different programs that in some way and at some time access the inventory file. If we added a single record or deleted one, or in any other way altered the physical residence of the file by mounting it on a different disk drive, all 100 programs would have to be changed—reprogrammed and recompiled, to adjust to the new "addresses" of the data.

Fortunately, we can delegate all that to the operating system and not worry about where things are when writing application programs. And, to make things fast and easy, we can endow the operating system with interpretive abilities—elaborate programming that enables it to adjust to changing file conditions "on the fly," without reprogramming and recompilation.

Supervision

Returning to the accounts receivable example, recall that the program requires record 13796 and has just passed on the request to the operating system; something has to be done with it. It can't just go on executing, because it doesn't have the data to analyze and update. So the operating system has the responsibility of suspending execution of that program, and reawakening it when the data has been successfully retrieved and delivered, which may be only a short time later or perhaps never, if the program has asked for a nonexistent record or some other error condition has arisen. In that case the operating system must notify the program so it can take alternative action or the system must take some action itself such as suspending the program and notifying the operator.

These and similar control functions under the heading of "supervision" are crucial to the execution of programs and the total operation of the system. Without the "traffic cop" functions at each crossroad, no programs could proceed without "crashing" into each other, into themselves or into other obstacles.

Device Handling

All of the fine details of managing and interacting with portions of memory and with the complement of attached peripheral devices are left up to the operating system. The application program wants to go from here to St. Louis via Route 66. The operating system (OS) worries about running the vehicle: meshing the gears, firing the cylinders in order, maintaining oil pressure and the like. The total management of the system, as a system, and the electrical interaction of all the attached devices is the province of the OS. It is the OS that makes it possible for the computer to respond appropriately to commands of the application program analogous to "go to St. Louis," such as "print a line from the contents of memory beginning at a given location," or "retrieve customer record number x from the accounts receivable file," and the like.

As complex and exacting as these tasks are when concerned with the management and control of devices directly attached to the computer, they become even more involved when dealing with *remote* devices via data communications. A key responsibility of the OS, when remote communications are involved, is managing the interaction between the applications programs and the telecommunications environment in a way that makes exchanging information with terminals hundreds of miles away as similar as possible to performing the same functions with devices in the same room. Operating systems vary widely in how well they accomplish this goal, and in how much technical expertise they demand of the user in programming for and managing a communications network.

Security

There's one last important operating system function that needs to be considered—security. Without stretching the traffic cop analogy too much further, think of the librarian in a blue uniform. Before initializing a program, the OS must check to see *who* the requestor is and whether he or she has *authority* to execute that particular program. And, before accessing a file, the operating system has to know whether the particular *program* is authorized to (1) read the file, and, even more critical, (2) read and alter the file. Sometimes, too, these factors interact. A particular file-maintenance program may have permission to read and write a file, but only if the operator currently activating the program at the terminal has the right security clearance. Some operating systems keep records of who accessed what files and when, and send out alarm messages if unauthorized accesses are attempted.

The identification of individuals is generally conducted by means of "passwords," secret identity codes known only to the individual, the operating system, and a few other people highly placed in the organization. For obvious reasons these codes have to be changeable because people come and go, and the information can become too widely known. The password is often a component of the total physical security system which may also include keylocks on terminals to prevent use by anyone not in possession of the key and to limit the use of certain terminals. For example, perhaps only the terminal in the accounting department can initiate and access payroll, and it has a lock for which only the controller and payroll clerk have a key.

Interaction with People

The precise way in which the operating system accepts commands and displays its answers to people determines in large measure whether the whole computer system is going to be easy to learn and operate, or whether it's going to be difficult. The first case involves a good deal of thought about human engineering, intelligibility and simplicity. Operating system designers, perhaps because of their own intellectual prowess, love a challenge for themselves and, often, for their audiences. Many poorly human-engineered OS's have been designed that are much kinder to the machine than to the operator or supervisor who is trying to figure out what is, or is not, going on, and what to do about it. Fortunately the situation is improving, and many newer systems have far better people-features than did the previous generation.

UTILITIES

The last category of systems software is generally referred to as "utilities." It includes commonly used, routine functions precoded and ready to invoke without much, if any, programming. The most common examples are "media-conversion" routines that read data from one medium and transfer it to another, usually without processing or reformatting. The nightly "file-save" routine noted in Chapter 3, in which the data base is copied to a removable medium for safekeeping is an example of a media-conversion utility.

Preprogrammed routines that sort or combine files, purge inactive records or print them out in "as-is" condition, print out the contents of the librarian's "card catalog" (better known as the "file directory"), and perform many other similar functions are supplied with the computer in the form of "utilities."

Importance of Utilities

There is nothing much in the utilities a user couldn't program for himself, but since these functions are common from user to user, there's no point in reinventing them. A good set of utilities saves time and money and generally operates with a higher degree of efficiency than most users could muster for themselves.

Some important and specialized utilities fall into the category of "information storage and retrieval" and "data base management" software, which go a step beyond the operating system in organizing and controlling files. The OS is normally responsible for cataloging, storing, and retrieving files and records as defined and called for by applications programs. The utilities go a step further, specifying the structure or format of files and their relationship to each other.

It's similar to the way some bosses do their filing. If they decide what goes in what file, leaving to their secretary only the responsibility of locating the folder in the right cabinet, that might be thought of as the standard approach. If, on the other hand, the boss expects the secretary to classify and cross-index all documents, and later issues requests like "Get me whatever we have on pollution control in Afghanistan," then we have a situation analogous to the use of information storage and retrieval and data base management software.

At present, most small business computers do *not* get involved in this kind of higher level, abstract information management. Most small business applications deal with files whose structures are simple and almost self-evident. However, one facet of file-management utility software that *is* becoming quite popular among small system users is a "report generator."

Report Generators

A report generator enables the user to code and input the specifications for an output report quickly and easily without programming. Obviously, the data must already exist in the system, and the user must know which fields of information he wants to print, where, from what files, and in what sequence. The report generator is itself a program that interprets the simplified user requests into machine-level programs that retrieve the asked-for data and display or print it in accordance with his specifications. Sometimes report generators include features that compare, select, sort and perform arithmetic on data. RPG-II is an example of one that in many cases goes far enough to substitute altogether for programming in the usual sense.

The usual case in the mini- and microcomputer field is for users to buy or create programs to handle routine input, processing and output of information, and then use a report generator, if available, to meet unanticipated or changing reporting requirements as they arise. Once a report becomes part of the established routine, it may be recoded directly in programming language and made part of the applications system. Why? Because report generators trade off generality for efficiency. Sometimes the generated programs leave something to be desired in terms of speed, efficiency and compactness.

EVOLUTION OF SYSTEMS SOFTWARE

Systems software, especially operating systems and file management utilities are evolving rapidly, getting better by the month. New and improved features are constantly being added, and efficiency is constantly being improved upon. User application programs have arrived at, or are nearing, the stage of *pure process,* nearly independent of the machine's physical environment.

A classic example can be found in data communications. Not very many years ago, writing an application program that communicated with remote terminals was something of a nightmare. The program had to make provisions for initiating and terminating electrical contact with terminals; take into account which destination was on what specific terminal, line and modem; and arrange for the handling of every conceivable kind of error condition and contingency that might arise in the vagaries of transmission.

No more. An application program merely composes a message, appends the code name of the addressee and hands it over to systems software. All the complex and messy details are taken care of by special "handlers" or control programs which are, typically, a part of the OS. The details of managing and controlling the computer itself, the supporting peripherals, data base and communications network will continue to migrate to systems software, becoming more and more invisible to the user and his applications. And that is as it should be. What better device could man invent to manage the resources of a computer on a split-second by split-second basis than a *computer?*

EVALUATING SYSTEMS SOFTWARE

How can the average small business computer user evaluate systems software? The answer is, he can't. Even programmers, analysts and consultants can't agree on the virtues of certain operating systems. Other than the obvious questions, such as, does a particular OS encompass particular features, the potential user is stymied. The real crux is not *whether* the various features have been implemented, but *how well.* The impact of a good language compiler that supports on-line programming, produces excellent error-diagnoses to help the programmer correct his mistakes and is well documented with reference and training material, or a compiler that doesn't fit that description is extraordinary. A programmer's work output is so dependent on the tools he uses that it could vary by a factor of several hundred percent betweeen the two extremes.

A deficient operating system can generate a phenomenal amount of waste. The amount of memory required to contain it is the first criterion. If it uses up half or three-quarters of the total program space in memory, leaving only a pittance for your applications, extensive justification is in order. (Some operating systems will pass the test, but others can't.)

Second, the number of program steps and memory-access cycles a particular operating system takes to perform a specific function, such as accessing a specified record, varies unbelievably from one to the next. Partly it's the skill of the designer, partly how well the architecture of the machine conforms to the requirement of an OS, and partly the extent to which a particular OS permits an applications programmer to blunder into an inefficient use of the whole system.

At the risk of disappointing readers and of angering people who make their living comparing systems software, I am compelled to state that there is no foolproof way for a user to evaluate systems software from published specifications. The best and only way to be *sure* is to see it in operation in your shop, running your programs and using your data under actual operating conditions. If that's impossible in advance, as it usually is, then the second-best way is to find a user operating with the same system under conditions very similar to your own, and see how well it functions in *his* shop.

A distant third-best alternative is to witness a realistic demonstration of a system similar to the one you are considering. In a demonstration environment you can experiment with various factors to see what impact they have on throughput. For example, see if the fastest operator can overwhelm the system by inputting a well-rehearsed order at top speed. Try two transactions in different workstations simultaneously to see if response or acceptance is slowed. Try inputting transactions, then printing a lengthy report, then both, simultaneously, to measure the degree to which they interfere.

The cautious buyer will do well to remember that no demonstration can approximate the exact environment of his particular operation or succeed in providing answers for all contingencies. And from his experience with other sales approaches, he will bear in mind that difficulties and shortcomings of any product tend to be minimized to make a better case. A certain amount of skepticism is required, but that is the case for any major purchase decision.

SUMMARY

Systems software, usually supplied with the machine by the manufacturer, consists of:

- Language Processors, which convert source-language programs into machine-level code which can then run on the computer. The choice of language is mostly a matter of who's going to do the programming and which, from among the available ones, the manufacturer has implemented really *well.*
- Operating Systems which control and coordinate the physical functioning of the machine in accordance with the road maps laid out by applications programming. The applications say where to go; the OS takes care of firing the cylinders, shifting gears, fueling the carburetor, and so on.
- Utilities, which relieve users of having to incorporate commonly used universal routines in their programs, like sorting, copying files from one medium to another, and, frequently, file structuring and information retrieval.

Evaluation of the completeness and competency of systems software is a tough job even for professionals. The best test is experience, your own or that of other users of similar systems under similar conditions. So-called benchmark tests under laboratory conditions are possible, but not without competent professional assistance.

7
Applications: What Makes a Good One

Any tedious, repetitive and costly task that involves processing and/or referencing information in a predefinable fashion is a candidate for computerization. High-volume, routine clerical jobs frequently qualify. Sometimes, however, jobs which are done infrequently but are extremely complex are also good prospects because of their high value to the business. Planning, modeling, forecasting and other analytical applications fall into the latter category. These seldom justify a computer by themselves, but they can become a bonus when clerical applications pay for automation on a day-to-day basis and provide the data to be analyzed as a by-product of the more mundane processing.

Two characteristics that absolutely must be present for an application to make sense are:

1. It must be possible to specify unequivocally and in complete detail what is to be done. Computers do not exercise independent judgment, learn or decide: they *execute* a predetermined program. Furthermore, no "loose ends" are allowed in the program: you can't tell a computer what to do for situations A, B and C and then expect it to react properly when D is introduced.
2. Second, there must be some *benefit* to be gained from automation such as reduced cost, greater accuracy, more information for subsequent decision making or the like. No benefits occur by themselves— they have to be defined, planned and strived for.

Sometimes benefits come from unexpected quarters. One small wholesaler doing less than a million dollars in annual volume needed a computer to replace his bookkeeping machines, although there was no money to be saved, he had all the product and customer data he needed and the current accounting operation was performing in an admirable and timely manner. Why? Because his building, having already been expanded to the limits allowed by local zoning ordinances, was crowded to the hilt. The addition of one more clerk would have forced an undesired and expensive relocation. Installing a small computer would enable the present staff to handle more business without additional office space.

ARCHITECTURE

A few years ago it would have taken a whole book to describe even briefly the various commonly used approaches to applications design. Today, with hardware components so much less expensive, and based on a growing body of a successful experience, applications designs are converging toward a common framework. The hallmarks of this commonly accepted architecture are:

· Interactivity
· Menu Control
· Integration

Let's examine these features one at a time.

Interactivity

It used to be very expensive, prohibitively so for all but a few very time-critical, high-value applications, to put clerks and operators directly "on-line" to a computer. Nowadays, large-scale computer systems can easily support dozens, sometimes hundreds and even thousands of on-line terminals simultaneously. Even the lowliest microcomputer supports at least *one,* and a minicomputer can usually handle from a few to several.

While these terminals (they're called "terminals" when remote from the computer and "workstations" when in the same room or in the immediate vicinity) are on-line, they share a portion of the resources of the computer, typically in round-robin fashion. The easiest way to visualize this "time-sharing" phenomenon is to look at Figure 7–1 and then think of the circus performer with all those plates spinning and balanced in the air on the end of sticks. Recall how he gets them all whirling and then just manages to get back to the first and subsequent ones in succession just as each one "needs service" (is about to fall).

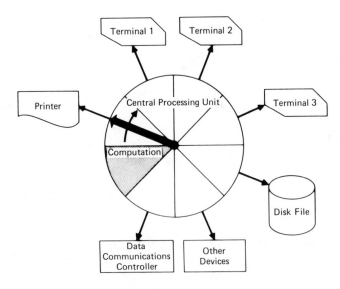

Figure 7-1. The Basis of On-Line Interactivity.

The systems software in a modern interactive computer works the same way. Each terminal (and other peripheral devices, as well) has the ability to spin a while on its own until it needs more service, that is, needs more data to display, or has accumulated a quantum of data to be read into the machine. The operating system directs the computer to provide the required service and then goes on to the next device. The efficiency with which it does this, and the degree to which it is able to "sandwich in" computing between these input/output control functions determines in large measure two vital characteristics of the end result: (1) the *response time* at each terminal, that is, how long it takes for the system to respond to an operator's action as he or she lifts his finger from the final key ending the message or request, and (2) the total *throughput* of the system, that is, the total amount of work actually processed during the day, counting all facets.

The beauty of this round-robin time-sharing technique is that each operator is able to carry on a running *conversation* with the system. Because keystroking and reading information is ponderously slow compared to the lightning speed of the machine, the system carries on multiple conversations at once, never actually responding to more than one request at a given instant, but moving fast enough overall to keep all the conversational plates spinning. We call this running dialog "interactivity." It's important for a number of reasons.

Prompting. Interactivity enables the system to prompt and guide the operator through an otherwise complex set of activities. The machine, under direction of its data-entry program, can direct the operator a step at a time to enter a transaction, much like filling in the blanks of a questionnaire. The difference is that dozens or hundreds of distinctly different questionnaires can be stored ready for instant flash-up on the screen, depending on what tasks the operator is attempting to perform. Furthermore, the electronic questionnaire can be *dynamic,* with subsequent questions or prompts dependent on previous answers.

For example, if the operator is vouchering invoices for accounts payable, the machine can be programmed to ask if the transaction involves distribution to a single or to multiple expense accounts. If multiple, the program asks for account number and amount repetitively until "end" is signalled. If single, the program might ask only for the expense account number and then immediately create the single debit entry by picking up the credit, reversing the sign and transferring it to the expense-entry field, saving time and duplication.

Prompting provides continuing discipline for operators, helping them to avoid confusion and errors, and reducing the time and skill required to reach a given level of proficiency at the keyboard. This is a valuable training aid.

In certain exceptional situations, where the variety of different input formats is quite limited and the stress is on continuous, steady production analogous to straight keypunching, prompting may be "turned off," reserving its use only for training new operators.

On-line editing. With or without prompting, one of the main advantages of interactive data entry is instantaneous editing and validating of input information. It is a simple matter to program the system to expect data in a specified sequence and format and to react if the data is otherwise. The customer-number field, for instance, can be declared valid only if it consists of 5 numeric digits. If the operator keys in a mixture of alphabetic and numeric characters or enters less than or more than 5 digits, the machine can be programmed to stop, display an error message, refuse to go further until a valid customer number is input, or whatever else is appropriate.

The concept of data validation can be, and often is, extended to actually referencing the inventory file or the chart of accounts to ascertain if the stock number or the charge number is not only of the prescribed format but *actually exists*. Logical checks can be performed comparing the debits to the credits, the sum of individual items to the total, the quantity-times-unit weight to the total shipping weight, and so forth.

Self-checking number schemes can be used to verify account, customer and item codes that are otherwise subject to clerical error. The various methods have one thing in common: they add an extra digit to the tail end of the regular number, which is an arithmetic derivative of it. Then, on the way into the computer, the arithmetic formula is reapplied to the number and the result compared to the "check digit." If the input check digit doesn't "compute," an error is signalled.

Batch totals of numeric data are often prepared clerically prior to computer entry and then input and compared to the sum of individual entries. If a mistake has been made, the batch will not balance, usually requiring the operator to find the error and correct it before proceeding.

Range checks and logical tests are often used. If the highest customer number currently in use is 65967, and no customer number begins with zero, it's easy to program an input-validation routine that rejects customer numbers smaller than 10000 and greater than 69999. (Notice, we saved a little room at the top for expansion.)

The overall effect of this instant editing and validating of input is a dramatic improvement in the quality and accuracy of data entering the organization's recordkeeping system. Discovering errors at the point of entry is so advantageous compared to letting them proceed into the system that benefits need hardly be stated. But we will review them anyway.

- Errors caught at point of entry are fresh because recently made. Operators have original source data still in hand and the transaction still in mind.
- There's a big difference between knowing *which* transaction is in error and simply that something is out of kilter. The difference might

mean spending a whole day tracking it down by tracing individual entries.

Errors discovered "later," after affecting records and reports, sometimes have extremely damaging effects, far beyond whatever expensive and time-consuming effort might be required to identify and correct them. Incorrectly registering the cost of a popular stock item might lead to selling it at an unsatisfactory profit margin over a considerable period of time. Finding the error only after the next shipment arrives may fall into the "spilt milk" category. Numerous other examples can be cited where incorrect data could lead to imprecise decisions in forecasting, ordering, production scheduling, customer relations, personnel and other areas.

Inquiry. Another almost universal feature of interactive systems is inquiry; that is, the ability to initiate an unscheduled look at a particular record or a portion of a file. Gone are the old dog-eared ledger cards that contained a running history of transactions, current status and a host of penciled notations and reminders in the margins. You know, the ones you could dip into, go right to the account in question by name or number, pull the card and make sense of it in about 30 seconds, while the question was fresh or the customer still on the phone.

Unfortunately, the old ledger cards had some drawbacks: they weren't always up to date; once in a while one got lost or temporarily misplaced; and, although an enormous fund of information was there in the ledger tray, there was no practical way of getting it out on a systematic basis. Certainly, examining a specific account, or a handful, was easy, but analyzing the entire file on a regular basis was almost impossible.

When computerization came along, accuracy, timeliness and the ability to analyze and extract management information from files improved, but at the expense of simple, ready access to data which was now stored as tiny magnetized spots on disks—neat and controlled, but not very readable.

Right behind computerized files came interactive inquiry facilities to make up the difference. Inquiry gives users the ability to "dip into" the data base, as needed, to retrieve information stored there. Obviously, it doesn't provide access to history or other information that isn't a regular part of the active data base, but that information in a well-designed applications system is available elsewhere: on computer printout sheets bound into books (or on microfilm) and cataloged by date and type.

The main purpose of inquiries is to obtain up-to-the-minute information: the amount owed, the number of pieces on hand, the unexpended balance, and so forth. Usually, these requests can be categorized and planned for; therefore, they can be programmed into the applications repertoire and, like other routines, called by name or number.

A few operating systems do not support any sort of multiprogramming that would permit execution of an inquiry without disturbing other ongoing processes in the machine. Most systems, however, (even those without multiprogramming capability) have an automatic "roll-in/roll-out" feature that suspends the program currently executing, removes it from memory, replaces it with an inquiry program, executes the inquiry and then restores the original process right where it left off.

In the majority of systems likely to be encountered, it's relatively easy and nondisruptive to initiate an inquiry, receive a displayed or printed reply and continue regular work. If, however, the volume of inquiries begins to usurp a workstation or constantly distract its operator, then it may be best to dedicate a workstation entirely to the task of handling inquiries. Many users have found this to be more cost-effective than delaying production work on other terminals. Also, from the office layout point of view, it may be necessary to dedicate terminals to inquiry work to avoid constant travel to the computer room or to the data-entry department.

Menu Control—How to Tell the System What You Want It to Do

There are numerous ways that applications programs, with the help of systems software, can be set up to respond to commands from people. People have to be able to instruct the system when to begin and end a particular procedure, what type of transaction to process, when to close out and balance various control accounts, when to add a new record to a file, when to print rather than just display the response to an inquiry, and so forth.

By far the most popular method, and perhaps the most effective, is "menu selection." This is an interactive dialog between the computer and someone sitting at a workstation or terminal that begins with the operating system displaying a "master menu" and asking, from among the applications listed, which one is to be performed. A typical master menu is shown in Figure 7–2. As you can see, some of the choices have to do with processing transactions, others with maintaining files, others with general control of the system. The categories are generally too broad to pinpoint exactly what is to be done. So, backing up each entry in the master menu is a subsidiary or second-level menu that lists all the main functions that can be performed within the selected category. Figure 7–3 illustrates what might flash up on the screen after an operator depresses the digit "4" in response to the master menu shown in Figure 7–2.

The person at the keyboard, by selecting entry 4, has indicated a desire to perform some task relating to accounts receivable. To narrow the field a bit, the system displays a more detailed A/R menu which asks, "From among all these accounts receivable programs, which particular one would you like to execute?"

In the sample menu in Figure 7–3 we have 13 choices. Suppose we

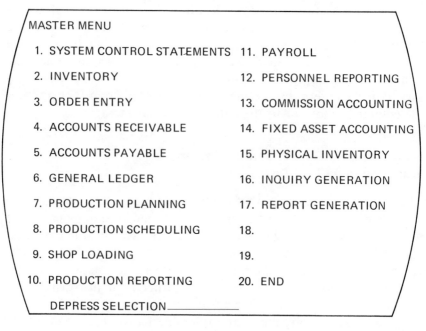

MASTER MENU

1. SYSTEM CONTROL STATEMENTS	11. PAYROLL
2. INVENTORY	12. PERSONNEL REPORTING
3. ORDER ENTRY	13. COMMISSION ACCOUNTING
4. ACCOUNTS RECEIVABLE	14. FIXED ASSET ACCOUNTING
5. ACCOUNTS PAYABLE	15. PHYSICAL INVENTORY
6. GENERAL LEDGER	16. INQUIRY GENERATION
7. PRODUCTION PLANNING	17. REPORT GENERATION
8. PRODUCTION SCHEDULING	18.
9. SHOP LOADING	19.
10. PRODUCTION REPORTING	20. END

DEPRESS SELECTION_____

Figure 7–2. Typical Master Menu.

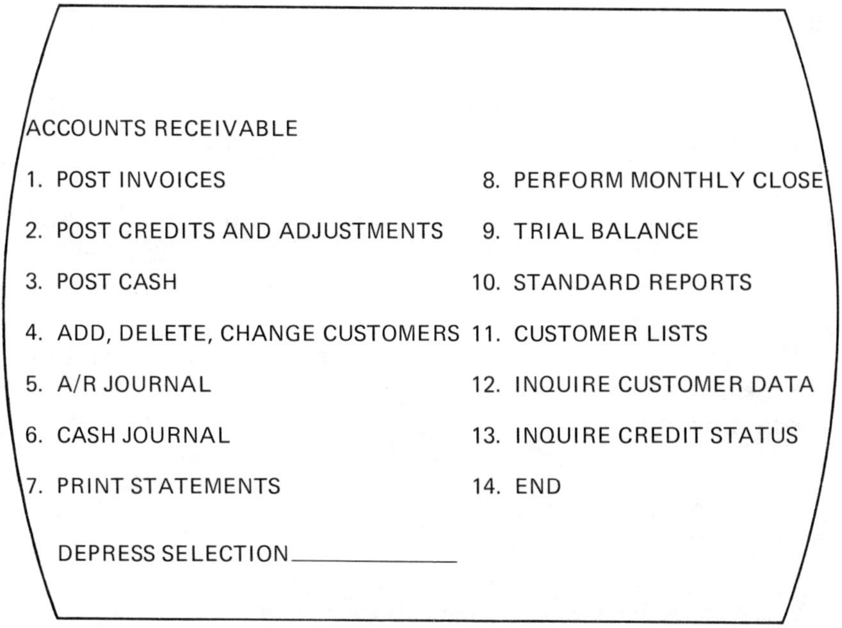

ACCOUNTS RECEIVABLE

1. POST INVOICES   8. PERFORM MONTHLY CLOSE

2. POST CREDITS AND ADJUSTMENTS   9. TRIAL BALANCE

3. POST CASH   10. STANDARD REPORTS

4. ADD, DELETE, CHANGE CUSTOMERS 11. CUSTOMER LISTS

5. A/R JOURNAL   12. INQUIRE CUSTOMER DATA

6. CASH JOURNAL   13. INQUIRE CREDIT STATUS

7. PRINT STATEMENTS   14. END

DEPRESS SELECTION_____

Figure 7-3. Typical Applications Menu.

choose to post cash. We depress "3" on the keyboard to activate the cash-posting program. (Selecting entry 14 would have caused the master menu to appear on the screen once again.)

If the choice had, indeed, been cash posting, that program itself might well have a menu or at least a series of questions to ask us about the particular batch of cash or checks to be posted, such as the "as-of" posting date, the bank deposit or batch number, perhaps whether we wish to flag or ignore unpaid service charges, unearned discounts below a given dollar amount, other discrepancies below x amount, and so on.

There are a few special cases where one might wish to bypass the menu-selection techniques by offering the operator the option of calling up a few specific procedures by title or abbreviated title. These would most logically fall into the high-production or key-punch kind of environment spoken of earlier, atypical of the way small business computers are used. In most cases the menu-selection technique turns out to be simple, foolproof and easy to learn, use and maintain.

Integration

One of the most useful and universal aspects of today's systems designs is data integration. By this we mean automatic, "built-in" interrelating of applications, one to another. A frequently used term is "interfacing," borrowed from the engineering realm where it means "compatibly interconnected." We speak of accounts payable being interfaced to the general ledger when accounts payable transactions in some way automatically generate the consequent entries to general ledger cash, expense and payable accounts.

The classic example used to illustrate integration is the order-processing application wherein the original entry of a customer order sets in motion a chain of events that:

- Checks the customer's credit
- Relieves inventory
- Posts accounts receivable
- Journalizes the sale
- Posts sales analysis and salesman's commission records

Two very important objectives are thereby achieved. First, the data is input only once, and subsequent copies or derivatives of it are posted to related accounts *without* further manual, clerical effort. Considering that clerical costs relating to data entry are going to be one, if not the *major* one, of the cost elements in a mini- or microcomputer installation, avoiding redundant entry of data is very significant.

Second, all affected records are posted with the *same* information. If the original entry was correct, then all related records are correct. One avoids receiving an order for 12 items, shipping 13, billing 15, relieving inventory of 10, repeating similar errors throughout the month, and then trying to make sense of overall financial and managerial information at the end of the period. Errors like that have a compounding effect, too. Think about the adjustments to be made when the customer returns the item he didn't order. It takes some fancy footwork to receive one, issue a credit for three and *subtract* two from inventory.

If the original entry turns out to have been in error, at least *all* related records are proportionally incorrect and unravelling or reversing the transaction is not more difficult than entering it in the first place. Almost all transaction-oriented applications are designed to include the facility to "reverse-enter" errors, automatically "backing them out of" interrelated records to clear the way for the correct data. Accountants will hasten to add that proper safeguards must be attached, including clearcut, permanent records of such reversals, so certain transactions can't be made to "disappear" from the system.

Integration can be accomplished in a number of ways, but by far the best is through a common data base, so that various applications can "communicate" with each other through their respective files. The interaction and cross-posting might occur instantaneously, as it does in a typical order-processing situation, or it might occur later, at closing time, as would typically be the case with payable records destined for the general ledger. The important thing is that the data has been entered only once, and that it is now under the care and protection of the system, stored inside the computer data base, where a great deal of electronic, accounting and systematic control will be exercised to see it doesn't get lost, altered, or forgotten.

Usually, in small business and departmental accounting systems, the general ledger turns out to be the central integrative and controlling factor. By posting all incoming transactions to *both* the relevant files and the appropriate general ledger (G/L) accounts as they enter the system, two benefits are achieved. First, the G/L is now posted. There's no further work to be done. Second, the G/L now provides "control totals" against which to balance the subsidiary accounts on a daily or periodic basis. If they agree, we can be reasonably certain that the detail has been properly posted and that it stays that way. Subsequent compensating errors in both the subsidiary application and the general ledger would be extremely unlikely because of program error or machine malfunction, but skillful human manipulation is still a cause for concern. That is why external manual controls over what goes into a computer and what comes out must be maintained, and why outside auditors are so necessary.

Your accountant or auditor will want to see that all the normal accounting and procedural safeguards are put in place. Adding-machine tapes of work batches taken by a department other than the one responsible for data entry will have to be reconciled with computer reports. Strict "audit trails" will have to be provided so that any transaction can be traced forward or backward to source and final effect throughout the system and so that no transaction or alteration of any kind can occur without leaving a written record. Other needed features might include provision for independent audit confirmation statements, assistance in the taking of, and provisions for later reconciliation with, physical inventories and the like.

Care in the design of applications, their integration and the provision for tight procedural and accounting controls will pay off handsomely in eliminating redundant posting, reducing errors, diminishing the opportunity for fraud and defalcation, and providing more and better information, available sooner.

ANATOMY OF AN APPLICATION

Just to give the reader a feeling for what goes on inside an application, let's take a highly simplified view, almost a caricature, of a portion of one. For this purpose we will examine, conceptually, part of the accounts receivable–cash posting procedure. We'll leave out most of the messy details that real programs have to contend with—like what to do if the customer record doesn't exist, the cash amount doesn't match the charges to which it is being applied, or there are discrepancies in invoice numbers, dates, service charges, or discounts. Instead, we'll concentrate on the basic functions of the program.

Figure 7-4, in "block diagram" format, depicts the fundamental sequence of activities in the program. Each block represents many individual logical steps which may ultimately require hundreds of program instructions to perform. To understand what will happen in the computer under the control of the program as a transaction is processed look at Figures 7-5 and 7-6.

1. The transaction is entered into the buffer memory of a CRT by an operator, perhaps filling in the blanks of a questionnaire-like form on the screen. The operator signals when the transaction is complete.
2. The operating system reacts to the signal by instructing the hardware to transfer the contents of the terminal buffer to a specific area of memory. The OS turns control over to the cash program, which was originally called up by the operator.
3. The cash program examines, for example, the first two characters of the transaction and, by comparison to a table stored in its portion of memory, now "knows" this is indeed a cash-posting transaction, as

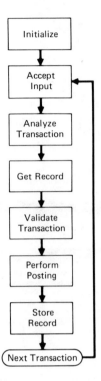

Figure 7-4. Cash Posting to Accounts Receivable—Block Diagram.

opposed to an adjustment, cancellation or some other related kind of transaction.

4. The cash program switches over to its cash-posting routine, which then examines the customer number field of the input record. We'll assume this field is the next 6 characters, which happen to contain the customer number 136790.

5. The cash program transfers that field to another area of memory, in effect delivering it over to the OS, and issues a "Get record" request. That request will also include a destination address, representing the beginning memory location into which the requested record is to be deposited.

6. The OS takes charge, suspends further execution of the cash program, looks up the physical hardware address of the requested data in its file directories and issues a command (or series of commands) to the hardware which finds the records on disk, reads it and transfers the data read to the desired area of memory.

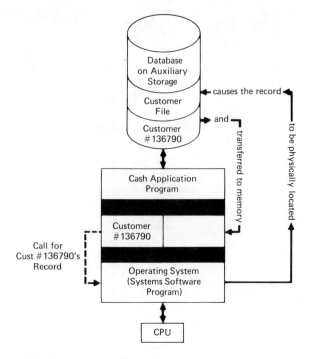

Figure 7–5. Cash Posting to Accounts Receivable—Data Flow.

7. After attending to the many housekeeping and error-controlling details that must be a part of the process, the OS returns control to the cash program at the point where it left off and restarts its execution.

8. The cash program examines the record to test if it is indeed an A/R record and that it belongs to customer number 136790.

9. If so, it then attempts to apply the cash amount to outstanding debit items it finds in the record, in accordance with the rules established in the program and any special instructions input by the operator.

As an example, this particular program might be set up to reject any cash item that does not exactly match the total of the designated charges—unless the input record carries a code from the operator that causes it to flag items as "paid," beginning with the oldest, until the next item in line would have exceeded the remaining unapplied cash, then post that remainder to the "cash-on-account" field of the customer record.

10. The cash program, after all cash items were posted and no additional input transactions remained for this customer, would tidy up a few control totals, "last posting date" field, status flags or indicators

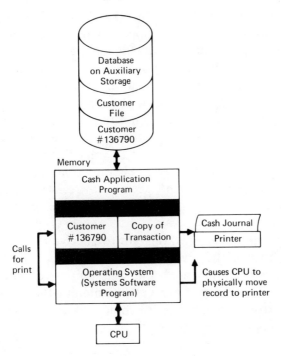

Figure 7-6. Cash Posting to Accounts Receivable—Journalizing.

and call the OS to restore customer number 136790's record to the file.

11. The OS, "remembering" where it got the record through its directories, would then cause the pathways of the machine to conduct the contents of memory containing the now updated customer accounts receivable record back to where it came from, and rewrite it in its appropriate place in the data base.

12. After completing this task, the OS returns control to the A/R program which would request another transaction, triggering the whole process over again. Or the OS might read a different kind of transaction record which signals the end of cash posting and triggers the loading and initialization, let us say, of accounts payable or some other application.

LONGEVITY

Of one thing you can be sure: any application will change through time, as business pressures, customer requirements, government regulations and general business practices change. Therefore, it is extremely important to construct applications in an open-ended fashion so they can be modified and extended, and, equally important, to be sure they're well enough documented so that this maintenance process can be accomplished without difficulty. Even the author of a program soon loses his bearings in it unless documentation is extensive, explicit and up to date. It is not unprecedented for a programmer to labor for days trying to fathom the esoteric methods he used to get around certain limitations of the machine in an old program, make changes, and then discover he's caused new, unexpected problems in the process that don't seem at all related to the changes. Finding these difficulties can be frustrating and costly, unless the documentation is there.

If your computer applications are to survive (and your business along with them), they will have to be flexible, modular, easily changeable, well documented and well supported. Otherwise they become a vise, putting you in an ever tightening "squeeze" and progressively narrowing your range of choices to meet new business conditions.

SUMMARY

Good applications are:

> Definable down to the last detail
> Clearly beneficial
> Probably interactive
> Probably menu controlled
> Integrated
> Written in a high-level language
> Modular, flexible, open-ended
> Extremely well documented

Within these strictures are a myriad of choices. The remainder of this book has mainly to do with the methods for making such choices.

8
Applications: Make or Buy, Custom or Packaged

Nothing else will ever rival applications software in its crucial impact on the success or failure of your business data processing project. Most of the hardware and accompanying systems software available today is solid, reliable and inherently capable of performing the kind of processing you are likely to need. Most computer systems can be upgraded; that is, if you've made a mistake and bought one too small or too slow, usually all it costs is more money to rectify the problem. A variation of a few thousand dollars in acquisition costs is worth taking a lot of time and effort to optimize, but it's not much compared to what you may be getting yourself into in terms of applications.

A well-crafted application can save money and time and dramatically enhance your business through better customer service, more opportune buying, scheduling, staffing, marketing and financing. It can provide the flexibility and "early warning" features needed to anticipate problems and opportunities ahead of competition.

A poorly designed application can fail to meet any or all of these objectives, add to the time and cost it takes to do business and put critical assets at unacceptable risk through loss of information and loss of control.

You probably don't need an automated system that reduces cash flow by getting out late and inaccurate billing, loses track of inventory and receivables, promotes tardy and inappropriate buying and scheduling decisions, alienates customers and employees and takes up all of your time, desperately trying to patch up the damage. Yet such a situation is an uncomfortably frequent outcome in the business-oriented small computer field, and when it does happen it results (99%) of the time) from a poor choice and/or unprofessional implementation of applications software.

Applications software makes the difference—in initial cost, cost of installation, operating effectiveness of the system and in its ongoing viability. Nothing is more important than making the right decisions in this vital area, so your attention wiil be well spent on the pages which follow.

MAKE OR BUY?

Good Programmers Are Rare and Beautiful

Almost anyone of reasonable intelligence, with a modicum of writing and arithmetic skills, the desire to succeed, a logical turn of mind and a willingness to attend to detail can learn to program. Native skill plus experience helps to make some of these people into real programming professionals. But even among the professionals there are tremendous differences in the quality and quantity of output. Some studies have revealed disparities of 11:1 in productivity of acceptable programming code between qualified individuals in the same department. There is unquestionably an art to making good programs.

There is even more mystery and art to *designing* good programs. After initial implementation, programs can be redesigned and reprogrammed with unbelievably improved results, in some cases running 2, 5, 10 or even 100 times faster than the original. Often the improved programs occupy far less space in computer memory and make far more efficient use of file storage space as well.

Designing programs requires special skills in communicating with potential users and empathizing with their needs. Structuring, coding and trouble-shooting programs takes almost inexhaustible perseverance and an aptitude for working at the minutely detailed level, without losing sight of the overall picture. Finally, a competent programmer must be as good at *documenting* what he has done as he is in doing it.

All this strongly supports a respect for professionalism in programming, leaving the job to the pros rather than taking a do-it-yourself approach.

The Do-It-Yourselfer

Many entrepreneurs and department heads are successfully doing their own systems design and programming. Several conditions have

to be met in order for this approach to have any reasonable chance
for success.

- The executive must be able to devote the extra time required. In any
  case, he or she is going to be called upon to spend many hours thinking
  about system needs, explaining them to analysts/programmers, and reviewing the proposed solutions in detail. The actual *doing* cuts down
  on the explaining but imposes a far greater amount of work in coding,
  testing and documenting programs, designing forms and CRT screen
  layouts, and planning and coordinating the physical data conversion
  and system start-up procedures. Not many active executives can afford
  to spend that much time away from regular duties without hurting the
  business in other ways.
- The would-be programmer/executive must be intellectually curious
  and highly motivated to investigate new subjects and areas of research.
  This type of individual characteristically takes on new hobbies and interests and devotes his best efforts to mastering what he wants to
  understand. He is often involved in several ongoing projects, operates
  at a high level of efficiency and can make the most of a 24-hour day.
  His motivation comes from a sense of personal challenge, and his
  commitment is intense and constant.
- The individual must have a limitless tolerance for detail. Most of us
  have wrestled with an office layout problem, wherein scaled cutouts of
  desks, chairs, cabinets and equipment are positioned and repositioned
  on a miniature of the available space laid out on graph paper. A
  number of constraints had to be considered including workflow, traffic, access to equipment for servicing, fire laws, aesthetics, phone and
  electrical outlets and, perhaps, building-floor load limits. The would-
  be programmer will have to work at that level of complexity and
  detail, *or below,* for weeks at a time! Not everybody can or wants to
  do this.

Your Place or Mine?

Even if the decision is to use professional systems design and programming talent, there are still big questions about whether to hire it
in-house or use outside services and whether to start from scratch or
use an existing applications "package."

The two questions are clearly related. If you can find a package to
buy that meets the needs of the business without further modification, the make-or-buy decision is pretty well settled. The package
is most certainly going to be cheaper because its costs of develop-

ment and support are being borne by several users, not just you. Secondly, the package holds promise of greater depth and seasoning than a from-scratch custom system, because the experience of others has helped and will continue to help uncover problems and refine the system. The catch is that the vast majority of packages are not installed without modification, and modification in this context means programming. So the question remains, who's going to do the programming?

A computer magazine, *Datamation,* mailed a survey concerning the use of packaged software to some 36,000 computer installations in late 1968. The survey showed that only 25% of the packages reported could be installed without modification, and two-thirds of the 75% that required tailoring were modified by the user organization rather than the vendor. This wasn't a small business study, per se, and it covered more systems software packages than applications, but a careful look at the details reveals that the mini-oriented applications results were not significantly different from those reported for the larger installations.

Packaged Applications

"Packaged" applications go back a long way in the computer business, but most of the present generation of small business packages began with a vendor, usually an independent software house, attempting to build upon an initial success or two with custom programming contracts. The attempts to piece together components of previously designed systems for each new user weren't always successful; many were unmanageable over time because of growing maintenance problems. A good many of the originators then went back to the drawing boards, returning with truly general-purpose systems that were more easily tailored and which retained a central "core" of programming logic that could survive from user to user. Others began on day one with a parameter-driven or generative concept and came up with general-purpose packages on the first try, not however without a thorough understanding of the full range of user requirements based on experience and/or careful research.

A recent edition of *International Computer Programs Quarterly* listed 1,600 mini- and microcomputer application packages available on the open market, so to speak, from vendors and users. Even this number is a small fraction of the total population of such packages, because many simply aren't listed and others are sold only with hardware in a single "bundled" unit, not as independent software offerings. Furthermore, user surveys and personal experience confirm that the level of buyer satisfaction with packages is good—not perfect—but good. All this bodes well for the future of packaged applications software and suggests that packages be afforded first-priority consideration.

On the other hand, a package remains a package only if it retains its basic identity and structure throughout the modification process. An absolutely uncomprising attitude on the part of a buyer can sometimes drive a business-hungry software vendor to undertake too much modification of a package. The result "looks like a houseboat with wings, and flies about as well."[1] Certainly, too, if the price of tailoring plus the cost of the basic license for the package is going to approach the cost of a completely customized development, then one has to think very hard about the pros and cons discussed below, before becoming committed to one or the other.

THE DOLLARS AND SENSE OF PROGRAMMING

There are three fundamental cost components to most acquired software: initial cost, including planned modifications; costs of unanticipated changes and adjustments; and ongoing maintenance expense. The first is generally a known figure, the others subject to wide and almost unpredictable variations. Let's take them one at a time.

Initial Costs

The size and complexity of each particular set of small business applications will obviously vary a good deal. In one article the author estimated from-scratch development costs for the "typical" set to fall in the range of $25,000-70,000.[2] In an attempt to escape such high initial costs, users as often as not employ preprogrammed pack-

---

[1,2] D. R. Shaw, "Software Costs in Automating Small Business," *ICP Interface: Mini-Small Business Systems* (Winter, 1977): 11–14.

ages. In order to make good use of a package, it must be a good one to begin with, must come reasonably close to meeting the need of the business, and whatever modification or tailoring is involved must not do violence to the basic integrity of the package or to the purchaser's pocketbook.

Within those constraints, the user can buy a set of minicomputer programs "through the mail," that is, with documentation but no personal assistance or modification support. At this writing, a representative complement (consisting of order processing, inventory, accounts receivable, accounts payable, payroll, sales analysis and general ledger) costs around $5,000. To whatever extent tailoring and/or unique installation problems are encountered, the user shoulders these responsibilities himself.

Another, perhaps more conservative, approach is to deal with a software house (or the computer vendor) that is willing to undertake modifications of the packages to fit them to the user's requirements and, usually, to assist in their installation. The prices for this kind of service, including license fees for use of the packages, tend at this point in time to run in the $6,000 to $10,000 range for a typical assortment of applications.

Some packages offer self-customizing features in the form of easily altered parameter tables that make it possible to specify titles, column headings, editing rules, computational formulas, discount factors, general account structure and titles, and a selection of options to control paying, purchasing, ordering and other operations.

IBM's Industry Applications Programs (IAP's) for Systems 32 and 34 are examples. Among many different industry packages is one called Construction Management Accounting Systems (CMAS) for contractors. Within fixed limits in terms of the size and number of records allowed and the specific recording, accounting, and reporting options offered, the contractor can, by filling out a questionnaire, cause a unique, tailored version of the programs to be generated for his use. Current CMAS prices are as follows:

Payroll:	$55 per month	
Job Costing:	32 "	"
General Ledger	32 "	"
Accounts Payable:	40 "	"

A contractor who required any programming whatever would need an RPG II compiler at $27 per month. Assuming the contractor sends two students to IBM's implementation school at $420 each and one student to both basic and advanced programming school for another $549, the outlay becomes $1,416 for training plus $186 per month for 5 years. That works out to about $12,000 over the 5-year period, not including any programing the contractor or his staff might do in the interval.

Univac offers a similar arrangement on their BC-7 machine, except that user parameters are interpreted "on the fly," each time the programs are executed instead of being generated into the program only once in a more or less fixed manner. Theoretically, there could be some loss of operating efficiency in Univac's approach, but the ability to alter parameters without a costly regeneration of the software system is an advantage. Univac's software pricing appears comparable but somewhat lower than IBM's.

Retail computer stores very recently have begun to offer "over-the-counter" business applications sets designed for "do-it-yourself" installation of a surprisingly comprehensive nature and at surprisingly low prices. It is not unusual to find a parameterized menu-driven complement of BASIC programs written for one or more of the popular "hobby" microcomputers (upgraded for business processing) including order processing, invoicing, inventory control, accounts receivable, accounts payable, payroll and general accounting for a price under $1,000. Of course, these programs are quite restrictive in the number and size of records accommodated, the complexity of logical operations available and in overall flexibility. And they usually come with little or no support from the seller: just an instruction booklet and interactive prompting within the software itself.

Not long ago it would have been possible to dismiss such programs as toys. Now, one should be cautious about eliminating the alternative out of hand. There definitely is a small but growing number of businesses, perhaps on the "low end" of the volume and complexity scale, making successful use of these micro-business systems; and the quality, variety and utility of the software is bound to improve still further with time. However, since there are so many of these systems making an appearance, most without any local technical backing, it is very difficult for the user to choose among them and to be certain that any particular one will meet his present and future requirements in actual operation.

A more conservative approach is the "turnkey" package wherein one vendor, usually a software house, delivers both hardware and tailored packages, installed and ready to run, at a single "bundled" price. The buyer, presumably, merely turns the key to commence processing. A typical price of $50,000 might include a minicomputer, which if purchased directly from the manufacturer would cost $35,000. In addition to the $15,000 difference, the turnkey house also typically gets a 30% or greater original equipment manufacturer (OEM) discount on the hardware, so his total margin is closer to $25,000 in this example. That is his price to analyze the user's needs, specify and carry out the agreed-upon modifications to the packages, confer a license to use the resulting software and take full responsibility for the result—at least in terms of meeting the written specifications ratified by the customer.

The next and final stage is completely custom, from-scratch development of a system to meet the exact, and possibly unique, requirements of the user. Whether done inside with staff professionals or externally by a software house, this kind of a development project is not likely to cost less than $25,000 and frequently runs in the $50,000–100,000 category, including design, development, installation and sometimes, but not always, data conversion.

Figure 8-1 summarizes the "ball park" ranges in which the initial costs of applications software are likely to fall, depending on which of the procurement options as described above are elected.

Last-Minute Surprises

As you, your systems analyst or an outsider begin peeling away the layers of your application needs in progressively greater detail, significant discoveries will be made, requiring new and sometimes difficult choices. Procedures which looked fairly simple and straightforward in the early stages will prove to contain complex and previously overlooked exceptions. You will have to decide which of the exceptions and complicated nuances to insist upon incorporating into the computerized procedures, which to continue to handle on a manual basis external to the computer and which to forego altogether.

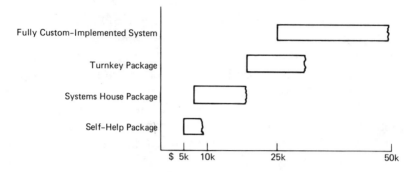

Figure 8-1. Approximate Ranges of Anticipated "Typical" Small Business Software Purchase Costs.

NOTE: D. R. Shaw, "Software Costs in Automating Small Business," ICP Interface: Mini-Small Computer Business Systems (Winter 1977): 11–14. Reprinted with permission from *ICP Interface*, a publication of International Computers Programs, Inc., Indianapolis, Indiana.

You might encounter a situation like this. Federal regulations require that a terminated employee be provided with an IRS form W-2 wage statement summarizing his earnings and taxes-to-date within 30 days of his termination. Normally, of course, W-2's are produced en masse at the end of each year. A proposed payroll package, let us assume, handles year-end W-2's but makes no provision for printing out W-2's on an exception basis throughout the year. Should you insist that the vendor modify the package to incorporate that feature? Chances are if you anticipate only an occasional midyear termination you'd simply decide to prepare the W-2 manually, typing from information contained on earning reports from the last pay period worked by the employee.

But suppose the question had to do with automatic triggering of backorders upon receipt of the awaited merchandise. If you're a candidate for order processing and happen to be in a business where backordering is prevalent and voluminous, then automatic allocation of incoming stock to backorders could be very important. Many order-processing packages don't do this automatically. Those that do may not employ the exact stock-allocation method you prefer. In this case you might decide to negotiate a rather major extension to the vendor's order-processing package.

Regardless of what occasions an extension or alteration, or what application it applies to, it is sure to be more expensive and traumatic the later it turns up. For example, if the issue arises during the initial proposal stages, while the vendor is still anxious to get a signed contract, he's likely to be more compliant (and at more reasonable prices) than if it comes up later as an unexpected addition. Also, the further the design and development moves along, the harder and more expensive it becomes to make changes. If the desired alterations aren't thought of until after *installation,* it's a little like altering the foundation after the concrete is poured. Perhaps it can be done, but perhaps also not without delaying the project and adding considerably to its cost.

This is certainly a good argument for doing the best possible job of analyzing requirements *before* detailed work on the system begins. Yet, it's impossible to think of everything. Some deficiencies and peculiarities simply will not surface until well into the implementation phase. Second, changes may occur in the business and regulatory climate after the system is specified. Not long ago, the IRS detailed a whole new category of payment advances for certain employees earning under $10,000 per year against something called "Earned Income Credit." These advances, when elected by eligible employees, are computed from special tables, are not subject to normal withholding taxes and are accountable in a completely new manner. No payroll program, no matter how well specified, could possibly have incorporated this complex new procedure prior to its recent introduction.

All of the foregoing is simply a way of showing that unexpected changes and extensions to any system will arise during design and development. These changes will in many cases fall outside the scope of the original design, be disruptive and add cost to the project. It's hard to put an estimate on such a variable factor, but it is not unusual for the user to spend an extra 10–30% beyond the contract price for additions or corrections of features that reflect peculiarities of his business.

Ongoing Maintenance

Another absolute certainty in the realm of applications software is *change* over time. Even if the system works perfectly and performs every desired function exactly as specified on the day of installation, not many days or weeks will transpire before new conditions develop requiring changes to the system. New government regulations, such as the payroll procedure described earlier, are notorious for throwing otherwise adequate, stable systems into disarray.

Changing business conditions can play havoc, too. Suppose you wholesale merchandise to retailers and your competitors begin delivering shelf-label and item-label stickers with each shipment, uniquely described and priced for each customer. Adding a label-writing system to your order-processing application which "remembers" each retailer's nomenclature and retail price for every stockkeeping unit you carry may be a tall order. Yet, this is exactly the kind of change that many wholesale drug companies have had to face recently to meet customer demands and competitive pressures.

Another example is the importer who made it a policy never to order more frequently than once per "lead time," which had the effect of creating one or at most two consignments en route from his overseas sources for a given item at any one moment of time. In specifying his purchase-ordering and tracking system he made allowances for a maximum of *three* in-transit shipments "to be on the safe side." During a recent Gulf Coast dock strike of unprecedented duration, this importer had as many as *twenty* different consignments of certain items tied up at sea in the holds of ships waiting to be unloaded, only three of which his computer was prepared to keep track of.

Mergers, acquisitions, new ventures and new product lines and services are a never-ending source of changing system requirements. Who can say with certainty that the nature and structure of his business will be the same even a year from today? Experience suggests that applications programs "turn over" in some stated time period (4, 6, 10 years); that is, as many new program steps are added or substituted in that period of time as there originally were in the total system. In terms of dollars, it probably means that the average user will buy his applications software at least twice during a 5-year period. Even if his "turnover" isn't 100% the changes over time will be piecemeal, so they will cost more than the first time around.

For example, assume a user has purchased a license to use a set of packages, which together with initially contracted modifications came to $15,000. During implementation and testing, let us say, he modified and extended his requirements for another $3,000 worth of design and programming, so his total cost is $18,000 for software. It's not unlikely that his total system now contains at least 10,000 "lines of code" (individual program steps). If he modifies or extends only 5% of it per year, which is decidedly on the low side, at the end of 5 years another 2,500 lines of program code would have been added or substituted. At today's going rate for programming, including testing and documentation, the cost would equal or exceed $18,000. And, if he had seen fit to retain only a single programmer, even part-time, during that 5-year period, his cost would have totaled several times $18,000.

In computerese, the sum total activity involved with keeping systems current over time is called program or system "maintenance." As has been established, program maintenance can be a substantial cost, no matter what. If done poorly, or if the original system doesn't lend itself to being maintained, then the user can find himself in big trouble. The importer referred to earlier had to "junk" his software sytem and start over for a number of reasons, including the one stated. The biggest problem in his case was that he didn't have rights or access to the original source code and program documentation, the supplier having relegated this responsibility exclusively to himself, and the supplier refused or was unable to perform the required program maintenance to keep the system alive. Without maintenance, systems rapidly deteriorate. Thus, maintenance is both expensive and crucial. Some concrete, reliable arrangement for ongoing program maintenance must be carefully thought out and arranged at the outset; otherwise, you will be figuratively lashing your business to the mast of a ship destined to sink slowly beneath the waves. Better make sure you have a crew standing by to patch the cracks, pump the bilges and keep the old tub in shape to respond to your commands from the bridge.

SUMMARY

Nothing is more crucial to the success of your foray into data processing than applications software. You must choose the right system, be it packaged or customized, make the proper arrangements for programming, both initial and ongoing, and make sure you are on solid economic, technical and contractual ground all the way.

Within these broad strictures are a world of choices. You can buy a preprogrammed package and modify and maintain it yourself. Or you can hire full- or part-time staff to do it. You can also purchase, or build, a completely custom software system exactly to your specifications.

The software, if anything other than a completely in-house effort, can be obtained from the computer manufacturer, from a software house, from a "turnkey" house that supplies both hardware and software or, literally, through the mail or off the shelf of a computer store. A package, if it fits, is generally a better and more economical choice. However, modification before, during and after installation is almost inevitable.

In order to undertake the long, possibly dangerous automation voyage, you are going to have to learn quite a bit about navigation so that it goes where *you* want, not the reverse. If you decide to "go it alone," you had better be, or had better become, at least a semiprofessional, and have the time to devote to it. Most of us will want to keep some experienced crew members involved, if not onboard, at least standing by for repairs and, perhaps, an occasional midsea rescue.

9
How Do I Know
If I Need One?

The author remembers calling on a wholesaler and servicer of a specialty equipment line who had actually ordered a computer and now wanted confirmation of his decision. After a few hours of conversation it was learned that this distributor had about 90% of the available business in his line within his market area, he personally knew every stockkeeping item in his warehouse and approximately how much of each he had on hand, his overhead costs were extremely low, his profits very favorable, his staff capable, stable and of long tenure.

Why did he want a computer? It turned out that the extremely comprehensive and well-thought-out manual reporting system he had devised for himself, although perfectly adequate otherwise, was running 18 days behind in posting. On further questioning it was revealed that the owner's wife, who formerly assisted in the office as both a quasi-office manager and bookkeeper was now at home awaiting the arrival of a new offspring. The answer was, of course, that she needed to be replaced by a competent, full-time office supervisor. Apparently the owner found it easier to order a computer than to think about facing his spouse with her replacement.

KNOWING THE PRESENT SYSTEM

Absolutely, without question or exception, the first step toward any new system is a thorough understanding of the present one. Nothing but good can come of such an effort. First, a painstaking analysis of the current system will reveal ways to improve it now, without waiting for automation. Second, the analysis may reveal that automation is unnecessary or impractical, or the improvements that can be effected immediately may render computerization superfluous. In either case, a great deal of money and effort may be saved. Third, a precise picture of current methods, forms, workflows and volumes is the foundation necessary for defining and designing the new system. Finally, understanding the current system implies tying down its costs, which forms the basis for cost-justifying proposed changes.

Preliminaries

Almost without qualification, it's a good idea to pursue the kind of rigorous, detailed analysis of the present system that will be recommended in the next few pages, regardless of whether automation is in the offing or not. Most people won't undertake it, however, unless there's an inkling or two that (1) a computer is probably justified and (2) verifying the fact requires such an investigation.

So, let us examine some of the telltale signs that suggest the likelihood of a payoff from computerization, one or more of which probably led you to begin reading this book in the first place.

1. Indicators. There are many measures indicative of the success of a business or institution. Not all apply to any one enterprise, and those that do, tend to be relative rather than absolute. But *something* may be making you uncomfortable about the performance of your business.

- *Disappointing revenue growth.* Either relative to the past, to the economy as a whole, or to competition, business growth is not keeping pace. The problem may be addressable with better customer service; faster response; greater accuracy; quicker restocking, production and/or manpower-deployment decisions; better management of the marketing function through more accurate, more comprehensive information available sooner; or, perhaps, pinpointed direct marketing support using computerized mailings or phone lists—any and all of which might result from the installation of data processing.
- *Disturbing profit trends.* Relative to history, the rest of the industry or the ambitions of management, profits (or cost-effectiveness, in the case of nonprofit organizations) may not be up to standard. The fault may be insufficient revenue growth or it may result from excessive costs. Cost factors addressable by

computer include direct displacement of current clerical and recordkeeping functions with lower-cost automation; more optimal buying and/or production decisions to lower direct costs; and the reduction of overhead through stimulating greater volume, better product or service mix and more optimal scheduling of resources.

· *Various financial and statistical indications of suboptimal operation.* Lengthening of the average age of receivables; increase in bad debt losses; excessive downtime, overtime, scrap and shrinkage; reduction in the ratio of earning to sales, equity, or assets employed; reduced turnover of inventory or other key assets; reduced dollars of revenue per order, per salesman, per customer, or per employee, and many other factors may be addressable by computerization. Just to take one area as an example, computers have been notably successful in improving the credit and collections function in many companies by policing credit limits more effectively, speeding cash flow through faster billing with fewer disputes over errors and inconsistencies, and by following up delinquencies sooner, with greater consistency and overall impact.

Also, computers are very good at scheduling limited resources, such as manpower, machinery and events, because they can be programmed to try all possible solutions, quickly identifying the one that produces the highest revenue, lowest cost, shortest elapsed time or whatever the desired outcome happens to be.

2. Other sources of dissatisfaction. There are problem symptoms which may be of a more intangible nature. While it's unlikely that any of these could exist without having an adverse effect on the indicators referred to above, the relationship may be subtle and difficult to pinpoint. For example:

· *A chaotic work environment.* Disorder, disarray, errors, omissions, missed commitments and an atmosphere of crisis in which people frantically rush from problem to problem—this kind of situation is usually rationalized as being the result of overwork and/or shorthandedness. One approach, certainly, is to lighten the load by putting some of it on a computer. As a general rule, however, one must be sure the chaos isn't more deeply imbedded in organization and methodology.

· *Personnel problems.* Poor morale, as evidenced by sloppy work habits, complaints, excessive turnover, and a negative atmosphere may be addressable by lightening the burden, providing more predictable results and introducing an exciting and interesting new tool in the form of data processing. But, this could also make things even worse, if the problem runs too deep.

· *Lack of information.* A very frequent management frustration in any business is simply knowing too little about what is happening and what is likely to happen. Not knowing one is overrunning the budget on a particular project until the money is already spent; failure to recognize a sudden shift in customers' ordering patterns; lack of awareness of adverse trends in productivity, margins, utilization and so forth are all amenable to computerization.

If there is one area in which computing systems shine brightest, it is in the information-management aspect, providing refined data, previously unavailable by any other means, with great accuracy and timeliness. The reason is obvious: computers are no better at originally posting data than many manual or mechanical systems, but when it comes to remanipulating the posted data, they have no peer. A typical system can read 10,000 records of 400 characters each in the space of about 5 minutes. Imagine how long it would take a bookkeeper to physically remove each of 10,000 ledger cards from a tray and copy down some information or visually scan each one to see if selected data is present and meets certain specified conditions. How many mistakes is the human counterpart to the computer likely to make as this fatiguing and boring task stretches on hour after hour?

A well-conceived data processing system makes maximum use of the *information* hidden in mounds of *data*. When the data is processed, analyzed, selected, summarized and presented in a digestible form, and somebody in authority looks at it, good things can begin to happen. As long as the important trends that spell *opportunity* and the telltale symptoms of loss and poor control that spell *risk* remain obscured in a welter of detail, nothing can be done to prepare for either. A computer can be readily programmed to filter out the random "noise" in any set of figures and highlight any change that represents a probable alteration in an underlying trend. Spectacular results are being obtained with computers, for example, in the realm of inventory and merchandising management, employing relatively simple statistical analyses of demand data.

· *Lack of uniformity.* A computer doesn't take coffee breaks, get absentminded, become easily overworked or exercise poor judgment. (The latter is true because it exercises no judgment at all: you do, through the logic of the programs.) Data processing procedures demand, and produce, the utmost in consistency; that is, when the equipment is in proper working order and the programs completely "bug free" the computer system puts out perfect work for days or weeks at a time.

Perhaps your business operates well for a time and then suffers one of its chronic, periodic, and unexpected crises in which everything seems to go wrong, fall behind schedule, overrun budget or turn out more scrap than product. The stabilizing influence of computer procedures could help, as could the computer's ability to absorb peak overloads with relative ease.

Getting to the Bottom of Things

Given some reasonable suspicion that all is not perfect in your present system, the next step is to find out what parts of it need to be changed, in what way, and at what tolerable cost. To do this, you need to assemble a diagram of the flow of information throughout your entire operation, together with copies of the forms and documents used, sufficient explanatory narrative to describe what's happening and why at each stage, and a count of minimum, average and peak volume levels of each component of the system.

One very good way of doing this is to paste actual forms posted with sample data on large poster boards, interconnecting them with lines to indicate flow and with boxes to indicate the various processes the data undergoes. Brief explanations should annotate each step.

Figure 9-1 is an oversimplified, small segment of a real system, but the basic principle is there. Once you have diagrammed the whole process of paper and information handling within your entire business you will probably be struck immediately by two impres-

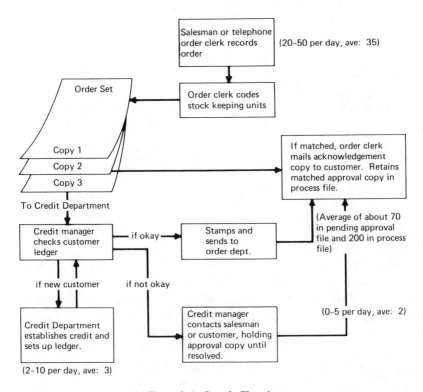

Figure 9–1. Sample Flowchart.

sions: (1) how surprisingly complex and voluminous it is, and (2) how many clumsy and/or unnecessary steps you can spot at once.

In Figure 9–1, why record the order, send a copy to the credit department, hold a copy, and go through a 100% match-up with credit-approved copies? Why not supply the order clerk with an alphabetical customer listing with stickers or notations on doubtful accounts? About 90% of the orders can then slide through without any further delay, and only new and doubtful accounts will be referred to the credit department.

The volume and complexity of the charts can be reduced considerably by condensing the procedures and flow diagrams onto smaller sheets, perhaps 8½" × 11", referring to the forms by name or number, with samples attached separately as a group, rather than as an integral part of the charts. Figure 9–2 illustrates how such a condensed chart might appear.

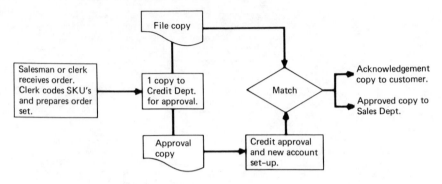

Figure 9-2. Condensed Flowchart Example.

Determining Costs

Equal in importance to understanding *what* is currently happening is knowing how much it's costing. High-cost procedures are good candidates for streamlining, and unless you know what the old procedure costs, you can't measure the relative merits of any proposed improvements.

Suppose you or someone in your organization comes up with the following suggestion: "Let's cut down on the number of parts in our expensive multiple-copy forms by purchasing a copier and using reproductions in place of the carbon copies." Good idea? Who knows? First of all, you have to know for what and how often it will be used. Reference to flowcharts, if you have them, will quickly identify the multi-part forms in use, and where and in what quantity they're being used. Looking at the workflow will readily tell you which procedures it is feasible to interrupt with a trip to the copying machine.

The volume or quantity counts will serve two purposes. First, they are the basis for determining the possible savings on forms. Reference to recent invoices from the supplier and to quotations on reduced or simplified forms will show the difference in the two prices for a given order size. This difference times quantity used equals potential savings. Second, the copier costs are probably volume related, too, so you need anticipated copy counts to figure out what the monthly expense of running the copier is going to be.

Now what about people costs? If you have developed some reasonably good estimates as to how much time each phase of the present procedure is absorbing, you have the final ingredient for an intelligent determination of how much manpower cost the proposed change is going to add or save.

Knowing who and how many people are spending what amount of time on each major element of the present system is crucial to all the subsequent analysis and decision making you will undertake. For example, how does an automobile dealer know whether it makes sense to install a computerized inventory-posting system in his parts department? Let's suppose right now that the personnel at the parts department counter look up the part in the catalog by model and year to get proper nomenclature and price, post to the work order or sales slip, retrieve the part and leave the inventory posting, reordering and other recordkeeping for subsequent batch handling by clerks.

Let's suppose there is a proposal before the house to use a weekly printout provided by a service bureau to which will be pencil-posted all receipts and issues by the countermen as each transaction occurs, bypassing any subsequent clerical operation by returning the marked printout to the bureau for week-end processing. However, this second look-up and the tallying of sales is likely to slow down service at the counter. Or is it? How much time is now being spent searching in the wrong bin for items or looking for items that aren't in stock? The printout will show which items aren't stocked and, among those that are regularly stocked, which are currently in or out of stock, and where in the parts department they can be found. How much time is now being spent updating catalog price lists with changes? Prices on the printout will be maintained automatically by the service bureau in response to the latest releases from the factory.

Any question of systems changes are going to come down to balancing the cost of the improvements against the benefits, and part of the calculation of both has to do with the cost of what is being displaced. In our auto parts department example, if the clerk who does the posting now has other essential duties but is not fully occupied by them, then there may be no clerical cost displacement. In other words, if 25% of Millie is going to be eliminated, but the other 75% remains, and vivisection continues to be illegal, there isn't much in the way of cost reducing you can do. If, on the other hand, the time freed can be productively employed in another area where changes are being contemplated, then it's logical to offset part of the cost of the proposed service with 25% of Millie's salary and fringe benefit expenses.

We could not have made any of these observations, however, until we knew who was performing the various functions involved and how much time was actually being spent on each. This leads to the subject of work measurement.

Work Measurement

As a companion to your workflow analysis showing forms, files and procedural flow of information, you need a catalog of costs for each major element of your system. Probably the largest single component of record-keeping costs is going to be people costs, so, for the moment, let's concentrate on that.

You need a reasonably accurate estimate of how many hours of each staff member's time is being spent on each major subdivision of the work during a given time period (daily, weekly or monthly as appropriate). For example, you may determine that, in the case of accounts receivable, daily posting of invoices and adjustments takes an average of 90 minutes and cash 30 minutes, except between the 15th and 27th of the month when the latter runs about 2 hours. In addition, at the end of the month, you might find that trial balancing and statement preparation take three full 8-hour days plus 4 hours of overtime, and that preparation of ageing and credit analysis reports takes another day after the monthly close. In a typical 22-day month, that works out to approximately 96 regular hours plus 4 overtime hours per month. If we know *who* is spending that time and how much the individual is being paid, we can calculate the labor cost component of A/R processing for the present system. Let's suppose that cost is $5.00 per hour plus 20% for fringe benefits. That gives us $6.00 times, for simplicity, 102 hours, or $612 per month.

Furthermore, if we know the amortization and maintenance costs of the posting machine and the costs of all the forms, ledgers and statements used, we can arrive at a total figure that pretty accurately reflects what it costs to process receivables. Let's say it's $775 per month. Now when a minicomputer or service bureau proposal comes along which would eliminate all or part of that posting and processing, we can quickly assess the resulting cost offsets (being careful to add back in the cost of any new preparation and manual control effort required to get the data ready for computer processing and to keep the computer honest).

If the service bureau wants to charge us $600 per month for A/R processing and we need to invest about 30 hours per month at $6.00 per hour in batching and totaling invoices and payments, we have a "wash" financially. In this particular case we needn't delude ourselves that the proposed service is going to save money, but there may be some other powerful benefits, such as greater legibility of statements, more detailed analysis of sales, or more useful credit reports that make the service worthwhile.

From another perspective, we now know how much A/R can "contribute" to the justification of a computer. If the computer is going to eliminate all of the current operation, substituting a new system which includes all the functions enumerated, then we have $775 per month to help offset the many and varied costs of the computerized system—including hardware, software, maintenance, operators, supervision, forms, space, power, and so forth.

Work Measurement Techniques

Libraries have been written on the subject of time and work analysis. For the typical small business office environment, however, the range of truly practical choices is limited to estimation, logging and observation.

Estimation. In some situations, people doing the work, their direct supervisor, or a combination of the two can provide a reasonably accurate breakdown of how each individual's time is being spent. This is especially true in highly uniform and repetitive jobs like counterman, cashier, service dispatcher, receiving clerk and so forth. In a more varied "back office" environment it may still be possible for bookkeepers or clerks to account for their time on an estimation basis. And, since precise accuracy is not required, this method may be good enough.

Logging. If people customarily do a number of different tasks, intertwined in varying mixes day to day, it may be necessary to resort to a more detailed and more accurate method of measurement. One of these is logging. The simplest method is to supply each person involved with some forms. Time periods should be marked across the top of these forms, and tasks performed should be indicated along the side. The time spent on each job can then be shown by drawing a line across the page. Figure 9–3 is an example of such a form. The functional categories apply to office secretaries. An accounting clerk or an assistant buyer would have an entirely different list, but the general format would remain the same. Note in the example that each instance of handling an incoming or outgoing telephone call was of such short duration that it was merely indicated with a check mark. Later, if important, an average time factor could be calculated.

What you're after is a rough estimate of how the work day, week

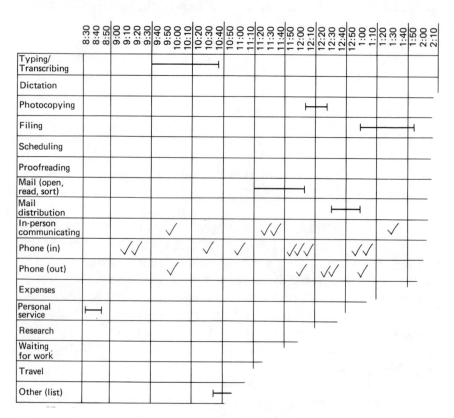

Figure 9–3. Administrative Time Log.

or month breaks down by function and applicational task. For example, you might discover that, on the average, your bookkeeping machine operator spends 77% of his productive time actually working the machine and the rest on miscellaneous tasks like filling in for the telephone order clerk when he's on a coffee break. What's more important, however, is how that 77% breaks down between receivables, payables, payroll and general accounting; and, perhaps, within one of them, such as payables, how much time is spent trial balancing and writing checks versus recording the original vendor invoices. It might be that in a new computerized system, the balancing and check-writing function will be completely replaced by an automatic procedure, but that each liability will still have to be recorded via a keyboard, perhaps with 20% improvement in speed compared to the old semiautomatic method. If that were the case, one could immediately identify all of the accounts payable balancing and check-writing hours plus 20% of the vouchering hours as potentially saved, hence as offsets against the total cost of operating the new system.

Observation. Reasonably accurate estimates of where your personnel expense dollars are incurred should be provided by estimating or logging. If those methods are judged to be inappropriate or of insufficient accuracy, then you can resort to the use of an independent observer—yourself, an industrial engineer, or a consultant, for example.

In an office environment the Statistical Work Sampling or Ratio Delay method will surely suffice. In this method, an observer takes a random route through the office at random times, based on a random number table. Statistical formulas specify how many times this must be done for what size office over what length of time to achieve statistically reliable results. The observer notes down what each person is doing as he passes each particular workstation on his rounds. At the conclusion of the study, the *ratio* between numbers of observations are a valid indicator of the *proportion* of effort spent on various tasks.

For example, suppose out of a total of 472 individual observations made randomly over a 10-day period, 126 notations were either "idle" or "away from desk" and the remainder, 346, were accountable to various tasks. We could deduce that 346/472 or 73% of the office time was being spent productively. Then, if the number of observations of "posting inventory" were 41, we could compute that 41/346 or 11.8% of the total *productive* effort in the office was being spent on inventory control. Other tasks would be worked out similarly.

This is a necessarily condensed explanation of the method to introduce the concept and help you determine if it might be appropriate to your situation. If you are interested, you'll probably want to seek more information and/or outside help in planning your study. Much more complete information is available from the *Industrial Engineering Handbook*[1] or from the numerous publications cataloged under the subject of Industrial Engineering–Work Measurement.

The payoff. If this kind of analysis seems like a big effort—it is. Nevertheless, it's something you should do in any case. It's a good idea to go through a complete systems and cost analysis of every major step of your present information and accounting procedure whether you intend to install data processing or not, just to see where the dollars and hours are going and where the problems are. Identifying problems and high-cost aspects is going to set off a chain of thought that leads inevitably to improvements.

Charting a Better Course

As a by-product of your procedural, volume and cost analysis of the present system, you are sure to identify aspects ripe for improvement. You're likely to end up with convictions like: "It's costing us too much to account for receipt of purchased goods!" or "We've got to speed up our quotation process for auto and home owners' coverages, either by automating it or better organizing it!" or "I can't readily see where to put our advertising dollars, but if I could draw from order processing an analysis of sales broken down by category of product and service for each territory and customer class, then I could begin to do some fine tuning."

Every businessman and administrator has a backlog of complaints, problems and unfulfilled needs regarding the methods he or

[1]H. B. Maynard, ed., *Industrial Engineering Handbook,* (New York: McGraw-Hill Book Co., 1963), pp. 379–398.

she presently works with. Analyzing the present system in detail will sharpen the perception of these limitations, bring them back to mind forcefully and will illuminate other previously overlooked opportunities for improvement. The combination will likely come down to a long list of desired improvements which can be classified into "must-have" and "nice-to-have" categories—the former for those things without which a new system isn't worth installing and the latter for those that should be included if at all possible.

An example of a "must-have" item might be: "a cash requirement statement showing total accounts payable liabilities spread by due date into at least the next three and preferably five biweekly periods." An example of a "nice-to-have" feature in a new accounts payable system might be: "the ability to automatically calculate due date based on invoice date and terms and to add a specified number of days beyond the calculated date based on general policy for non-discountable items."

Systems specifications. At the very least, what you will end up with is a complete anatomy of your present system together with a list of desired improvements. That in itself will be an enormous help to whoever is going to bid on or design your new system. Once you've come this far, it's not much more difficult, however, to develop your own design specifications, at least at the broad conceptual level. Ideally, you should chart the flow of procedural steps in your new idealized system, showing forms, documents and reports, the data they contain, volumes and a description of the functions that need to be performed at each stage. If you're not quite enough of a systems analyst to go that far, or perhaps are still somewhat undecided about exactly how the new system should function, then the very least you should do is prepare a formal list of required features and functions, *including those you wish to carry over from your old system;* there will be many such desired carryovers. This combined list will define what you want out of the new system and which aspects of the current method are to be supplanted by it.

For example, suppose part of your new specifications includes: "Invoice preparation will use essentially the same invoice form as at present, but with the addition of total weight and estimated freight charge calculation based on the following formula." You have told a prospective supplier exactly what you want, and pretty much in what form or format you want it. You've also told yourself about two things you're no longer going to do after the *new* method is implemented—extend and type invoices and manually calculate and add transportation charges in the shipping department. You should, by this point, know how much it's costing to perform those two functions, so the dollars saved can be calculated to show how much of the costs of the new system they offset.

In the same way, you should go through the entire procedure, application by application, until you have specified what is wanted from the new system and how much offsetting cost will be saved thereby. Keeping specifications and savings segregated by application and by function within application will be helpful later in making possible adjustments and compromises in your idealized plan, in the event some of what you want proves to be impractical or uneconomic. Following along with the cited example, it may turn out that size and weight factors for each stockkeeping unit are too variable or require too much recordkeeping to permit accurate estimation of transportation charges. In that case, one might give up on the particular feature, add in the cost of a computerized postbilling adjustment procedure for adding actual shipping charges, and take the shipping department's weighing and posting costs back out of the savings offset total.

Figure 9-4 is an example of a basic requirements statement by one company regarding one particular application. Notice that the offsetting savings are spelled out. This statement would normally be backed up with more detail, including flowcharts, descriptions, volumes and copies of forms in use and, perhaps, rough layouts of desired new forms and reports. Thus have we defined the old system, the new system with desired improvements and the various tasks that will be displaced from the old to new.

TANGIBLE AND INTANGIBLE SAVINGS

At this point we're a long way down the trail of identifying the savings and benefits from the new system, at least by reference to the tasks it will replace. The tangible, directly measureable savings are fairly easy to price out; however, its wise to go through a checklist to see that nothing has been left out.

SYSTEM NAME: ORDER ENTRY/BILLING

DESCRIPTION:

- Order entry through CRT (Cathode Ray Tube)
- Automatic preparation of picking tickets
- Automatic preparation of invoices (including taxing, discounting, pricing, and extending)
- Automatic backorder capability
- Automatic posting to the General Ledger
- Automatically generates commission data

	ANNUAL RECURRING BENEFITS	
	Unmeasured	Estimated
BENEFITS:		
· Reduced Xerox costs		$ 5,800
· Elimination of billing clerk		9,600
· Gross profit by line item or invoice	---	
· Legibility and appearance of invoice	---	
· Improved speed of mailing statements	---	
· Reduced clerical time required for copying statements	---	
		$15,400

SYSTEM NAME: ACCOUNTS RECEIVABLE/CREDIT AND COLLECTIONS

DESCRIPTION:

- Automatic preparation of open item statements
- Aged report ordered by customer name or number
- Listing of customers exceeding credit limit
- Overdue report by number of specified days or dollars
- Credit and collections department could use CRT for inquiry rather than updating records manually
- Computer preparation of past due notices
- Interactive on-line inquiry to any account
- Recording cash automatically updates accounts receivable and general ledger

	ANNUAL RECURRING BENEFITS	
	Unmeasured	Estimated
BENEFITS:		
· Elimination of NCR 395 maintenance		$1,800
· Elimination of service bureau		1,700
· Reduction of bad debt through more timely and accurate reporting		1,400
· Personnel time savings on review of customer aged balances and elimination of need to update cash receipts postings	---	
		$4,900

Figure 9-4. Sample System Requirements.

Tangible Savings

Obviously, the wages directly attributable to tasks that will be displaced are derivable directly from the work-measurement data described earlier. It probably makes sense to allocate fractions or percentages of an individual's time to various tasks first, without worrying too much about whether that whole person can be eliminated or employed elsewhere under the new system. That comes later when the whole picture is clear. For the moment, 20% of a clerk earning $5.00 per hour is worth $176 per month in direct costs, *plus* a lot of other things. The pluses include payroll taxes and fringe benefits, which realistically run in many companies to 25–35% and sometimes more. But what about other overhead?

Supervision. If the individual reports to someone, he or she takes up part of that supervisor's time in directing, problem solving and related administrative duties. If the total supervisory and executive wage bill (plus fringes) is divided by the number of nonsupervisory employees in the organization, you have some idea of how much this overhead item is costing per employee. For our example, let's say it's another 15%, although the figure will vary from organization to organization.

Space. If an employee is going to be displaced, the effect will be to free some space which may be saved or used by the new system. Credit the value of the free space to savings. Later, we'll charge whatever of it will be used in the new arrangement to costs of the new system. The net may turn out to be substantially positive and, in today's real estate and construction market, of great value, either currently or for future expansion.

Sometimes a business reaches the point where continued expansion with proportionate increases in clerical staff will literally drive it from house and home. The cost of expansion, renovation or physical relocation may be so high that avoiding that alone may justify computerization.

Substitution cost. When employees are sick or on vacation, you may be incurring substitution costs in one of three ways: using "temps" from a personnel placement agency, having employees from other areas fill in, or backlogging the work until the employee returns. In the first case, the cost is obvious and should be added to the total annual expense of the employee. In the other two cases, the cost is harder to pin down, but it may very well be there in the form of overstaffing or excessive overtime. It would not seem unreasonable to add another 6% (3 weeks/52 weeks) to 8% (4 weeks/52 weeks) to each employee's basic wage cost to cover this contingency in your calculations.

Replacement costs. What is your annual turnover rate for the job classes concerned? Is it zero, on average? Unlikely. Chances are that history will show some definable rate, such as 10%, 20% or more, among the clerical and bookkeeping ranks. Whenever an employee does leave, expenses are incurred to recruit a replacement and, after hiring a person, to train him or her. Recruiting costs include advertising, agency fees and the time spent interviewing and screening applicants. Training costs include the time spent in orientation and on-the-job training both by the new employee and by the person who is actually conducting the training. When it happens, breaking in a new clerk, administrator or bookkeeper can be lengthy and expensive. Let's suppose it turns out to cost an estimated $1,750 to recruit and train an employee for a particular position. Further assume that, based on experience or anticipation, a 25% turnover rate is reasonable to expect. Therefore, we should add 25% x $1,750 or $438 to the annual wage cost calculation for the position. Basically, what this says is that, on average, every 4 years we're going to incur an additional $1,750 expense to maintain the position, or an average of $438 per year—another factor for the savings offset total.

Equipment. If the task in question involves equipment that will be replaced or retired by the new system, don't forget to include the rent or purchase cost amortization, annual service cost, insurance, cost of the space it occupies, and the cost of supplies.

Supplies. If any part of a job that is to be eliminated consumes forms, documents, stationery, ink, ribbons or other supplies, then the annual cost of these items ought to be taken into account—just as the cost of such items coincident with the new system is going to be accredited to *its* cost of operation.

Outside services. Present service bureau charges for work that will be absorbed by the new system are a perfectly obvious candidate for inclusion in prospective savings under this heading. But what about some portion of current outside auditing fees assuming less time will be spent under the new system to produce confirmations, trial balances, physical inventory cards or lists and so forth? Fees paid for other outside services, such as cash management and lockbox fees to banks, fees to collection agencies, fees paid for periodic mailings which can be done in-house under the proposed setup, and so forth, may be among those affected by the new system.

Reduction in assets employed. If it can be firmly established that the new system will definitely improve machine scheduling, thus postponing the purchase of additional capital equipment, or reduce inventory by some percent, or facilitate closing down a branch distribution point or something of the sort, then the value of the resulting reduction in capital costs ought to be taken into account. An anticipated 20% reduction in a $300,000 work-in-process or finished goods inventory is worth something like $1,000 per month. (20% x $300,000 = $60,000. Capital cost @ 15% = $9,000 per year. Insurance might be another 2–3% or $1,500. Shrinkage and obsolescence could easily account for another 2.5%, so the total becomes $12,000, or $1,000 per month—enough to cover a major share of computerization costs.)

Intangible Savings

Among the possible benefits of automation are many that fall into the intangible category, to which it is extremely hard to ascribe a finite dollar value. For example, an anticipated improvement in customer service is worth something, but how much? If part of the improvement will derive from filling a larger percentage of items demanded, a fill-rate improvement of, say, 2% translates directly into a 2% increase in sales. That certainly can be further translated into annual earnings.

If, on the other hand, the improvement is to be manifested in faster response to customer inquiries, quicker turnaround of orders, better image and an unpredictable improvement in cash flow due to faster, neater and more accurate billing and/or statements, then coming up with a monetary value may be very difficult. And, if the benefits are to be found in better management through more accurate and more timely information, then the task of establishing a solidly defensible dollar return may be almost impossible.

Most businessmen end up taking the attitude that a new system, to justify the risk, must be economically justified by clear-cut, direct (tangible) offsetting cost savings. Any intangible benefits are just extras, bonuses that may have to make up for disappointments and miscalculations in case all of the anticipated tangible savings don't materialize, or computer costs turn out higher than projected. Such a prudent, conservative approach is diffcult to criticize. The trouble is, there may be situations in which the *main* benefits of automation are intangible, and where actual operating costs may even *increase* with the installation of data processing.

One approach to this problem is to calculate the dollar impact of achieving certain assumed levels of improved operation and then factor the assumed saving or profit increase by the percentage likelihood of achieving it. For example, one might come up with the following table of events:

(A) Benefit	(B) Annual dollar value if achieved	(C) % likelihood of reaching goal	(D) Adjusted value (B X C)
20% reduction in inventory	$12,000	90%	$10,800
2% improvement in fill rate	$4,000	75%	$3,000
15% business expansion without staff increase	$15,000	50%	$7,500
		Total	$21,300

Another approach, especially suited to the improved image, faster turnaround and better management kind of factors, is based on convening a panel of experts and having them each make independent assessments. In this case, the experts would be yourself and your key staff members, possibly your accountant and banker and perhaps a consultant. The idea is to lay out a series of "what ifs" regarded as likely outcomes of computerization, get everyone's independent estimate of what the "high," "low" and "most likely" value would be for each one, average the results and then pick a figure representative of the best thinking of the group.

For example, if you were a distributor and had convened your key jobbers or salespeople, you might pose the following question: "What if our computer enabled us to definitely confirm availability of stock on items and commit same or next day shipment while the customer is on the phone. How much would our sales increase, if any, in the first two years?"

Answers from five people familiar with the business and the marketplace might come back like this:

Response	Lowest possible	Most likely	Highest possible
1.	$50,000	$100,000	$150,000
2.	65,000	100,000	200,000
3.	0	5,000	10,000
4.	25,000	60,000	100,000
5.	50,000	200,000	300,000

Response 3 seems too far below the others and might be eliminated; response 5 might be discounted by some amount. Determining the average from the remaining responses would yield a figure in the $100,000 range.

Total Value of Benefits

Cost reduction and profit improvement estimates will allow you to calculate a total offsetting value for the planned computerized systems. The figure you derive can then be used for comparison with the automation costs, allowing you to evaluate the impact of your investment decision.

COSTS OF AUTOMATING

How much is it really going to cost to automate your business? That obviously depends on what tasks you're going to perform, how, the volume of work, what particular means you'll employ and a whole host of other factors. The next three chapters take you through the entire procurement process, a part of which involves getting proposals and price quotations from a number of different vendors. The recommended procedures go to great lengths to elicit as many of the cost factors in as realistic and uniform a fashion as possible from each vendor, so honest comparisons can be made.

The basic cost of the system you select will vary. It may be a $750-per-month, on-line, remote computing service or a $5,000 microcomputer from the local computer store, accompanied by a 75-page mimeographed programming guide. It could be a $40,000 customized turnkey hardware-software package from a systems house. Perhaps you're ready to contract for computer and applications separately to the tune of a hundred thousand dollars or more. No matter what price is quoted, there are a number of cost components that will not be explicit or apparent in the vendor's proposal, but about which you should be aware.

Add-Ons

The vendor will, at best, meet the specifications you and he agree upon. If you come up with a steady stream of last-minute changes and improvements to those specified and agreed-upon requirements, you are going to pay for the resulting add-ons. If extra systems design and programming is involved, you'll pay for it either by the hour or on a fixed price basis for each major add-on. If the changes require augmenting the hardware, in the form of more memory, larger disk storage capacity, a faster printer or another CRT terminal, then you'll be asked to pay the toll for that, too.

The trick is to do a sufficiently exhaustive job of analyzing your requirements up front, at the outset, so there are few if any add-on surprises later during development and implementation. Once fully committed and heavily into the project, your leverage in negotiating additional treatment and terms with the vendor is drastically reduced—almost to the vanishing point.

Yet, despite the best of intentions, you will encounter overlooked requirements and, perhaps, changed requirements based on some new government regulation, shift in the market, or reorganization move affecting your company. So be it. Nothing in the systems field is ever completely static. Try to minimize the add-ons, have a clear-cut understanding with your vendor regarding how add-ons will be handled and, perhaps equally important, budget for some reasonable percentage of additional charges. For instance, if the total software bill is going to be $7,500, it might be well to set aside 10–30%

extra against possible add-ons, in the event such are encountered. If the bill for changes and additions begins to look like more than that, say 50–100% of the original estimate, then it's probably time to reshuffle the deck, begin a whole new negotiation or perhaps even a new procurement.

Operating Expenses

One thing your vendor is not going to take great pains to emphasize are the expenses you will incur to operate the system once installed. If it's an on-line service or even your own interactive computer system, chances are you will not have to add a "computer operator," per se, to the staff. Someone will have to turn on the system in the morning, load and unload paper for the printer, perform a shutdown procedure in the evening, handle problems and coordinate service calls. In most cases this will be far from a full-time job, and may combine nicely with some other assignment like lead data-entry clerk or data-entry supervisor. The heavy personnel expense component of your day-to-day operation will be found among the people who sit at the CRT screen, keying in the data that represents the fundamental transacting of business.

The vendor will argue that there are no personnel costs associated with the new approach because the same people who operated the old manual or mechanical system will be retained to operate the new one. In many cases this is basically true. However, there may be some hidden pitfalls in this simplistic assumption.

First of all, the new system may involve much more work, either because it encompasses functions that aren't being performed at all under the current system or because it collects and centralizes work that is now being done, perhaps poorly, elsewhere. As an example of the first case, the present accounts payable system may record liabilities simply by entering the amount via posting machine on a ledger and dropping the vendor's invoice itself into the file right behind it. What to pay and when, may be subsequently decided by you or an equally tightfisted subordinate.

Now, if that process is getting too big, too complicated, too hit-or-miss to continue by hand, and is going to be committed to a computer, recognize that the data needed by the computer will have to be keyed in, and that the posting process will now consist not just of a

4-, 5- or 6-digit amount, but will probably require keying into the computer: vendor number, total credit, account number and amount of each distribution debited to expenses, invoice number, date and, possibly, terms if other than the vendor's standard terms. That's a whole lot more, and more complex, keying than required under the old method. The payoff in terms of better cash management, accuracy, control, and fuller and more timely analysis may more than justify the extra effort. But the responsible clerk *is* going to spend more time at the keyboard than previously.

An example of the second case might be a situation where pricing is currently done by, let us say, countermen in branch outlets. Priced and totaled sales slips might then be collected and posted centrally to receivables. Under the new system, the counterman will key stock numbers into a keyboard printer and get back a printed and accurately priced and totaled invoice, and receivables will be posted as an automatic by-product. It's very likely that the counterman will take longer under this system to obtain an invoice, but it will be accurate and legible compared to the present quick handwritten scrawl. Second, by centralizing control of pricing in the computer, we have created a price *maintenance* problem that may never have existed before in the central office. Somebody is now going to have to enter prices into the system and keep them up to date on a daily basis via the keyboard. This function was previously performed by countermen replacing sheets or making notations in catalogs. No countermen are going to be released as a result of relieving them of this responsibility; therefore, the net effect will be an *increase* in personnel expense attributable to the computer.

Thus, it is entirely possible that the computerized system, regardless of its great merits and benefits, may end up *adding* to the size of the office staff. It is very unlikely to reduce staff. That may seem like a heretical statement, but experience bears out the fact that most small businesses do not end up displacing or reducing staff with the installation of data processing: they wind up doing more work, faster and better and are able to absorb additional growth in volume and complexity without a commensurate increase in people, but net reductions are rare.

Don't forget, too, that a computer, if you own it, will add to your property and casualty insurance bill and, in any case, will consume electrical power and occupy floor space, all on an ongoing basis.

You can obtain precise costs for the first two factors by consulting your insurance agent, the power company and the vendor's site-planning representative. The third one, floor space, is probably your best guess of what the space you and the site representative pick out is worth now (or perhaps at some time in the future when the organization runs out of room).

Conversion Costs

A big area of trauma and misestimation of costs is to be found during conversion to the new system. This period, often stretching over many weeks or months, is the one in which overtime and "live-in" temps often become a way of life. The reasons are obvious. The new system is totally foreign and unfamiliar; it must be exhaustively tested for "bugs" and oversights; the data base, usually millions of characters of information, must be partly transferred from the old system and partly created from scratch; and everyone who uses the system or handles any of its input or output must be retrained—all this while the existing system continues to percolate along as if nothing at all unusual were happening. No one has yet discovered how to accomplish all this without considerable cost in time, effort, expense and an extra supply of headache remedy.

As will be pointed out in Chapter 14, the conversion and installation phase must be planned very carefully to avoid complete chaos, and part of that planning process is estimating in detail the costs involved. These include: overtime; vendor training and support charges; pre-installation computer time charges for program development and testing; service bureau charges for data-entry services, if any; temporary office help; cast-off of obsolete forms and supplies once the new ones are instituted; and, of course, the costs of physically installing the computer-related facilities including shipping, handling, electrical wiring, partitions, air conditioning, fireproof vault for tapes and disk packs, relocation of desks, telephones, file cabinets and so on. It is a rare case when these one-time conversion and set-up costs do not run into the thousands of dollars.

Hardware Maintenance

Chances are, whether only terminals or an entire computer system is to be installed on your premises, you will want to enter into a hardware maintenance contract with the supplier, or a third-party maintenance company that offers comparable service. Undoubtedly you will be presented with firm quotes for this coverage. In the case of terminals only, it will run in the vicinity of 1.5% of the purchase price per month, and in the case of a whole computer system, will probably run from 0.75% to 1 + % of the value of the system. That's really not a whole lot of money—$200–300 per month for the typical minicomputer—and is a pretty good bargain from the "insurance" angle alone, because the contract usually includes parts, too, so that no matter what breaks, no matter how expensive, and no matter how long it takes to fix or replace, it costs you nothing except your regular monthly contract fee.

Alternatively, if you decide to buy maintenance on an as-needed basis, you'll probably pay $40–50 per hour, with a 2-hour minimum per service call; and there are a few parts (disk drives, memory boards, and power supplies, for example) that could run into a major expense if they fail beyond the warranty period, usually 90 days.

Software Maintenance

Maintaining the software component is a major ongoing expense so easily overlooked that virtually no small business computer buyer *ever* budgets for it. Chapter 14 attempts to detail this challenge and possible approaches to meeting it. But, depending on the dynamism of your business, its marketplace and its regulatory milieu, your programs will undergo constant evolution and, not unlikely, a revolution or two now and then. Who is going to design and implement these inevitable changes? Larger companies who regularly do their own programming employ large staffs of programmers. Nationwide studies reveal that 50–60% of the man-hours expended in these programming departments are devoted to maintaining (fixing, modifying or enhancing) existing applications, instead of developing new ones.

Portfolios of programs "turn over" on average every 3–5 years. That is, if a business uses x number of lines of program code, over a 3- to 5-year period it will generate another x lines of code either replacing or supplementing the originals. Thus, it is unsound to ignore this source of ongoing expense. To be on the safe side, one should probably budget 20–33% of the original software costs each year, including the first, for maintenance. How to spend that money wisely will be dealt with in Chapter 14.

THE BOTTOM LINE

This chapter has covered a lot of ground; from the faint stirrings of dissatisfaction leading to an investigation of the feasibility of automation; through an exhaustive analysis of the present methods; to a determination of present costs, deficiencies and unfilled needs; leading to more or less detailed specifications of the proposed new system; to a rough idea of what the new system will cost to acquire and operate.

If, when comparing the costs to be displaced in the present operation to the anticipated costs of the new system, you come up with a positive number, a savings, then you are well on your way. If not, attention needs to be refocused on intangibles: have you given enough weight and value to the unmeasureable benefits of computerization? What about future expansion, competitive pressures, anticipated inflationary increases in labor and service costs, your own ability to cope with increasingly complex and voluminous business issues? Does having a computer or comparable service now represent an essential stepping-stone toward the kind of modern methods and information systems required in a company of the size and capability you intend yours to be?

If any or all of these answers are yes, and the net costs and risks of moving ahead are reasonable, then, "full steam ahead!" But *don't sign anything yet.* There will be plenty of time for that after you've gone through the steps of a sensible procurement procedure designed to uncover all the variables, precipitate the right decision and protect you morally and legally every step of the way.

10
Steps to the Right Decision

One way to guarantee confusion in deciding on the right form and selecting the specific brand of automation for your company is to passively allow vendors' sales representatives to run rampant through your shop, each loudly proclaiming his solution as small business nirvana. Unsurprisingly, each vendor will "discover" that the particular approach which especially favors his product or service vis-à-vis the competition is the "correct" one. Each will stress the virtues of his offering and conveniently neglect to mention its weaknesses and limitations. Each will endeavor to find out which of its competitors are in serious contention and then, as often as not, sow seeds of dissension and doubt with respect to these rival offerings.

As a result, each vendor will propose a different approach to the problem. Each will estimate timings and monetary savings on the basis of a different set of procedural, volume and other assumptions. Relevant facts, particularly those that might reveal flaws; potential problems caused by lack of depth of analysis, experience or organization; financial risks; and even the determining positive factors will be scattered and buried at random, if they appear at all, throughout the proposals.

Because the automation decision ranks with the most important and far-reaching ones you will ever make with respect to your business, you cannot afford to take a passive approach to it. You must take the lead in structuring and controlling the process leading to a final decision, and you must make that fateful decision *yourself*.

A STEP-BY-STEP GUIDE

The following sections describe ten cardinal points in a procedure leading from where you are to where you need to go down the automation trail.

The first three have already been discussed in detail; the remainder are covered in the chapters which follow. The important thing is to have a plan, a method to the mini-micro madness, which spells out exactly what is to be done, by whom, and when, and which shows you exactly where you are on the scale at each stage and what remains to be accomplished.

1. Define the Present System and Identify Costs

The point has been made. You need to know in detail what is now being done, how, how much it's costing and what is wrong with it. This is the foundation upon which everything to follow is constructed. Descriptions of inputs, outputs and functions, and accurate counts of the low, average and peak volumes of work involved are absolutely key to designing and sizing the new system. Peak volumes and maximum record and file sizes are crucial in determining what size (hence price) equipment or service will be required to do a day's work in the time allotted. Present costs will help determine how much can be spent in performing similar functions on the new system. Defining problems will suggest solutions.

2. Define Improvements Desired

In Chapter 9 we argued that a meticulous look at present methods would bring to mind a long list of needed changes and enhancements, which, when coupled with the already extant list of long-standing frustrations and unfulfilled desires, would comprise a statement of requirements for the proposed computerized approach.

This process can be as simple as stating, in writing, what functions the present system performs that are to be retained and what new or altered functions and features need to be added. There really isn't any need to distinguish between the two—just enunciate what the new system has to do, in total.

The chief value of this process is to create an aggressive positive stance toward what is to be proposed, and to insure the results meet the real requirements of the business and that all vendors bid comparable systems if they expect to qualify for selection. A second benefit of this approach is that it often reveals important improvements that can be made *now,* without waiting for automation, and which may postpone or even obviate the need for automation. The case of a particular chemical packager, frustrated by misleading production data, is a good example. An "automation" study revealed that the real source of the problem was inaccurate production counts from each packaging machine on each production shift. Merely transferring these erratic numbers into a computer wasn't going to make them any less erroneous. The solution was found in the installation of improved photoelectric unit production counters on each machine and the institution of a more foolproof method of recording and checking readings. And no computer was needed.

3. Derive the New System and Its Benefits

The further the user goes in crystallizing the details of his intended new system, the more certainty and fullness will surround the realization of its benefits. Chapter 9 ardently espouses the idea of specifying the features of the new system in as much detail as practical and of identifying and attaching dollar values to the benefits, insofar as possible. Even intangibles can be quantified based on judgment and a sound set of assumptions, although, as was pointed out, it may be well to collect and average the estimates of a number of knowledgeable people rather than just one or two.

Having specified the system in writing, the buyer now has the edge on prospective vendors; he can take control of the situation. Having solidified and quantified the benefits, he knows exactly how much he can afford to spend to achieve them. Some exotic aspects may prove to be of modest incremental value, yet entail disproportionate cost. These can be easily and intelligently traded off for lower prices while negotiating the final specifications with the selected vendor. Agreeing on the fine details of the proposed specifications will be somewhat give-and-take in any case, but the more visible the consequences, the better.

4. Prepare an RFP

Chapter 12 mounts a powerful set of arguments in favor of issuing a formal Request For Proposal (RFP) to prospective bidders, describes how to do so and how to evaluate responses. Suffice it to say here that the RFP is the culmination of your careful analysis and the formalization of your statement of requirements. It forces the vendor to bid on what you want rather than on what he thinks stands the best chance of getting him an order. And it minimizes the "apples-to-oranges" kind of comparisons so typical of small computer proposal evaluation by reducing everything to a more or less common brand of fruit salad.

5. Evaluate RFP Responses

As will be seen, we take a strong stand in favor of a formal rating and numerical evaluation plan for estimating and comparing the merits of the various vendor proposals that are elicited by an RFP. Having a rather rigorous procedure in mind for this function makes sense when one considers how much effort will have already gone into achieving objectivity and how ludicrous it would be to abandon it in favor of an emotional decision at this late stage. All this assumes, of course, that you haven't already decided what you want to buy and are simply looking for window dressing to justify that decision, pacifying your conscience by having "looked at a number of other alternatives." If you find yourself leaning in that direction, don't feel bad; many computer consultants used to make an excellent living in the 1960's and 70's constructing elaborate studies to "prove" to Fortune 500 companies that the computer vendor they had already selected was the best choice. Yet, your perseverance in coming this far demonstrates there's hope you will see it to the end—perhaps arriving at a conclusion startlingly different from the one with which you began.

6. Choose and Negotiate

A combination of hard facts, subtle judgments and commentary from other businessmen who have had experiences with different vendors will lead you to a decision, but that is only a beginning not an end. Next come specifications and contract terms, a rather arduous negotiation in most cases, but well worth the trouble in preventing and curing trouble. Chapter 13 is devoted in its entirety to the fine points of contract negotiation, probably the single most important activity the small businessman can undertake with respect to assuring the success of his computer project. A rather poor system, strongly supported and implemented, can succeed; a much better one can fail if all concerned do not go all out to make it work. One way of encouraging the vendor to make the required effort is to create conditions that penalize him severely if he doesn't.

It is amazing to note how quickly some vendors lose interest in a procurement once the order is signed. It is our task to build in attention-getting provisions that keep the vendor interested, even fascinated, until the proposed system is installed and working at or beyond the promised level of perfection.

7. Plan the Implementation

Many vendors offer at least a surface assault on the issue of implementation planning as a part of their standard proposals. It will be the mission of Chapter 14 to help you round out and refine the proposed plan to:

- Make it more realistic.
- Add the details that make the difference between a real plan and a ritualistic bow in the direction of one.
- Clarify responsibilities: who is responsible for each element and when is the deadline?

Special pains must be taken to arrange for the inevitable psychological trauma accompanying automation. Steps to inform, train and enlist the cooperation of employees are a key part of implementation planning and deserve much more care and consideration than is usually the case. Employees can and do defeat excellent, valid automation programs; it happens every day. The reader will, it is hoped, take precautions that will reduce the casualty count by at least one.

8. Verify Performance

An integral part of the implementation plan is tracking progress against it. A plan without recognizable check points is no plan at all; it is merely an ardent wish and carefully articulated hope. And, as each check point arrives, there must be a defined, tangible expected outcome that can be reliably determined as having been met or not met, as the case may be. Further, the plan should illuminate the consequences and suggest steps to be taken in the event the goal has not been achieved.

Admiral Hyman Rickover is credited with having fathered the atomic submarine, an incredibly complex task fraught with human and scientific uncertainty and potential delay, on time and within budget—mainly on the strength of a scheduling system that forced each one of thousands of military units and contractors involved to report progress against fixed targets every two weeks! Goals were defined with such detail and precision that no one could "wriggle off the point of the sword" if his piece of the entire drama was falling behind. Since the atomic submarine was designed to submerge, here the similarity to your automation project must end. Yours must be kept afloat by keeping track of what's happening and plugging leaks as they occur, before the orchestra begins to assemble on the fantail to play "Nearer My God to Thee."

9. Complete the Installation

Choosing, planning and verifying performance against check points and milestones is, of course, all aimed at bringing off a successful installation. But just what is *installation*? To the shipper it means dropping off crates on your loading dock. To the computer manufacturer it means physically connecting the hardware units and verifying their performance by means of checkout routines equivalent to electronic "tic-tac-toe." To the people responsible for application programs it may mean demonstrating that three sample transactions found their way to a hypothetical accounts receivable record.

To you, on the other hand, it has to mean performance of all, or the most important, of the tasks you contracted for, on your premises, operated by your employees, using your data, live, in regular day-to-day- production. Anything short of this is interesting, encouraging, a step in the right direction—but it's not *installation*. The final and most important milestones set up in your implementation plan will involve testing to see whether installation has been achieved, application by application. The most important provisions of your vendor contract will entail retaining financial and legal "leverage" over the supplier(s) until installation has been achieved and verified.

Yet, installation is not the end of the road, either. Problems can and regularly do develop *post*installation. Chapter 15 deals with some of the likely ones and makes suggestions on what actions to take.

10. Follow-up

A planned follow-through program, periodically reviewing your automation project, will serve two vital purposes: (1) to ascertain whether the benefits that were planned and upon which the new system was justified have been realized and (2) to recognize when and where the system is falling behind or getting out of step with respect to current needs and opportunities.

In the first case, if the score is too low in relation to expectations, then corrective action is in order. Sometimes it's a question of people falling down on the job. Sometimes ideas that looked good in theory just aren't working in practice. Perhaps programs need "tuning" to improve running speed. In any case, pinpointing problems will go a long way toward motivating remedial activity.

The author is reminded of a situation where inventory consisted of a number of item families, each one of which had a basic item plus variations. The variations all carried the same cost price as the "mother" item except where otherwise designated. File-creation programs were so arranged that they "borrowed" the unit cost figure from the parent for each variation as the whole family was being set up. A systems review after installation revealed that gross profit figures were being consistently inflated and inventory valuations were unrealistically low. A quick check revealed that new variations of an existing item family were getting into the system with a zero cost figure, because unless they happened to carry an explicitly different cost, the program looked for the parent, found it absent from the input (naturally, because the parent had passed through the setup procedure at an earlier time) and therefore assigned no value to the cost field. The problem was as easy to correct as it was to recognize—once somebody went looking for it. But, you'll be surprised how many little problems and inconsistencies can sneak by in the design of a computer procedure and how difficult they can be to spot sometimes. Incidentally, this one would have come to light very soon anyway because of an upcoming physical inventory reconciliation.

The second case, keeping the system current with evolving needs and changing conditions is a never-ending process, but, fortunately, one that moves leisurely enough in most organizations to permit something less than hour-by-hour concern. In most cases once- or twice-a-year review will reveal areas in need of improvement without allowing them to fester into the crisis stage. There will come a time in the life of any system, however, when it must be significantly upgraded and, sooner or later, replaced. Periodic review will provide ample warning of the approach of such an eventuality.

THE MOST ESSENTIAL INGREDIENT

You!

None of the previously described steps are likely to be successful without your active participation. Why? Because it's your business or department at stake, you're the final arbiter of what's really needed and you're the real source of organizational priorities, direction and assurances.

First of all, innumerable trade-offs are going to be called for in adjusting to the realities of computerization, some of which will have a profound impact on the way you do business. You have to make these judgments: no one else is as concerned or as qualified.

Second, neutralizing employee resistance and enlisting their wholehearted cooperation is much more likely to be achieved if you make it clear by word and deed that "We're really going to do this thing, no ifs, ands or buts, because (1) we really need it, and (2) I'm personally committed to it, all the way!" Personal assurances to people that they'll have a job, won't be hurt and won't be embarrassed by the new system have much more meaning from you than from one of your subordinates. Further, your assurances will be more believable if you're visibly involved, in there "pitching" and making the real battlefield decisions that will put force behind public statements and policy intentions.

Assurances

If the passengers are jittery about their first flight into automation or, as is almost certain, once off the ground the ride gets bumpy at times, the captain needs to come back out of the cockpit to calm things down. It just won't do to send a flight attendant, because everyone knows who's flying. (If it's *not* you, that is likely to set off even more unrest.)

The participants in this threatening, previously uncharted voyage need a powerful, steadfast leader to rally around and draw comfort and courage from. If this rallying function slips away from legitimate, constituted authority, namely you, it's likely to reappear informally and *il*legitmately in the form of a "ring" of during- and after-hours complainers and subconscious saboteurs. People tend to draw closely together, engaging in endless gossip and self-assuring chatter during crises. You can channel that tendency into useful teamwork and substitute reassuring fact for frightening rumor, if you're part of the process. If not, this rather tribal-like leadership role may fall to a disgruntled ringleader who, let us say, is less interested in establishing a flourishing data processing function in your shop than you are.

It is possible that assurances from you may be false, deliberately so. Your plan might be to hold everyone's nose to the old grindstone until the computer is safely installed and then fire or demote half the staff. Chapter 14 explains some of the reasons why this strategy may not work, and why as a general statement of policy the author feels that guarantees and assurances should mean what they say and that people with no future in the new, computerized organization should be displaced long before the event.

Activity versus Passivity

This chapter, and, indeed, the whole recommended approach to automation, elects the active rather than passive role both for the user organization vis-à-vis vendors and the decision maker with respect to *everything*. The decision maker is urged to take charge; to structure the analysis, decision-making and procurement process; plan the implementation; intervene in the personnel relations aspect of motivating, training and reassuring the staff; and to actively manage these projects from beginning to end.

The headman may, in a few lucky instances, be able to delegate the entire process, but not always, and not without serious risk. In a few cases, the whole thing is better out of the hands of the top manager because of his lack of time or interest or his personal idiosyncrasies. So be it. Whoever has the responsibility *is* in effect the top manager.

11
Major Alternatives

Presuming the reader has established a likely need for data processing, where does he look for solutions—a computer store, service bureau, major computer company, minicomputer manufacturer, software house, his cousin's brother-in-law who majored in computer science at Cornell and recently installed a computer in his family's business? Does one elect an outside service and stay with it, use a service as a stepping-stone toward eventual installation of an in-house computer, or go directly to the actual installation? If the answer is an in-house machine, should it be purchased outright, leased, or rented?

Answers to all of the above: yes, possibly. It all depends. As is so characteristic of the computer business, there are no simple answers, and every alternative has its pros, cons and trade-offs. Let's examine these main alternatives conceptually to see which are most likely to apply to any given situation.

IN-HOUSE EQUIPMENT OR SERVICE

Although the sale of in-house small business computers is spreading like wildfire, this phenomenon is relatively new and still multiplying from a relatively small base. In absolute dollars, the service bureau industry is still a bigger business and continues, after many years, to grow at an annual compound rate of 20–25%. So the service bureaus must be doing something right. What is it?

The Basic Service Proposition

The service bureau industry actually predates computers; it began back in the punched card tabulating days, catering to a number of different classes of users:

1. People who wished to avoid the responsibility of owning and operating their own equipment

2. Those who wanted to try out data processing without becoming irrevocably committed to it

3. Companies awaiting delivery of their own equipment who wanted results in the interim

4. Organizations with a workload so variable that a given complement of equipment would constitute either too little or too much at various times

Then gradually, as the idea began to take hold in the late 1940's and throughout the 50's and 60's, service bureaus began to develop specialized industry and applications expertise tending toward prefabricated solutions to the problems of certain classes of users. In the beginning, a unique system was designed and "programmed" (programming consisted of wiring up punched card "plug boards") for each individual client, but experience and know-how made the job quicker, easier and more certain of success with each successive iteration. Some bureaus remained generalists, but many focused on specific industries or applications. Soon "packages" began to emerge wherein the solutions were pre-established and preprogrammed, applying the same solution, or one with minor variations, to all users of a given type. Automatic Data Processing Inc.'s payroll package, General Electric and McDonnell-Douglas Automation's hospital systems, Reynolds and Reynolds and Service Bureau Corporation's auto dealer packages are examples.

Thus, to the list of four basic classes of service bureau users, we have to add a fifth:

5. Users who want to minimize development costs and risk of failure by adopting a generalized set of programs and procedures already in use by similar organizations.

Certain vendors of small computers, not suprisingly, began somewhat more recently evolving down the same road. Today, one can buy software packages and "turnkey" hardware-software packages which are every bit as prefabricated as the most firmly established service bureau package. The bureaus do retain one major difference, however, concerning who operates and maintains the packaged system after installation: they do—or do they?

Service Bureaus Enter the Hardware Arena

As mini- and microcomputer vendors forage in the traditional $500–1,500-per-month service bureau bailiwick, and as the cost of hardware continues to decline, the service bureaus find their safe market niche and secure customer bases under serious attack. As a perfect manifestation of "if you can't beat 'em, join 'em," the data services industry is responding by offering mini- and microcomputer hardware as part of their services, and at competitive prices.

This movement represents an evolution that began back in the mid-1960's with so-called on-line services. Many users of batch services wanted faster turnaround and a degree of applications integration and comprehensiveness virtually impossible to achieve on a batch basis. The alternative was a big, complex and sophisticated system too expensive for most users to justify on their own. Solution: shared usage over the telephone. As long as the distance to the nearest connecting point was not too great, and usage remained fairly low, businessmen found themselves able to purchase what would be called today a "turnkey" service via terminals connected through the telephone to the vendor's data center. Originally the cost of a minimum application set was around $1,200–1,500 per month for the small business. Subsequent reductions in hardware and communications costs have served to lower this threshold for the minimum user to around $800 per month. (It's hard to imagine this trend continuing much further though, because so much of the remaining expenses are communications costs, which have stabilized, and people costs, which are going up.)

To this economic dilemma, bureaus have responded by moving the service right into the client's office in the form of a packaged, turnkey small business computer, cutting out all or most of the communications expense, taking full advantage of the latest advances in mini- and microtechnology and reducing the user's dependence on the bureau's labor-intensive operating services to an absolute minimum.

A growing number of service bureaus are joining the hardware derby. A number now offer compatible upward growth from simpler, lower-cost on-line and batch services. Reynolds and Reynolds, headquartered in Dayton, Ohio, is a prominent example. R & R actually began with paper forms sets and "one-write" manual accounting systems designed primarily for auto and equipment dealers. Back in the 1950's, they instituted batch punched card tabulating services to complement use of their forms sets. By the early 1970's they were into on-line time-shared computer services from a handful of regional data centers using terminals and dial-up telephone connections. Users were allowed only certain rigidly scheduled time periods each day. When the time was up, each group sharing the machine had to get off, regardless of where the work stood, to make room for the next group.

By 1975, Reynolds and Reynolds introduced another more advanced version of the service based on dispersed time-shared minicomputers. Nearly 100 separate centers were set up, serving an average of 25 users apiece, each of whom could go on-line whenever he wished and stay on as long as desired. Then, in 1978, R & R released a full-blown in-house turnkey version of the system on similar but smaller, lower-cost minicomputers. Within a year or two, the success of this offering placed R & R within the first tier of turnkey minicomputer sellers in the United States, yet it was confined to a single, rather small market segment: auto and equipment dealerships. Undoubtedly, this narrow specialization was far more of a help than hindrance to R & R in carving out an important position in the marketplace.

The Stairstep Approach

The Reynolds and Reynolds story would be significant enough just in terms of the magnitude of its success, but it represents a major departure for service bureaus and an interesting new "stairstep" approach for users. Potential customers of R & R and of service bureaus taking the same path can try some data processing with a batch application or two at modest cost, perhaps $200 or $300 per month, with little risk or obligation. Then, depending on how things go, more batch work can be undertaken. Once the learning process is well in hand, the user can elect to upgrade to a terminal-based on-line service which, in itself, can be as much or as little as the user is prepared to pay for and profit from. Then, after the whole system has been installed, one piece at a time apace with his ability to absorb it, the user can choose to take delivery on his own computer at comparable or even reduced cost, but with the added flexibility and control that comes with running one's own shop.

This gentle "stairway to computing" approach appears to offer some attractive advantages for users to whom it applies. First there is the logic of paying only for what is used, as opposed, possibly, to buying a whole computer system and having a major part of it idle during the installation, start-up and learning phases. Second, there is the seemingly clear advantage of being able to walk away relatively unscathed, at least in the early stages, if things aren't working out. The graduated approach deepens the user's involvement and financial commitment in progressive stages, each one dependent upon the success of previous ones. Presumably the user never finds himself "out in left field" without having played short stop and second base successfully.

Drawbacks are, of course, that the buyer may be prolonging the eventual realization of important benefits, and he may be paying a premium along the way in terms of what the same quantity of work would have cost on his own machine had he successfully installed it and made full use of it. The latter "if" is a big one for many first-time users, and it is precisely this element of risk and uncertainty which may justify the service approach for many prospective users.

Responsibility to the User

One other advantage service bureaus enjoy in addressing the small or first-time user is their fee-for-service orientation. Service bureaus have traditionally engaged in "hand holding" clients more or less on an ongoing basis, because they're dependent upon continuing customer satisfaction and goodwill to keep those monthly checks coming in. Many, though not all, hardware vendors are used to the idea of demanding payment up front and allowing the user to fend for himself once the system is installed.

On the other hand, service bureaus entering the hardware arena have difficult problems to solve, some of which have already been succesfully dealt with by the hardware companies. Service bureaus have traditionally conducted their business and performed operational, technical and maintenance activities in one or, at most, a few locations—their own data centers. It remains to be seen how well, overall, they can adapt to the support and maintenance of dozens, hundreds, or perhaps in a few cases, even thousands of computers scattered over a broad geographic territory.

Also, many bureaus discourage or even prohibit programming to meet the specific requirements of each individual user, preferring to stick with a generalized, uniform package. What will happen when user requirements in a particular industry or applicational segment begin to diverge beyond the reach of a single software framework? The resulting fragmentation of the support effort is likely to put a severe strain on their ability to keep everyone happy.

Pro and Cons

The general advantages and disadvantages of buying data services versus hardware can be characterized as follows.

Advantages of services:
- Low initial "threshold" costs.
- Pay-as-you-use plan.
- Service is usually thoroughly tested and proven, entailing less risk.
- Generally well-supported packages including good training, documentation, customer service and conversion assistance.
- Overall approach tends to be customer-oriented on an ongoing basis to keep revenue flowing.
- Commitment is less to begin with and can be built up gradually in step with needs, ability to assimilate, and with "proof of performance" of prior stages.

Drawbacks of service:
- More expensive on a per-transaction basis than a well-run, fully utilized in-house system.
- Somewhat inflexible, difficult if not impossible to deviate from the vendor's prefabricated package.
- Often not as fully or efficiently integrated as an in-house system, because the various pieces are designed to be sold separately.
- User is relatively more dependent on the continued support of the vendor as compared to owning, operating and supporting his own computer.
- User is not in full control. Someone else is piloting his ship, though presumably in possession of greater technical and professional skill.

Advantages of in-house equipment:
- When fully occupied and well managed, the in-house system is clearly most economical.
- User can, at commensurate expense, take full responsibility for operational and technical support, freeing himself of outside dependency.
- Full user priority control over scheduling and program modifications.
- Systems usually upgradeable at reasonable incremental cost to accommodate growth.
- If purchased, or leased long term, eligible for Investment Tax Credit.

Disadvantages of in-house equipment:
- All or most of the investment and commitment is up front, prior to successful usage.
- Can entail a slow buildup to reach full operating status, hence payoff may be accordingly deferred.
- Ownership and operation is a heavy responsibility, demanding time, effort and professionalism.
- Hardware and software are subject to premature obsolescence if technology and/or business requirements change more rapidly than anticipated.

A Not-To-Be-Ignored Alternative

With respect to service versus hardware, the competing factors do not clearly favor one over the other; each case must be examined on its own merits. One thing is clear, however: the prospective data processing buyer should at least consider service, and, even if he becomes firmly convinced that hardware is the way to go, he should investigate purchasing it from service bureaus among other sources.

SOURCES OF EQUIPMENT

We have already discussed service bureaus as a source for small business computer hardware. There are, of course, several others.

Traditional Small Business Suppliers

One prime source is the traditional small business equipment supplier: companies like IBM, NCR, Burroughs and Univac which have catered to the bookkeeping machine and/or computer needs of this marketplace over the years. These companies generally provide an all-inclusive service including hardware, software, and maintenance, based in company-owned sales and service offices.

In the mini- and microcomputer field, these companies typically offer proprietary software packages for a fee which can be modified to some extent for the purpose of tailoring them to more closely match specific requirements. Modifications are sometimes carried out by the vendor, by a recommended subcontractor or by the user himself, depending on the situation. If a subcontractor is involved, some of the vendors will assume a prime contractor role, shouldering the technical and financial responsibility for the programming firm's performance.

Among the main advantages of dealing with this class of vendor are their size, stability and financial responsibility, their proven record of past performance in satisfying the small business market, their expertise and established software in many industry and applicational specialties and, generally, the greater array of financial arrangements available, up to and including short-term rental of equipment (and software). The latter is considered in greater detail toward the end of this chapter.

It used to be possible to state that the traditional small business offerings were significantly more expensive than comparable offerings from other sources without fear of contradiction. As of this writing, the distinction is no longer clear. It *is* true that many vendors offer lower-cost computers than the major suppliers; it is not necessarily true that these lower-priced offerings really *are* comparable. In an increasing number of real-life situations, the author is finding the majors bidding at thoroughly competitive prices in terms of hardware, software, support and service.

Make no mistake about it, though; the user who simply puts himself in the hands of one of these suppliers without developing a demanding, competitive atmosphere is still taking an unacceptable risk. The accuracy and detail with which requirements are analyzed, the degree of support committed, and, very frequently, the price depend on what the vendor's representative feels he has to do to get the business.

Another caveat has to do with the availability and quality of personnel in the local office and how well they're managed. Computer company X may provide excellent results in Cleveland and Ashtabula but regularly fall on its face in Akron. Chapter 12 discusses the importance and methods of determining the capability and perform-ance readiness of the local branch office.

Minicomputer Manufacturers

The emergence of the minicomputer has spawned a whole new group of companies typified by Digital Equipment Corporation (DEC), the oldest and largest of the category, Data General, Wang, General Automation, Microdata, and about a hundred others. These com-panies manufacture mini- and microcomputers and, typically, sell them to large companies directly and to smaller users through dealers, systems houses and so-called OEM's, a misnomer that stands for Original Equipment Manufacturers but really means those who resell equipment from original manufacturers, presumably with some value added.

One major advantage of dealing with this class of vendors is that they tend to be at or close to the leading edge of new technology, manifested by high-performance gear at low prices. The other side of this particular equation is, however, that these companies tend to be engineering- and manufacturing-oriented, preferring to leave the messy details of satisfying users, particularly the fussy and less self-sufficient ones like small businesses, to others. Quite often the mini-computer hardware manufacturer will provide a list of "qualified" software firms to a computer buyer but take no responsibility for the success of the resulting implementation. In fairness, however, let us point out that responsibility for turnkey-type systems is not without cost and risk, and a vendor who does not include it in his price can-not be expected to provide it. Chapter 12 addresses the risk of being caught "in the middle" between separate hardware and software procurements and how to deal with it.

Start-up Situations

Manufacturers of data-entry equipment and intelligent terminals are beginning to broaden their product offerings to include "stand-alone" small business processing capabilities. We use the term "stand-alone" to distinguish actual processing from merely acting as a terminal or communications funnel for the data to be processed on a computer elsewhere, perhaps at a service bureau or at corporate headquarters. When acting in this role, terminal and key-to-disk companies like Datapoint, Four-Phase, Applied Digital Data Systems (ADDS) and others tend to use marketing and customer service techniques similar to the previously discussed mini- and microcomputer manufacturers and can therefore be lumped into the same category. One difference, however, may be that some of these newly instituted diversification efforts are not as far along or as thoroughly established as the largest and oldest of the minicomputer manufacturers.

Among the newer offerings, many from start-up companies, are very attractively priced and packaged microcomputers with complements of packaged applications software. Hardly a week goes by without an announcement of one, two or three such new offerings, usually at progressively lower prices. Some of these really do represent innovative design "breakthroughs," but two important reservations must be set forth: one, generally speaking, there is no "free lunch." Users will not get $20,000 worth of analysis, design, programming, training and support thrown in free of charge with a $5,000 computer. Second, not all such ventures are going to stand the test of time. Many are long on optimism and salesmanship and short on capital and prudent management. Some relatively large ones, even subsidiaries of large, established companies, have already "bit the dust." Great caution should be exercised in attaching a value to projected, committed services from *any* vendor, but particularly from those of this class.

Turnkey and Systems Houses

Another relatively new branch of the data processing industry, growing at a prodigious rate, are turnkey vendors and systems houses which do essentially the same thing—provide contractual applications software and related services to the end user. The only difference between them is that the turnkey vendor supplies the hardware along with his other services; the systems house works through, or in parallel with, a hardware vendor. As a general rule it is easier to deal with one vendor than several, but often a very satisfactory set of arrangements can be worked out among multiple vendors, so long as the various responsibilities are clearly defined and each vendor has the desire and the ability to fulfill his part of the bargain.

Systems houses and turnkey vendors do place the main emphasis where it belongs: on solving the customer's data processing problem, which means applications software and support, not just hardware. Obviously, they extract a price for doing so (see Chapter 8 for representative prices). If the user elects to go this way, he must assure himself that he will actually receive the value-added for which he's obligated to pay. Typically, this means careful reference checking to test the vendor's ability to perform and some very dexterous negotiating and contract writing to make sure he is properly *motivated* to do so. These topics are upcoming in the next chapter.

The Computer Store

Another brand-new phenomenon in the mini- and microcomputer field is the "computer store" which sells CPU's, peripherals, accessories and software right off the shelf, in mix-and-match combinations very much the way high-fidelity stereo components are sold. The buyer may walk out of the store with an assortment of components that he then interconnects on his own in his home or business and "fires up" or "puts on the air," as the lingo goes, by means of a set of systems software contained on a diskette or a cassette tape. Typically, the systems software consists of an operating system, one or more language processors, some utilities and a self-help instruction guide and reference manual. Most computer stores also offer a variety of packaged applications programs which can be used as is or with modifications (usually undertaken by the user himself). The *really* intrepid gadgeteer can even buy his machine in kit form as circuit boards and integrated circuit chips ready for assembly and wiring. This, of course, adds still another dimension of thrill and challenge to the do-it-yourself computer approach, saving money to boot.

If the buyer needs help along the way in bringing his off-the-shelf computer components together and making them function properly as a problem-solving system, he can get a certain amount of assistance from the store, often by phone, sometimes in person, and often at extra cost. Those computer stores that are moving heavily into business computing, as opposed to continuing to ply the hobby trade, are beefing up their application programs and documentation and adding professional systems analysts and programmers to their staffs to handle problem-solving, training and software-customizing assignments on behalf of business users. In that respect, many computer stores are beginning to look suspiciously like systems houses with showrooms. This is a thoroughly predictable and positive development in the eyes of most observers.

Many stores have developed an "upstairs-downstairs" kind of operation wherein the showroom is run as described, but orientations, training sessions, problem-solving workshops and one-on-one consulting and programming activities are conducted "upstairs," mainly for business clients.

Hardware service, as was the case with sales, is often handled like hi-fi equipment. The offending unit is brought into the store where the trouble is diagnosed and defective components replaced. Sometimes considerable delay is entailed, and, sometimes, the store is able to provide a comparable component on loan until the user's unit is repaired. In the case of larger, standard systems purchased through a store, the user can contract for regular manufacturer's maintenance service, the same as if he'd bought the equipment direct from the maker. And, if the store happens to be manufacturer-owned he has, indeed, bought from the maker.

There is no question that the computer store concept represents a "low overhead" approach to delivering computer power to the small business user. There is also no question that some of the overhead reduction is reflected in reduced services. Whether the typical user can be as effective in his use of the equipment under the more spartan provisions of this type of procurement remains to be seen. It's simply too early to generalize. Going back to the "free lunch" thesis, there has to be a difference between a $5,000 product from a computer store and a $20,000 or $25,000 equivalent from a more traditional source. If the difference turns out to be mainly useless overhead and unneeded services, then the user may well achieve a big savings by going this route.

USED EQUIPMENT

What about used gear? If the buyer knows exactly what he wants, aren't there bargains to be had through dealers and brokers and direct from users who have outgrown their equipment? The answer is most assuredly yes.

As a general rule of thumb in the industry, minicomputer systems with a typical complement of peripherals, if from a first-rate manufacturer and consisting exclusively of components of that make, will depreciate in market value at around 25% of the remaining value per year. In other words, a $32,000 system from a well-known manufacturer may be worth $24,000 after a year, $18,000 after two years, $13,500 after three and so on. If the configuration is unusual, nonstandard, or of mixed vendor origin, the depreciated value may be even less.

Why? Simple arithmetic. Computers have a finite life span, reflected in depreciation schedules for accounting and tax purposes ranging from 4 to 7 years. Even 7 years, on a straight-line basis, implies 14.3% depreciation per year. Now, to this add the fact that small computers have been exhibiting a 15%-per-year improvement in performance/cost on average for many years, leading us to assume that this trend will continue for some time into the future. These improvements have come in the form of lower prices for comparable equipment or more capable equipment at the same price or a combination, as each vendor tries to leapfrog the others on the strength of higher-volume production, better design or lower component costs, particularly of integrated circuit devices, or all three. If one adds financial depreciation of 14% to a technological degradation factor of 15%, it's a wonder that only a 25% erosion in market value stands up. Yet it seems to.

To this must be added an adjustment for remarketing costs. Computer brokers, for example, usually charge the seller a 10% commission, thus further reducing the net amount salvageable from a used small business computer. And finally, amounts paid for software licenses, program modifications, training and support are typically of no account whatever in the transaction (that is, totally lost), because they usually have no value to the next user. The licenses may not be transferable, and even if they are, the new buyer probably wants to do different things on the machine than did the previous owner.

Two Sides of the Equation

The rapidly decaying value of used equipment spells danger for the first-time, small business user. It simply means there's no cushion to be found in the resale market for mistakes. Don't assume you can unload your error on somebody else with only a modest penalty if you've bought the wrong system. You can't.

The other side of the coin, however, is opportunity—the chance to find a complete hardware system on the used market at a fraction of the original price. And, for the buyer who knows exactly what he wants, who is totally self-sufficient from a systems-support point of view and who is able to protect himself in certain ways enumerated below, the opportunity to pick up a bargain is very real.

Vendor Support of Used Equipment

For subsequent purchasers of small business computers, support provisions simply don't exist. If the vendor has sold the system once and has already taken his revenue and profit, he can't be expected to perform his original sales and support routines all over again for the next buyer, this time free of charge! You may not even be able to *purchase* the equivalent of first-user support, because quite naturally the vendor wants to spend his precious and, typically, overcommitted manpower resources in generating new business, thus keeping his production line and not just his sales department busy.

The exception will be the manufacturer's service department, the division that performs on-call and contract maintenance on the hardware. This unit is typically a profit center in and of itself, independent of the factory, to which one dollar of service revenue looks as good as any other. This company within a company will be anxious to perform maintenance on your previously owned computer system, but only on condition that it costs them no more than the normal amount to accomplish it.

If you are outside the regular geographic coverage area of one of the manufacturer's service centers, you can expect to pay more than the advertised price for service, and response time will be extended in proportion to the distance. But more important, if, in the sole judgment of the local service department, your machine has not been maintained to full factory "standard," they may refuse to take it under maintenance at all or until some amount of "refurbishment" has been undertaken. The amount required is established by their sole judgment and is entirely at your expense.

To protect yourself against such an eventuality you should write into your purchase agreement *legal recourse* against the seller, giving you the right to demand payment for manufacturer refurbishment from him and, in the event he refuses to pay or the manufacturer refuses maintenance coverage altogether, providing the right to return the equipment to the seller for a full refund. If not, then have the equipment inspected and *certified* by the manufacturer as eligible for normal maintenance coverage before executing the purchase agreement.

RENT, LEASE OR PURCHASE?

The vast majority of sellers in the small business marketplace do not themselves finance equipment and software, either because they lack the financial resources or because they once lacked them and have never seen fit to alter the policy. The only exceptions are the major old-line small business equipment companies like IBM, Burroughs, NCR, Univac, Honeywell and Olivetti. The others will either sell you the equipment outright or recommend a "third-party lessor," usually a bank, finance or insurance company, who will, under separate simultaneous agreement, repurchase the equipment from you and sell it back to you at a monthly fee for the term of the lease. In the case of the old-line suppliers, these latter options are also available but added to them are various short- and long-term rental arrangements.

Purchase

Buying a computer is like purchasing any other piece of capital equipment. You'll obviously have to acquire the capital, charge the cost of that capital to the automation project and account for depreciation. The allowable life of the asset for Internal Revenue Service purposes is typically no less than 5 years and, to qualify for the full Investment Tax Credit (ITC), 7 years or more. Various accelerated depreciation plans are usually allowed, too. Almost all leases in the small computer field are written for a 5- or 6-year term.

Sometimes, also, principals in a small business can purchase the equipment themselves, through a separate limited partnership or Subchapter S Corporation, lease the equipment to the business and then benefit personally from the resulting tax shelter effects, if applicable. Very specific rules apply to this and the other aspects of de-

preciation and ITC, so to be absolutely certain of the potential consequences in your particular situation, you should consult your
accountant, attorney or other taxation authority.

As a general rule of thumb, in the case of a purchased machine,
most purchasers end up depreciating the small computer on a 5-, 6-
or 7-year schedule and assume only a nominal salvage value at the
end of the period.

Lease

The typical lease is practically no different in cost impact than what
would have applied had the purchaser financed the transaction himself. The leasing company charge is simply equal to monthly depreciation, usually on a 5- or 6-year straight-line amortization schedule,
plus interest. The interest rates charged are usually not much different from the cost of money available to small businesses at the
time of the purchase. Usually there is a down payment of 10–15% involved and sometimes a provision to purchase title to the equipment
at the end of the lease for a nominal amount, typically 10% of the
original purchase price.

The main difference is, of course, that the leased item is financed
"off balance sheet" from the company's point of view and the impact on other capital commitments is only indirect. From any other
standpoint a full-payout computer lease is little different from a se-
cured loan and is certainly no less *binding* on the buyer than an outright purchase. Putting things another way, a leased machine cannot
be returned to the manufacturer or the leasing company if the user
gets tired of it or if the machine is no longer functional. The payments continue until the end of the lease regardless of what you do or
do not do with the machine, so the risks are the same.

Rent

Rental plans are a different matter. Where available, and they are far
from universal, they do offer somewhat reduced risk, but at a commensurately higher cost. To make this clear let's take a concrete example.

The following options were offered recently to one of the author's clients by a major small business machine supplier regarding a proposed $34,000 minicomputer:

Purchase	$34,000
Monthly maintenance	$300/mo.
Rental (including maintenance)	
1-year plan	$1,200/mo.
3-year plan	$1,100/mo.
5-year plan	$1,000/mo.
Lease (*not* including maintenance)	
66-month plan	
1st, 65th and 66th payment in advance	
10% purchase of title at end	
	$800/mo.

100% "pass-through" of ITC on purchase and lease, 5/7ths of ITC on the 5-year rental plan and 3/7ths on the 3-year rental plan.

That is one large collection of perplexing options. The vendors usually, and unsurprisingly, offer a computerized analysis service using various interest rates, depreciable life and other assumed factors to calculate and compare the projected financial impact of each alternative.

Table 11-1 shows the potential financial outlay for this equipment projected through time, giving full effect to the Investement Tax Credit and imputing a 9% opportunity cost to capital as calculated for this particular buyer at the point in time involved. For this buyer, assuming maintenance rates remained at the $300 level, and that he planned to replace the equipment at the end of 5.5 years, his lowest cost option would have been to rent on the 5-year plan. If, however, he planned to use the equipment for 7 to 8 years, then purchase or lease would be optimal, and virtually equivalent financially. The

Table 11-1. Comparative Financial Impact of Various Options in a Sample Situation.

		Cumulative Expenditures			
	Purchase		Rental		Lease
		1 yr.	3 yr.	5 yr.	
end of 1 year	$36,950	$ 14,400	$11,740	$ 9,570	$10,010
end of 3 years	49,662	43,200	38,140	33,570	36,850
end of 5 years	65,550	79,200	71,140	63,570	70,390
end of 7.5 years	78,260	108,000	97,540	87,570	78,200

lease figures assume, of course, that the user exercises his 10% purchase option at the end of 66 months.

Note that if the suspicion exists that things are going to go wrong, and that the user may want to "get out from under" within a year or two, any of the rental plans look more advantageous. In this case, the vendor happens to allow longer-term rental plans to be converted "backward" into shorter ones for a small penalty plus the difference in what the price would have been under the shorter-term plan.

And, to put the final ornament on the cake, this vendor allows conversion from rental to outright purchase with recapture of 50% of the first year's rent and 40% of subsequent year's rent, not to exceed, in total, 65% of the purchase price. Remembering that the 1-year rental plan calls for $1,200 per month and that the current maintenance rate is $300 per month, 50% of the amount paid under this plan equals two-thirds of the cost over and above maintenance.

Therefore, in this situation, under this set of assumptions, the user can rent for one year, then if all is well, convert to purchase with little loss in equity.[1] If the productive life of the machine extends another 5 years or so, he will have achieved the impossible: the lowest initial risk, together with the lowest long-run cost.

Only a few vendors offer the array of different plans depicted here and, of course, every user's situation is different, so no general rules can be prescribed. However, a rental arrangement, especially one convertible to purchase, could be a definite plus in a given situation and will probably have an assignable, though probably not overwhelming, weight in the decision-making process.

One other miscellaneous point, subject to change in law or interpretation, is that, as of this writing, the IRS allows buyers to take the applicable ITC on the entire system, *including software,* if purchased as a single unit from the same vendor. This could mean as much as an extra 10% of the value of the software off the company's tax bill compared to a separate software procurement, which at this moment does not qualify for ITC. If available, this could be an important economic consideration as part of an overall evaluation, so the buyer is well advised to ascertain current practice with respect to ITC on software at time of purchase.

---

[1] There is one complication, however. Under this plan, the ITC will not apply to the original purchase price but to some allowable "used" value in accordance with the rules then in effect. Consult your tax expert for details.

SUMMARY

Automating is not simply a case of determining which is the "best" computer and phoning in an order for one. Even if there were one "best" machine and identifying it were easy, which is most certainly not the case, there are still a number of other options to consider:

- Buying service rather than equipment, using the auspices of a professional service bureau at less risk and perhaps lower costs in the short run.
- Buying service as a stepping-stone toward a compatible in-house version of the system, thus achieving somewhat lower risk at the outset coupled with the economic benefits of ownership in the long run.
- Electing in-house equipment from the start, on the basis of a solid evaluation, lowest projected costs over the life of the project, desire to maintain complete control, develop in-house expertise or other factors.
- Then, within the last category, deciding from among various acquisition options including purchase, lease and, at least in certain cases, rental.

The services of an accountant, tax lawyer and/or management consultant could be helpful in sorting out these alternatives and helping to determine which one best applies to a particular situation.

12
The RFP (Request For Proposal)

Having established a presumed need for data processing, a solid cost base from which to measure its effects and the broad outlines of the desired new system, you are now ready to do something about it. Generally speaking, the wrong thing to do is to begin entertaining vendor sales presentations and proposals. If initiated and controlled by the vendors, these importunings are bound to confuse both you and the issues. The vendor representatives go to school to learn how to get orders, not perform objective analyses. It is best that the user take control of the situation, rigidly legislating the rules by which the game will be played, if he is to have any hope of coming up with an unbiased decision.

There are at least 2,000 mini- and microcomputer systems vendors in the U.S. as of this writing and an equal number of service bureaus. Yet, according to an International Data Corporation study published in *Fortune,* most small businessmen in the market for a computer contact two competing vendors, and the average contact only three. The survey found that "Generally it takes a salesman 5-6 visits to close a sale. . . ."[1]

Other surveys and the author's experience confirm that few buyers perform any kind of systematic comparison of one vendor's offering to another, and few perform a financial analysis to determine if automation is even warranted in the first place.

And, as this author asserted in another computer industry publication, the user "frequently makes no provision whatever to protect himself against the failure of the software supplier to adequately maintain the system in the future by (a) analyzing the financial soundness and survival potential of the vendor in the first place and (b) protecting himself physically and contractually so he can take

[1]International Data Corporation, "Computing for Business Into the 80's," *Fortune* (advertising supplement, 5 June 1978).

control of the software in the event of bankruptcy, default or nonresponsiveness of the supplier."[2]

This chapter presents a methodology whereby the relevant issues cannot escape attention and, to the greatest practical extent, can be evaluated objectively, alternative by alternative, vendor by vendor, with the goal of arriving at sound conclusions and minimum risk.

RATIONALE FOR THE RFP

A Request For Proposal, or RFP, as it is customarily called, is nothing more than a written statement from the prospective buyer telling prospective sellers what is wanted, under what conditions the buyer intends to do business, and what information the buyer requires of the vendor in order to make an intelligent decision. It has to be in writing because that way each vendor gets the same message and can at leisure and in detail study the requirements fully and develop a thoughtful reply.

Although a formal, written RFP sounds like overkill—something more appropriate for the federal government or a multibillion-dollar corporation—it is the only way to achieve comparability between proposals. Each vendor sells toward his strengths and away from his weaknesses and limitations. Left to himself, he will propose what he thinks has the best chance of getting him the order, not what does the job the the way you want it done or in the same way other vendors will propose.

The vendor must be *told* what to propose, so his offering can be compared on an "apples-to-apples" basis with others. If he then wants to go on to propose alternate approaches which do not conform to the exact requirements of the RFP, he may do so in a separate document; but the burden of justifying the deviation is his. He must explain how his proposed system accomplishes the equivalent result. In other words, the RFP is a proclamation in which the user says loudly and clearly: "Here is the kind of system I want. Here's what it has to do for me, in what volumes, over what space of time. Here's a list of questions I want you to anwer. Fill in the blanks. Your answers will help me determine how well your products and services fill the bill."

[2]D. R. Shaw, "Who Needs a Formal Software RFP? You Do!" *Interface: Mini-Small Business Systems* (Fall, 1978): 6–7, 12.

And, perhaps, the proclamation may go on to say: "If you take serious exception to what is demanded, then you may separately propose alternatives; but remember that proving your method is better than mine is an uphill battle. I may choose to ignore your suggestions altogether."

Conserving Time and Energy

By taking the lead and spelling out exactly what is needed, the user avoids having each bidder "traipsing" around his place of business, making independent studies, interviewing the same people and asking of them the same questions that two or six or a dozen other vendors have done or will shortly do.

It is unquestionably a great deal of work to prepare an RFP. And, no matter how well executed, an RFP will still leave unanswered questions in the minds of prospective bidders which will have to be answered, briefly, by phone, letter or in person. Yet, all of this represents but a fraction of the time that might be spent, in total, considering all the people involved, in assisting each vendor separately in the development of his proposal. To escape this problem, users typically compromise either by arbitrarily limiting the number of vendors to be considered or by giving vendors short shrift, hurrying them through the process, providing vague statements of what is wanted, thereby not only permitting but positively encouraging a slipshod job. The former runs the risk of bypassing a truly outstanding solution simply for not having considered a broad enough range of possibilities. The latter results in a babel of incomparable, inadequate proposals from which it is impossible to objectively select a winner and which sets the stage for increasingly uncomfortable and expensive surprises as the detailed design and implementation of the winning system unfolds (which may cost more time than would have been invested in a proper RFP at the outset).

In general, then, your time and that of your staff will be conserved by doing a proper analysis and RFP up front, rather than dealing piecemeal through time with numerous vendors, entertaining proposals that miss the mark and choosing one that appears reasonable but, through faulty communication between the parties, ends up wide of the target after the action is underway.

Comparability

A well-structured RFP asks questions of each vendor in a format and sequence that facilitates comparing one to another. Left to themselves, bidders will choose their own styles, scattering facts and fancies in a wide profusion of material. They will carefully avoid stating damaging information. They will paint other factors with an unnaturally positive and seductive glow. Some will compose original literary works. Some will create a brief cover letter to which is appended "boiler plate," that is, brochures, stock paragraphs and other prefabricated material. Some will attach operator's guides, user's manuals and other technical references. Some even mass-produce proposals via computer by inserting a few user-specific parameters into a generalized program that prints out a customlike proposal on a high-speed line printer.

The only practical way of picking out the relevant facts, rating them and comparing them across all the various alternatives is to demand that the vendors answer each question fully, in writing and in the prescribed sequence.

Suppose, for example, you are interviewing aspiring copywriters for your cosmetics advertising department. The race is between William Shakespeare and say, Harold Robbins. Not an easy or obvious choice, since both have their strengths, though in different genres. It might be well to ask questions about experience specifically related to selling beauty aids, request samples of their work and, perhaps, ask each to write an essay in 25 words or less on "How I can 'crank up' the effectiveness of your current ad campaign."

Less facetiously, how would you go about comparing two offerings, the first from a "Fortune 500" computer giant and the second from a local 15-man turnkey house doing under $1 million per year in sales? If you considered only the giant's reputation and stability versus the local firm's flexibility and eagerness you still wouldn't have a basis for comparison, and the decision would likely be an emotional one. On the other hand, if you reduce the evaluation to a point-for-point comparison, giving each contender a fair and honest score on many factors, including the ones mentioned above, and assuming you have attached the proper weight and emphasis to each factor, then at least you have some chance of making an objective choice.

Specificity

Computer salesmen are justly famous for implying much, committing little and falling noticeably short even of *that* when it comes to delivery. As a breed, they prefer to talk reassuringly about users' legitimate concerns rather than to make pledges, commitments and guarantees in writing. If a miscalculation or, shall we say, overly optimistic representation has been made, it's those made in writing that can come back to haunt, to embarrass, to get one in "hot water" with the home office, even to generate legal action, which is sure to bring headquarters to a boil. Written commitments are second only to being below sales quota in the lexicon of sins to be avoided by computer salesmen.

The written response to a well-conceived RFP is the first step toward putting the vendor's "feet in the fire," getting him to be specific about the issues about which he'd rather verbalize and "arm wave." The RFP should leave little or nothing to chance or good faith when it comes to specifying what is to be done, with how much equipment or service, at what price, how long it should take and what the vendor must do about it if the requirements aren't met.

Put that way, the user leaves no doubt about what he wants in terms of specific information and binding commitments. This has the effect of warning off any computer "con artists" and putting the rest on notice that they'd better be scrupulously accurate and, perhaps, even a little conservative in their claims making. Just to narrow the field a bit and put a little extra pallor and teeth clenching into the otherwise glamorous and glossy sales routine, you might include a notification in the RFP of your intention to incorporate the winning vendor's response to it in the contract you and he will eventually sign. That's a little like etching glass or metal with an acid bath. Only the pattern that's fully covered survives; the rest washes away quickly. Some vendors' slates may come up completely blank under such circumstances.

The specificity angle works both ways. Not only does the RFP demand it of the vendor, but it helps the vendor immeasurably by being specific about what the buyer wants. Too often, selling is a guessing game in which the vendor tries to estimate on the basis of a brief and inadequate investigation. This is necessarily so, because the prospective vendor cannot afford to make as thorough a study of your requirements as *you* can, just on the faint hope of getting an order. So he crosses his fingers and guesses what will do the job and at the same time will look good enough and low enough in cost to get the business.

Most vendors prefer to work on the facts rather than these rough estimates. If you provide them with solid data, they are much more likely to propose the right solution and to feel confident about it. That confidence, in turn, can manifest itself in a lower price (less hedging against the unknown) and in firmer commitments and performance guarantees than would otherwise be the case. And that, in turn, bolsters *your* confidence and pocketbook and reduces risk.

ANATOMY OF AN RFP

There is no set formula for constructing an RFP. A great deal depends upon how complex your particular situation is, to what level of detail you've analyzed it, and how far you've gone toward constructing a detailed design of the desired solution. The wording and format depend on what you think will communicate the best in your situation. However, there are some categories of information that should be included and, probably, in the suggested sequence, unless you can think of a better one.

Introduction

A little background on your company or institution and its previous experiences with manual, mechanical and electronic systems will be helpful to the bidder. Size, number of employees, type of business, organization structure, past history and future projections of business growth and diversification will be very useful in proposing a system with sufficient expansion potential.

It wouldn't hurt to state why you think you need automation and what you hope to gain from it. The bidders may honestly aver that some of your expectations are unrealistic. If so, you should know about it.

Finally, the introduction should state the "rules" under which bids will be accepted.

- To whom questions are to be directed and when.
- To whom proposals are to be submitted and what the final deadline is.
- When you plan to make a decision.
- When contract negotiations will begin and end.
- When you intend to install the system.
- If detailed specifications are required, apart from the proposal, (which is normally the case), when they are expected.
- What portions of the RFP response and/or the specifications are to be appended to the contract.
- What the basic contractual arrangements are under which you intend to do business; for example, if you require performance guarantees and penalties, say so. Why waste time with vendors who can't or won't conform?
- And, as a matter of information and courtesy, you might explain to bidders how you intend to evaluate proposals and go about reaching a decision.

Description of the Present System

The buyer should define in as much detail as is reasonable, along the lines discussed in Chapter 9, what is being done *now,* how, and, if you're willing to be totally open with the vendors, how much it's costing. An open approach helps the vendor make better judgments about what to propose because he can understand the related cost trade-offs.

Copies of the forms in use, flowcharts of procedures, volumes and file sizes concerned with the present system aren't absolutely necessary if the new system is fully specified later in the RFP, but such information can't hurt, and it might help. No vendor will ever be offended or put off by receiving too much information about your job.

System Requirements

The statement of your requirements can take many forms, ranging from a narrative describing what is wanted in concept, to a listing of desired functions and features of each application, to an elaborate quasi-design document that spells out the new system in quite a bit of detail.

In any case, tell all you know or are reasonably sure of. Most RFP's classify wants into "must-have" and "nice-to-have" classifications. That way the vendors know what features they absolutely have to propose, the lack of which will either disqualify them or put them at a serious disadvantage in the bidding. A vendor who can also incorporate many of the "nice-to-have" options without unduly complicating or cost-escalating his proposal will do so, thereby increasing his chances of getting the order.

It's hard to conceive of too much information in this section of the RFP. Especially important are input, file and output descriptions. If you already know the approximate formats of key documents and reports, by all means include them. One common means of depicting such requirements is shown in Figure 12-1. The 132-column layout forms for this purpose are abundantly available from computer vendors, forms companies and consultants throughout the industry. Table 12-1 shows a sample file description. Listing each field with its composition—alphabetic, numeric or mixed, right or

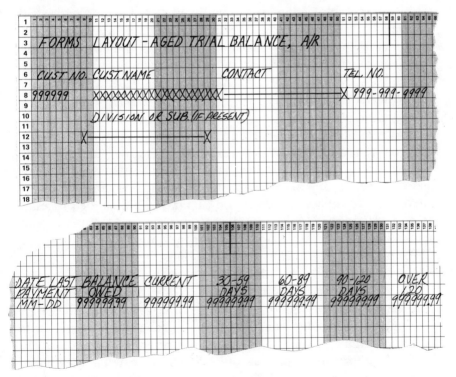

Figure 12-1. Sample Document Format Using Standard 132-Column Computer Layout Forms.

Table 12-1. Sample File Description Showing Composition of a Hypothetical Accounts Receivable Master File.

Accounts Receivable Master File (One occurrence per active customer account)

FIELD	SIZE AND TYPE	COMMENT
Indentifier	2 Numeric	Record type code 06 = A/R Master
Account number	6 Numeric	Sort and access key
Customer name	21 Alphanumeric	Company name
Division or subsidiary	21 Alphanumeric	Used only if applicable
Street address	22 Alphanumeric	
City	15 Alphabetic	Standard abbreviations if necessary
State	2 Alphabetic	Standard state code
Zip code	9 Numeric	New postal code
Contact name	21 Alphabetic	Used only if applicable
Telephone number	10 Numeric	Format: xxx/xxx/xxxx for area, exchange and number
Date of last activity	6 Numeric	Format: xx/xx/xx for month/day/year

left justified, with leading or trailing blanks or zeros—together with its size, if you know all these specifics, will be helpful. If not, the vendor will make assumptions about the details and check them out with you later.

There are four other items essential, or at least highly desirable, in this segment of the RFP.

Volumes. File sizes, transaction counts and exception counts for each major application area with expected high, low and average occurrences are essential. It's one thing to know that company X handles 20 orders a day on average. It's quite another thing if 90% of the orders for the week come in on Monday and must be processed by noon Tuesday. It's also another matter if the business is seasonal, generating, say, four times the average volume during the pre-Christmas rush. These volume vagaries must be spelled out clearly.

Processing rules. Decision rules (or "algorithms" as some of the unrepentant vendors up from the scientific leagues call them) are very important. Under what conditions, precisely, is a customer to be denied credit, a small balance to be written off, an item to be backordered or substituted, a cost item to be allocated among multiple departments and so on? The more you say about these functions the better the vendor can determine which of his systems is capable of performing the desired functions and how much programming or adjustment is required to match your need.

A serious mistake here could have a profound impact on the appropriateness of a packaged software approach versus a custom system. If the vendor assumes, in the absence of fine detail, that the package fits, and it later turns out not to, then trouble is in store for all concerned. Considerable redesigning and added cost may ensue. Or, the user may have to give up certain important features in order to avoid excessive tailoring of the package. At worst, he may decide to give up altogether and begin again with a whole new procurement. (Of course, if the user has signed a contract without specification approval rights or has approved specifications without being aware of the short-fall, then it's too late for anything but raising one's heel in a swift arc from the rear and upward, making sharp contact with the corresponding hemisphere of the gluteus maximus. This form of exercise, though regarded as harmful by some authorities, seems to be gaining steadily in popularity and frequency among computer buyers. Perhaps this book may, in some small measure, help reverse the tide, channeling buyers into more acceptable forms of recreation.)

Critical timing considerations. If there are sharp cutoff times pertaining to certain input, processing and output, these must be put forth. Not only do such constraints influence volume and speed determinations, but also the fundamental design of the applications and whether such important systems functions as multiprogramming will be required.

For example, if monthly financial statements must be in the hands of management by the seventh working day after month-end, but branch receivables cannot be closed until after the tenth day because of local processing plus mailing-time requirements, this tells the systems designer two important facts: (1) some subsidiary ledgers have to remain open after regular closing, and (2) the system must accommodate accrual entries that are subsequently adjusted.

Or, if parts-requirements processing can be deferred until day-end in a manufacturing-control environment when the entire computer can be given over to it, rather than at a time when other processes such as order entry or production reporting must proceed in parallel, the size of the computer, its memory and the complexity of the operating system needed may be reduced considerably.

At this point you should be able to clarify to the vendor which applications, such as payroll, can be processed in batch rather than a transaction at a time and which files are subject to unscheduled inquiry and/or reporting. This information will tell the vendor what files must remain on-line at all times and whether some kind of ad hoc data base reporting system is warranted.

Archival records. If period history from prior years, for example, is to be retained, it's a good idea to specify what, how much and how it's going to be used. These requirements could suggest the addition of a magnetic tape storage facility to an otherwise all-disk system. Subsequent manipulation of the data might require a distinctly different complement of numbers, speeds and size devices, depending on what you intend to do with the information.

Mandatory Information

The RFP will include a list of questions to be answered and information to be supplied by each bidder. Make it clear that every question or issue must be succinctly addressed in writing and in sequence with the item numbers and headings provided. This is going to make analysis and evaluation of responses very much easier.

Some of the issues you may want addressed are:

Hardware.

- Configuration proposed. Description of each component, including quantity, speed, capacity and special features.
- Maximum size, quantity and capacity to which each of the above may be expanded.
- Other devices. Detailed description of other separate items required such as data-entry devices, remote terminals, communciation lines and equipment, along with their maximum expansion potential.
- Environmental requirements. Complete description of site, power, air conditioning and other requirements.
- Reliability and maintenance. Repair manning, spare parts stocking and response time policies. Details of various contract maintenance plans. Historic, factual data on average mean time between failure (MTBF)

and mean time to repair (MTTR) for similar equipment in similar applications.
· Costs. Prices, under whatever purchase, lease and rental plans are available for each element of the above, including additional equipment for future expansion.

Applications software.

· Specifications and features. A reasonably detailed list of features and functions of the proposed applications software, showing point for point how it matches the requirements set forth in the RFP.
· Other features. Additional functions not asked for, which could be beneficial.
· Sample inputs and outputs. Illustrations supporting the claimed features and functions.
· File design. A complete layout of each file in the system showing content and format.
· Running time estimates for the major applicational procedures (which the vendor is willing to guarantee).
· Prices under various plans for the above.
· Maintenance. A discussion of application program architecture, language, parametric control, if any, and other features bearing on future maintainability. Description of program documentation. Determination of ongoing rights, responsibilities, recourse, prices and guarantees with respect to future correction and enhancement.

Systems software.

· Description of each element of systems software proposed, including operating system, language processors, data base and communication management systems, query and report generators and utility programs. Listing of features and functions.
· Any limitations of the above with respect to memory size, number of concurrent activities, number of terminals, and so on, indicating minimums, maximums and level proposed (if not maximum).
· Description of documentation to be supplied.
· Prices and terms for the above. Description of cost versus performance trade-offs, upgrade potential and costs thereof.
· Maintenance provisions for all systems software proposed.

Support.

· Responsibilities of each member of the bidder's organization who will directly support the buyer.

- Organization chart and brief resumés of key individuals.
- List of all the other accounts for whom these individuals play similar roles.
- Training facilities, methods and materials, with samples and training class schedule.
- Identification of all the costs associated with support: systems analysis, design, programming, consultation, training, start-up and ongoing problem solving and enhancement.

Contractual obligations.

- Sample contract and other agreements.
- Description of how sales proposals and written specifications are incorporated into equipment and/or service agreements.
- Position with respect to performance guarantees and remedies covering hardware, systems software, applications software and remedial maintenance.
- Buyer's options in the event of seller default through each stage of development, test, delivery, acceptance and ongoing operation.

Acceptance tests.

- Description of the location, duration and nature of demonstrations, tests and formal acceptance procedures to which the system will be subjected.
- Statement indicating whether formal written specifications are a part of the overall acceptance procedure and where they fit.
- Relationship of all payments, deposits, progress payments and payment of the balance to the specification and acceptance process.

Financial responsibility.

- Audited financial reports showing current and historical performance of the bidder's business.
- Credit and bank references.
- If private or closely held firm, background and financial status information regarding principals.

Record of success.

- Names of (number) customers whose systems have been installed for at least one year.
- Names of (number) customers in this locality.

· Names of (number) customers in buyer's type of business.
· Name, address and phone number of decision makers in above roster.
· Other evidence of expertise, customer satisfaction and seller's willingness to perform.

Integration. If more than one organization will be involved in developing or supporting the proposed system:

· Description of each one and its role.
· Statement of how coordination is to be effected and precisely how control is to be exercised and by whom.
· Full financial, organizational and background information on each company participating.

Implementation plan.
· Proposed plan of action leading from vendor selection through final acceptance and full implementation of the system, showing each step, with the individual or organization responsible in a timetable or Gantt chart arrangement.

WHO SHOULD BID?

Finding the right vendors and the optimum number of them is a very difficult problem. Certainly no less than three bidders for a given approach to the problem should be considered: that is, three service bureaus, three hardware manufacturers, three turnkey systems houses, and so forth. If the user is already certain of the type of vendor he wants to do business with, then he may not go to the trouble of soliciting bids from other categories of companies. But this may turn out be a mistake. How can the user be really certain that the service bureau, or the in-house mini or the off-the-shelf micro is the right approach until he's had the opportunity of comparing each side by side on the basis of common bid specifications?

If the buyer has gone to the trouble of preparing a more or less formal RFP, then it doesn't cost much more to consider a broader range of alternatives. After all, the work of proposal preparation from this point on is mostly the vendor's. If the vendor thinks he has something special to offer, why not let him have his say? The pros and cons can then be weighed not only within but also between each alternative approach.

Assuming, then, that the buyer wants to consider at least three potential suppliers of each acceptable approach, the question remains as to where to find qualified bidders; or, if the company is fairly large and visible, how to select which ones from among a host of aspirants of each type to allow to bid seriously. Among 100 manufacturers, 2,000 or more systems houses and 2,000 or so service bureaus there are bound to be more contenders than can possibly be considered. In general, you might wish to include on your selected-bidders list vendors who meet one or more of the following criteria:

- The current supplier of manual or semiautomated equipment or outside services if he
  (a) has done a good job
  (b) appears to have something to offer in a more advanced system
  (c) has some special knowledge of your needs, based on past exposure
- A vendor who has been calling regularly and
  (a) has made a good impression and
  (b) has picked up some understanding of your requirements in the process
- A vendor with a particularly notable reputation in your industry, field or geographic locality; someone who is known to be doing lots of business with organizations like yours, or in the same neighborhood
- Suppliers recommended by friends, business acquaintances, bankers, accountants and/or consultants
- Companies that have come to notice based on advertising, trade shows, direct mail promotion or general reputation

A rather concentrated exposure to a broad range of companies representing a cross-section of different approaches can be obtained by attending a computer industry trade show. Annual affairs like the National Computer Conference, Western Electronics Show and Convention, Data Processing Management Association Conference, National Mini-Micro Computer Conference and many, many others can be quite useful in this regard.

Watching the ads, product announcements and news stories in one or two popular computer industry publications can be a source of information about potential vendors and will provide details and dates of upcoming computer conferences in your area. It's very difficult to single out a few of the many excellent magazines and newspapers devoted to data processing, but the two with the greatest circulation are

Datamation, a controlled-circulation monthly magazine from Tecnnical Publishing Co., (circulation department) 35 Mason St., Greenwich, CT 06830. And *Computerworld,* a weekly newspaper published by Computerworld Inc. 797 Washington Street, Newton, MA 02160.

Research reports published by professional industry watchers can be a rich source of inspiration, ideas and specific information about vendors. The two most prominent such sources are Auerbach Publishers Inc., 6560 North Park Drive, Pennsauken, NJ 08109; and Datapro Research Corporation, 1805 Underwood Boulevard, Delran, NJ 08075.

Seminars on subjects related to small business data processing are a regular feature of today's landscape. The American Management Associations, various universities, trade associations, accounting and consulting firms and, of course, the vendors themselves are constant sources of user education for a fee and, in some cases, for free. The no-charge sessions are subject to suspicion that the hosts hope to achieve some direct or indirect benefit for themselves. Nevertheless, the prospect well fortified with caution and totally immunized against infectious sales contagion is probably safe in exposing himself to "free" educational sessions now and then. It is wise, however, to leave your checkbook and the corporate seal at home when attending such conferences.

EVALUATING PROPOSALS

The most important principle in evaluating vendor proposals in response to an RFP is to break the process down into small enough segments so that each component can be judged pretty much independently and on merit. It's impossible to read through a dozen thick proposals and objectively answer the question: "Which one is the best deal?" However, by putting a microscope on specific elements, one at a time, it's fairly easy to figure out which one has the closest service facility, or to rank the vendors in order from most to least on the basis of how many computer installations are claimed in a particular line of business.

By separating the evaluation into a number of clearly defined subevaluations, one escapes the well-known "halo effect" which asserts an overall emotional tone to most rating methods if the categories are too few, too broad and nonspecific. Then, by reassembling the subcomponents into an overall score, a much more meaningful, objective and sometimes surprising result is achieved.

Things like the neatness, readability and professionalism exhibited in the proposal itself are factors but not decisive ones. By measuring and rating such items separately, and combining them into the overall scoring formula on the basis of the weight they deserve, they become just some many criteria, each in proper proportion to the others.

The Framework for Rating

The RFP itself spells out the basic framework for a proposal rating scheme. Under each of the major topical headings are a list of important questions and information requirements. Some of these may need still further analysis to be useful, but the outline is already established. For example, under the heading of Hardware, you may already have the data on maximum growth potential for the proposed system in terms of maximum memory size, auxiliary storage capacity, number of terminals supported, and so on. It would be a simple matter to rate each offering on a scale of 1–5 on the strength of this factor by assigning the value 5 to the system with the greatest expansibility, 1 to the lowest, and all the others proportionally in between. But cost of expansion may vary, too, so you may decide to calculate the cost, from the prices supplied, of some arbitrary amount of growth such as: doubling the size of memory, adding the next increment of disk storage closest to 20 million bytes and adding four more CRT's. Now you have a new list, ranging from high to low. This time assign the value 5 to the *lowest* vendor and 1 to the highest.

By the time you have rated all the factors you will have constructed a spread sheet similar to the one shown in Table 12-2. By assigning weights to the individual factors, or at least to groupings of them, the rest is simple arithmetic. Multiply the ratings times the weight and then sum down the columns to arrive at an overall score for each vendor. In Table 12-2, a greatly simplified version, you see that vendor C won by a narrow margin, mainly on the strength of price. If some other factor, such as customer support, had been more heavily weighted by giving it a 40% weight instead of 30%, then the results would have favored vendor A. Thus, you see how easy it is to manipulate the results: but establishing the rating scheme and the weights *in advance, objectively,* is not manipulation—it's good business. It allows you to judge what's important to you out of the atmosphere of an emotion-charged, high-powered sales presentation. There's no law against choosing a vendor other than the best scoring one, but the score itself should be unbiased.

The example in Table 12-2 is an unrealistically simple one compared with an actual situation. A real evaluation would, first of all, probably encompass more than three vendors and, frequently, several separate offerings from each of some of those vendors. In other words, vendor A may propose a system that conforms closely to the specifications and also propose a different, perhaps less expensive, alternative which conforms less closely but which the vendor contends will do the job. Both alternatives would be set up as separate entities in the evaluation table, as if they had come from different companies. (Of course, some of the factors would be rated in common, such as nearness of service, quality of proposal, vendor's reputation and financial stability.)

Secondly, there are many more factors to consider, rate and score than the handful illustrated. The example shown doesn't separate hardware from software, systems software from applications software, the various applications from each other, and doesn't touch on such vital aspects as ease of use, reliability, the vendor's experience and track record in the industry or the geographic area involved, detailed examination of specifications, acceptance testing, contracting procedures and so on.

The weighting factors will be much more finely distributed in a real-life situation, too. Perhaps "functionality" in the applications sense *is* worth 30% in a given instance; but, of that, inventory control might be several times as important as accounts payable to a manufacturer, for example. So the multiplier factor for payables might be 1% as compared to 15% for inventory. In an insurance agency, however, the exact reverse may be true; payables (and/or accounts current) might be of overriding importance whereas inventory control may not even be under consideration.

In general, the more precise the breakdown and the more powerful the microscope put to the minute factors, the more accurate and unbiased the result. But the result is still just a number, a numeric

Table 12-2. Sample Simplified Vendor Rating Sheet.

Factor	Weight	Vendor A Rating	Vendor A Weighted Score	Vendor B Rating	Vendor B Weighted Score	Vendor C Rating	Vendor C Weighted Score
(1) Ability to perform specified functions	30%						
(a) Conformance to mandatory features		5	150	1	30	4	120
(b) Conformance to additional features		4	120	3	90	3	90
(c) Guaranteed timings		4	120	5	150	5	150
(2) Customer support	30%						
(a) Nearness of sales and service		4	120	1	30	5	150
(b) Commitment to ongoing software maintenance		5	150	1	30	1	30
(c) Quality of training and documentation		5	150	4	120	3	90
(3) Cost	40%						
(a) Initial price		1	40	2	80	5	200
(b) Estimated operating costs		4	160	1	40	4	160
(c) Cost of future expansion		3	120	2	80	5	200
TOTAL	100%		1130		650		1190

score. The process of picking the winner isn't quite as mechanical as that.

SELECTING A WINNER

The numeric scoring system described above will bring the prospective buyer of a computer or computer-based services as close to an accurate, unemotional decision as possible, yet much work and thought may remain to be done. For one thing, the factors that have been evaluated are those contained in the proposals in accordance with the instructions contained in the RFP. There are others. Also, there may be some very important last-minute "jockeying" among vendors that goes on after the proposals have been rated and the leading contender(s) identified.

Tentative Selection

Typically, all but one, two or three leading contenders are effectively eliminated by the time the user is able to distill proposals down to the level of numeric scoring. Some fall by the wayside because they haven't responded fully and honestly to the questions raised in the RFP. Others may exhibit lack of interest. Others may be priced out of line with the leaders. Others may exhibit a take-it-or-leave-it, ironbound attitude toward contract terms, specifications and acceptance testing. Others may simply score consistently low overall compared to the leaders.

At any rate, with a handful of contestants left in the race, it is then practical to (1) check references and (2) engage in preliminary negotiations. The quicker the pack can be reduced to a few front runners, the sooner can this next important phase of selection begin.

References

Not only will vendors freely provide names, addresses and phone numbers of satisfied customers, they will, apparently unknowingly, supply the names of a few restive, doubtful and sometimes dissatisfied ones, too. Unless the vendors take very special pains to "check the temperature" of each account periodically and to "reference their references" themselves, perhaps by posing on the telephone as a prospective buyer, they really never know what a user will say to a prospective one at a given point in time. The author's experience suggests that users are much more candid in their assessments than vendors would like them to be, and quite often a customer touted as a major "success" may with little provocation tell some damning tales about the vendor which would chill the very soul of the salesman who provided the reference and dim the enthusiasm of even the most ardently convinced prospective buyer.

Why does this happen? First of all, almost every vendor who has been in the business for any length of time and has done any significant number of installations has undoubtedly left a few "clinkers" along the way. Secondly, small businessmen, as a breed, tend to be rather open with each other about their successes and failures and their likes and dislikes compared to their counterparts in larger businesses. Fortune 500 companies may be very hard on vendors privately but refuse to "wash linen" publicly. However, most small businesses feel no obligation to coddle, educate and protect vendors, particulary those who have done less than the promised or expected job. They know what their customers expect of them and what happens if they don't deliver. They give the same as they get.

Point one, therefore, in checking references is not to be put off by a few negatives. Practically every vendor has a few skeletons in his closet. If fact, if you check a half dozen references and still haven't heard a single discouraging word, something may be wrong. You may, indeed, be in possession of one of those rare, up-to-date "purified" lists from which all but the most complimentary customers have been eliminated. It would be best for you to do some further checking by asking some of the originally listed customers for the names of others they may have heard about who are not so satisfied.

Second, don't just exchange bland and superficial generalities: probe! Ask questions about areas of crucial importance like what was delivered compared to what was promised, whether the vendor lived up to his support commitments, how the reliability of the products or services stack up against expectations, how smoothly the conversion was effected, whether hidden costs and unexpected operating expenses have surfaced, whether the system has been kept up to date with changing needs, how the vendor has handled problems, bugs, power outages, mechanical breakdowns, human error, and so forth. What about quality of vendor personnel, turnover, training and continuity with the user through time? How much longer did development, conversion and break-in take than originally planned? Why?

Like any good investigator you should zero in on key issues in your questioning, coming back at suspected weak points again and again from different angles. When you finish with an interview—face to face whenever possible and at length by phone, if not—you should know a great deal about the vendor's actual performance on the account in question, what went wrong and, perhaps, what steps might be taken in dealing with that vendor to guard against similar mistakes in your company. After sifting through the details, it should not be difficult to develop a simple rating scheme that yields another numeric score reflecting the degree of customer satisfaction and vendor performance evidenced by the reference visits or calls.

Preliminary Negotiations

During the reference-checking process, or immediately upon its conclusion, the buyer will probably begin "serious" discussions with one or more likely winners with respect to contract terms and price. It may even make sense to negotiate in parallel with the finalists so that the moment a decision is made an agreement can be signed. Certainly, if there are any significant concessions vendors have been quietly holding back for the "end game," now is the time to draw them out. You should know just how far each contestant is prepared to go on the key items of price, guarantees, specifications and contractual obligations so that if the winner begins to back away from his prior promises during final contract negotiations, you can quickly transfer the winner's crown to the runner-up with only a momentary flicker of embarrassment.

There is a very great reservation to be stated with respect to price negotiation. Some companies simply will *not* negotiate price. Some will who shouldn't. One has to be a good enough practical psychologist and business strategist to recognize when concessions are either not going to be forthcoming or will be counterproductive if they do. For example, the degree to which a vendor is willing to make price and contract concessions is roughly proportional to his desperation for business. Too much flexibility in this respect may denote actual or incipient instability on the part of the vendor. Furthermore, negotiating him into a position of negligible profitability on your deal runs two risks. First, this one could push him over the edge, so to speak, into a precarious business situation if he's new, small, weakly capitalized, or all of the above. Second, even a solid company gets quickly fatigued answering distress calls from a marginal or unprofitable account. Your sharp negotiating talents could push the vendor into a corner from which his only profitable escape is to shortchange you later. The "no free lunch" theory says that a deal that looks too good is too bad for somebody—either the buyer or the seller. And either way, you could be the loser.

On the other hand, let's not get overly solicitous for the vendors. Most of them do have some extra negotiating room in whatever they propose, saving a few aces and trumps for the last few tricks of the game. And most will not walk away from a sure sale just to uphold ceremony, policy or the sanctity of "fair trade" pricing. How far you go is a matter of judgment.

SUMMARY

An RFP and associated numerical rating scheme is essential if a large number of different vendors and/or alternatives are going to be considered. Such consideration cannot be applied without analyzing and objectifying the decision-making process.

- Take the lead in specifying what is wanted, both from the system and in the proposal.
- Demand precise, written answers to an exhaustive list of questions and information requests.
- Break down the evaluation process into a large number of factors that can be rated independently.
- Assign weights or emphasis multipliers to the factors roughly proportional to their importance.
- Sum up the weighted scores for each offering.
- Zero in on a few finalists and for these few check references and conduct tentative negotiations.
- Don't just check—*probe* references. Get behind the banalities.
- Tighten the "iron boot" a little on the finalists during the final selection stages, but don't cripple the winning contestant: he has to remain at least ambulatory to do your job properly.

13
Negotiating the Contract

The title of this chapter should really be "Wherein It Becomes Less Expensive for the Vendor to Perform Than Not," for that is the objective of negotiating the contract. That formulation may seem overly cold and cynical. After all, isn't the vendor a citizen of the business community like the rest of us? Doesn't the vendor want to do a good job, gain a loyal customer, get good references, avoid squabbles and complaints?

Of course. But there's something else the vendor wants more, and that's to meet his sales quota (which translated means keep his job or stay in business). Today's frenetically competitive small business computing marketplace virtually guarantees that the vendor will often overreach himself in order to stay alive. He will oversell, underspecify, make unrealistic promises, overcommit his resources, oversimplify and/or conceal problems to get the business, and then hope against hope things will work out later. Those are the facts, like it or not. We can perhaps offer some excuses for the vendor based on mitigating circumstances; the market is fiercely competitive, extremely price-sensitive and basically naive. It's also a relatively new business that hasn't yet settled down and found a sensible equilibrium.

The task at this juncture is to make sure that when a "crunch" of one kind or another comes, if it does, that the cards are stacked in your favor; that if someone gets short shrift it isn't you; that if unanticipated expenses are incurred through no fault of yours that someone else pays; and that the vendor never feels comfortable in taking calculated risks and muddling through with respect to *your* installation. It can be done. All it takes is extra effort, careful preparation and a cast-iron constitution.

Negotiating a contract can be as important as choosing the right system or service. You can do everything right all the way along and lose it all at the negotiating table.

Roy N. Freed, an attorney and founder of the Computer Law Association says, "There are opportunities to negotiate with practically all suppliers, especially if customers create a situation in which they have bargaining power and then use it effectively."[1] Freed asserts, and this author emphatically agrees, that most users throw away this opportunity out of ignorance, timidity or failure to allow sufficient time for negotiation within the procurement process.

VENDORS' NEGOTIATING STANCE

Fundamentally, the user is outgunned when he sits down at the contract table because:

- Vendors negotiate computer contracts for a living. They're well prepared and very professional about it.
- The vendor's contract is a very impressive, preprinted document that looks inviolable on the surface.
- The vendor will avow that "everybody" signs the standard contract and modifications are highly irregular and will complicate and delay the realization of the benefits which now appear so tantalizingly close at hand.

"You don't have to believe what the sales rep tells you. Nor do you have to sign the standard contract that you're given. You can negotiate. Vendors are going to be aggressive. But you can be just as hardnosed and get what you want," says Larry Lettieri, an editor of *Computer Decisions* magazine.[2]

Many vendors will readily agree to changes in their standard agreement if they're convinced that the buyer knows what he wants and that failure to give in to him will likely lose the order. Even this opportunity, begrudgingly granted, is easily lost if the buyer hasn't begun the process early in the procurement, allowing several weeks for it in his timetable, because the vendor may argue as follows:

"Look, ordinarily we might be able to work something out, but it would involve our home office legal department and possibly weeks of negotiating and exchanging drafts between your lawyers and ours.

[1]Roy N. Freed, "Computer Contracting Is Changing For The Better," *Computer Decisions* (June, 1979): 93.
[2]Larry Lettieri, "Negotiating The Contract Maze," *Computer Decisions* (April, 1977): 21.

There's no way we can do that and still get your order in and accepted in time to meet your January start date. Anyway, hundreds of other customers have signed our agreement, avoiding delays and legal expense, with no ill effects. . . ."

At this juncture, if you haven't previously fortified yourself with a list of demands and, perhaps, a suggested draft of a modified agreement and you have failed to initiate contract discussions in an earlier phase, you may be tempted to go ahead and sign as is. There are two other options that should be considered, however. One is to issue a purchase order stating that it is conditional upon completion of successful contract negotiations by such and such a date, after which time the purchase order is null and void if a contract between the parties has not been signed. The salesman may say that such an order unaccompanied by a signed contract is of no consequence, that company policy does not permit commencement of design or development work or placing firm orders into the production schedule without a contractual commitment from the buyer. However, it does at the very least put a bit of heat on the negotiating process and might speed it up, especially as the deadline approaches.

Another alternative is to delay the planned implementation until such time as a sensible agreement has been worked out. Is it really all that bad? What was the hurry in the first place? You've gone all these years without a computer, so why must you have one in the next 90 or 120 days? If the conversion is linked to a specific cutoff point, such as the beginning of a fiscal year, consummation of an acquisition, physical relocation, commencement of a new product or service, what were you going to do if the conversion happened to be delayed by one of a thousand other likely problems? If conversion is all that one-way, all or nothing, perhaps it is too risky a proposition to begin with. No data processing implementation should ever be planned without a whole series of fallback options of the "If we miss January, here's what we'll have to do to get started in February" variety.

Limitations of Liability

One of the provisions found in almost every vendor's standard contract goes something along the lines of "no warranties, express or implied, of merchantability or fitness of use whatever . . . ." This is usually coupled with some positive statement about a 30- or 90-day warranty on workmanship and materials, in the case of hardware, under which the vendor is obligated to replace or repair defective components. Baloney! That's 100% for him and zero for you!

The author has had the extreme displeasure of being in the courtroom as an after-the-event expert witness at the conclusion of an arduous trial in which it was conclusively proven that a system, due entirely to failure and incompetence of the vendor, never performed any useful work whatever and in fact nearly bankrupted the plaintiff, only to hear the judge find in favor of the defendant (vendor) on the grounds that the wording of the contract excluded performance as a condition for payment. That's what the contract says, that's what the buyer agreed to, so case dismissed!

Another famous, universal clause in vendor contracts states something to the effect that "the present agreement constitutes the entire agreement among the parties and excludes all other representations, verbal or written. . . ." On purely technical grounds, the contract *should* be the entire agreement. But what the vendor really wants to do with this clause is to sidestep the proposal, salesman's promises and even written specifications of the system if there are any. The user must insist that these promises, commitments and performance specifications *are* a part of the agreement, either by writing them into it, making specific reference to them as appendixes or by specifying a procedure by which they are developed and incorporated subsequently.

Another notorious provision of standard contracts has to do with the definition of the phrase "ready for your use" and linking payment terms thereto. It's doubtful that any reasonable buyer would object to paying the final balance owed on a computer system, for example, after it was, indeed, incontrovertibly proven to be "ready for your use." The problem is that the vendor's definition has to do with passing some predefined engineering tests which assure that for a few minutes the newly set-up system did actually compute, print, read, write, and so forth in accordance with factory standards. But what does that have to do with creating a bill of materials or writing payroll checks? About as much as saying that because his tools are sharp and in working order a carpenter is competent to build cabinets. Let's see a few mitred corners and tongue-and-groove joints before we make that judgment.

Brinkmanship

The vendor may put up quite a fight over some or all of your suggested contract changes, and, if they are vague or unreasonable, he may be perfectly justified in doing so. He may resist phrases like "in a timely manner" or "to the buyer's complete satisfaction." What do these purely subjective phrases really mean, and aren't we setting the stage for possible endless argument over what's timely and satisfactory? Fine. Let the vendor suggest something more specific and objective. If the vendor understands that you won't sign without written protection against possible default, he'll either come up with acceptable language in the contract or lose the business.

Is it all that bad? Assuming the RFP shook a number of viable contenders out of the bushes, why not fall back on number two or three? With more than 4,000 vendors competing for the business, it just doesn't stand to reason that only one can do the job. As a matter of fact, if the task is so constructed that only one vendor submits a viable bid, you should go back to the drawing boards: something is drastically wrong with your approach.

The best advice is to "hang tough" with respect to most of the suggestions contained in this chapter. You may be surprised at the last-minute creativity an otherwise recalcitrant vendor may exhibit once he's convinced you're really serious.

BASIC PROTECTIVE FRAMEWORK

What the user really wants to accomplish is to build in guarantees that the system will perform the proposed tasks, as advertised, and that all the value he is paying for is actually delivered in a *usable* form. In the more draconian condition, he wants out of the contract, his money back and, perhaps, payment for damages if the terms are not met and the situation is irremediable. But the user hopes never to be forced to invoke such sanctions, because to do so may literally take years of litigation, will certainly cost a great deal of executive time and legal expense dollars, both of which are far better spent on running the business rather than punishing recalcitrant computer vendors.

"Remedies should be picked more for their value in goading the supplier to perform than in helping the customer recover from a default," says lawyer Freed. Secondly, Freed says, "the trick is to identify significant performance obligations of the supplier promptly after the agreement becomes effective and to enable the customer to end the relationship as early as possible if the supplier turns out to be unreliable."[3]

There you have the basic negotiating strategy: to build in identifiable performance milestones which enable you (and others, if necessary) to determine whether or not the vendor is really delivering the goods and meeting his commitments, which carry penalties along with them strong enough to deter sloppy performance and, finally, which provide escape as painlessly as possible from the situation if the sanctions fail to turn the tide.

The Buyer's Obligations

On the other hand, let's not be guilty of as much one-sidedness on our account as the vendor originally attempted to foist upon us on his account. The buyer has clear and crucial obligations regarding the success of the installation that should be just as explicitly spelled out in the contract as the vendor's. The supplier is foolish if he doesn't insist on them; and the buyer's interests are not served by omitting them, because the buyer needs a clear statement of his responsibilities and, perhaps, a bit of a legal goad to keep his part of the joint venture in solid working order, too. Furthermore, if the buyer's obligations are clearly enunciated, and he can demonstrate that he has met them, the vendor doesn't have a leg to stand on in claiming that his default is by reason of the buyer's failures.

Some of the assurances to which a supplier is reasonably entitled are:

- A sensible, spacious, properly conditioned environment in which the equipment can function. The vendor should define for you exactly what this means for his particular brand of equipment or service.
- Access to the site. The vendor representatives must be allowed to get at your equipment, data and people, as reasonably necessary.
- Proper power and, if required, common-carrier communications facilities in support of the system. The vendor should specify exactly what is necessary.

[3]Freed, "Computer Contracting," p. 91.

· Proper staffing and full cooperation with respect to systems analysis, definition of requirements, approval of specifications, acceptance testing, provision of to-be-converted data, reasonable accuracy of that data, and ongoing operation of the system.
· Willingness to pay the going rate for additions and changes to the agreed-upon system.
· Agreement to refrain from misappropriating the vendor's property, stealing his trade secrets and, perhaps, recruiting his employees.
· Prompt payment for services rendered.

RECOMMENDED PROVISIONS

The following sections itemize some of the key provisions a user should consider for incorporation into his agreement with the seller of computer equipment, software and/or services. This does not constitute legal opinion, nor does it substitute for it. The reader needs to carefully consider the relevance to his particular circumstance of each of the ideas expressed and is strongly advised to consult with an attorney before drawing conclusions and undertaking definitive negotiations.

Specifications

The key to any user's contract is specifying what constitutes vendor performance in terms of quantity, quality, cost and timing. Foremost in any sensible agreement must be some means of specifying what it is that the delivered system is supposed to do for the user. One very simple approach is simply to append a copy of the proposal or RFP response to the contract, making appropriate reference to it in the text of the agreement. It may be, however, that the proposal merely states how the system specifications are going to be developed rather than defining them in advance. This is more likely to be the case in larger, more complicated or highly customized systems. There is much to be said for an approach that:

1. Incorporates the proposal in so far as broad, general commitments, dates and "not-to-exceed" prices are concerned
2. States the means by which detailed specifications are going to be developed and ratified

3. Inserts provisions to nullify the contract if ratification of the specifications is not accomplished by a certain date
4. Makes provisions to incorporate the specifications into the agreement once prepared and ratified

It is absolutely unacceptable to name applications and a few generic features in the contract and leave it at that. My idea of what constitutes "inventory control" or the proper format for an aged trial balance may be entirely different from yours. If I deliver my idea to you and you don't like it, do you take it as is or, if not, which one of us pays to change it? All of that should be worked out as far in advance as possible.

The modern, professional technique is for the vendor to prepare a very detailed systems description containing all functions, features, input formats, output documents and reports, the structure of all data files and other relevant formulas and descriptions, and then to have the buyer initial each page to signify his agreement. That way, the buyer knows exactly what he's buying, the seller knows what he has to deliver, and, if there is a deviation later in what is provided, the vendor is responsible, or in what is required, the buyer is responsible—a neat, simple and unequivocal as possible approach.

Developing specifications to such a level of detail implies designing the system, a time-consuming and costly procedure. It isn't reasonable to expect the vendor to totally underwrite that process himself, unless the proposed system is nearly 100% "canned" and uncustomized. It might be appropriate to provide in the contract for a down payment to the vendor which is partly refundable if the resulting specifications are not acceptable to the buyer.

At this stage the greater the level of detail is, the better. First of all, the vendor needs a document from which the system, or changes to it, can be programmed. It's dangerous to come to an agreement with the buyer on the basis of one document and hand a different one to the programming department. The fidelity of communications and the chances for strong conformance to the actual requirement are greatly enhanced by using the same documentation for both purposes. Secondly, many subtle discrepancies and some not so subtle ones don't come to light until the participants get down to the "grubby details."

The author recalls another expert witness after-the-fact situation, this one having stopped short of the courthouse, in which the vendor proposed a "two-step" order-processing system, among other applications of lesser importance. Buyer and seller each thought he knew what was meant by the term; namely that incoming orders would be entered into the system, picking and shipping documents prepared automatically, the order information stored until updated with any necessary changes, adjustments and shipping cost data and then invoiced. The two main steps being: order entry and adjustment, if any, and then invoicing.

After the hardware was "installed," meaning the manufacturer's engineers certified it to be in running condition, the user paid for it. Then the "two-step" order-handling system was installed. It was indeed two step, two big ones. Orders could be entered as long as desired, then adjustments entered and then the invoicing command issued. The problem was that all open orders were automatically invoiced whether adjusted and shipped or not. The program merely cleared the open order file, *in toto*. Since it wasn't the nature of this user's business to ship all orders received the same day, the system was totally useless. As it turned out, the changes needed to correct the logic of the order-processing programs were not trivial, and, worse, the vendor seemed unable or unwilling to make them.

The chances of uncovering an anomaly like this in advance of delivery and payment would have been materially improved by availability of detailed systems specifications. Even that wouldn't have provided 100% insurance in this case, unless the user happened to notice that the specifications made no mention of a cumulative open order report and the invoicing routine lacked provisions for indicating which orders to bill; but the chances would have been much better than the zero they turned out to be.

This brings up another important point: it is incumbent upon the buyer to read the proffered specifications thoughtfully and to compare them carefully with his original statement of requirements. He should be in a position to explain them to subordinates; if he can't, then either they aren't explicit enough or he doesn't understand them well enough. In either case, it's back to finishing school for more preparations prior to the big debut.

Schedules

Committed dates arrayed into a detailed schedule of events are an integral part of the total performance picture. Specifications, yes, but by when? How long after that before key parts of the system will be demonstrated? When will the hardware be delivered? What about site preparation, electrical and air conditioning arrangements? Data preparation and data conversion? Formal acceptance testing? Various types of training: management, technical, operations? What about design and ordering of forms and special supplies?

All of these items and more are still to be discussed in Chapter 14 under the heading of implementation planning, but the major events, especially as they involve performance and delivery by the vendor, need to appear in the contract along with the appropriate remedies in the event of nonperformance. In each case, the user must agree to perform his part of the bargain promptly and as specified. But if he has upheld his end of the contract and the milestones are not met, then the fault is clearly ascribable to the vendor, and he must correct the problem or suffer the penalty. Acts of God excepted, the vendor should be "on the hook" to meet promised dates. And even in cases beyond the seller's control, the user may still require a graceful exit which is reasonable and fair to both parties but which gets him out from under a hopelessly bogged-down situation.

Acceptance Testing

If the contract attempts to hold the vendor to specific deeds, acts and accomplishments, some means of determining whether he has indeed performed such feats is required. Usually, this acceptance and certification procedure, which should be spelled out clearly in the contract, takes three different forms, all three of which may apply at different stages of implementation.

Demonstration. If the vendor is developing a system or modifying an existing one, much of the work takes place long before "installation" in the user's establishment. Much of it, sometimes all of it, is ready for demonstration prior to the availability of the user's data and forms, training of his operators, proper reorganization of his procedures and so forth. Yet, using made-up sample data in place of real input, plain computer paper instead of forms, the vendor's premises and people instead of the user's, a fairly realistic demonstration can be performed which illustrates the features of the system.

There is one very important "plus" about such a demonstration: if the vendor *cannot* perform it, there is very little chance of his being able to go on to subsequent success. This also provides an easily perceived basis for getting out before the really big damage is done. He will of course in this situation avow that the failure was bad luck, hardware malfunction, a misunderstanding or whatever. Okay. Give him two weeks to get his act together and try again. Perhaps even a third strike might be permissible, but at some point the game must be called and everybody take their bats, mitts and balls and go home.

The demonstration, however important an early qualifier it is, is *not* conclusive in the positive sense for two reasons. First, it's not exhaustive. It is merely a sample, carefully chosen to illustrate the main features of the system and build up everyone's confidence that the final product has a decent chance of turning out well. It is not a laboratory experiment under controlled conditions to test all the possible side effects and ramifications of the system. It is merely illustrative and indicative, but a strong early warning if it goes poorly.

Second, demonstrations are almost always artificial in one way or another. It's very easy for a programmer to code in some instructions that will give the illusion of processing a transaction when, in actual fact, the transaction wasn't processed at all: the program merely referenced a file of prepared results to make things look right. To some extent even the most honest and objective demonstration has to resort to a few shortcuts to illustrate certain procedures— or else the demonstration would go on for months. "Faking" elaborate month-end closing and consolidation procedures to illustrate financial statement production might be an example.

The point is, a quick flyby over the Grand Canyon by airplane may serve to convince you that something very big, wide and deep is indeed there; but you haven't counted the rocks until you've been to the bottom, and getting there will take a lot of work.

Acceptance test. The next, and more conclusive stage in certifying the performance of the system is generally conducted in the user's shop, under quasi-realistic conditions, using data, forms and procedures very much like that of the finally installed production version. This *is* intended to be a laboratory test. It tries to duplicate as many of the realistic, live conditions the system will have to meet as possible.

This test is not "live"; that is, actual orders, vouchers, production decisions, or paychecks are not being produced; but, usually, data which was live in the recent past is used to determine if the system reacts appropriately and to see if results are comparable to what actually happened when the same transactions occurred in real life. Sometimes it's possible to run the system, or parts of it, in "live parallel," that is at the same time, using the same data, as is actually being handled by the old system it is designed to replace, and compare results point for point. Sometimes not. Obviously, if the new system does things the old one doesn't do or does them in some radically different way, then a strict "parallel" may be impossible to achieve. Common sense dictates how far to go in insisting on a point-to-point, transaction-by-transaction comparison.

The goal at this stage is to put the system, or parts of it, through rigid enough tests to determine the following:

· Does it conform virtually 100% to the agreed-upon specifications in terms of feature and function?
· Does it work reliably; that is, does it handle a mix of work over a protracted test period (two hours, a day, two days) with consistent, trouble-free results? Or does it stall and get "hung up" in an irrecoverable state of limbo or produce errors that neither operator nor developer can explain?
· Does it produce the specified volume of work in terms of lines per minute printed, transactions per hour input and processed, records output, files sorted, inquiries responded to and so forth?

It is absolutely foolhardy to allow the project to proceed further toward installation if these targets are not being met, because after "going live," time to correct deficiencies becomes a luxury—sometimes an unattainable one. It's a little like discussing swimming lessons with a drowning man; "It's a fine idea, and one of these days, as time allows we'll certainly put it on the agenda."

The acceptance test should be a prearranged experiment under agreed-upon conditions which attempt to simulate as closely as possible those of actual operation over a limited time period. The better defined it is, the less chance of ambiguity concerning results. The best acceptance test is one that has an unequivocal result: either pass or fail.

Definition language should run along the lines of the following:

"Process 20 actual orders, chosen at random from past work, with customer and stock numbers manually recoded to fall within the range of a sample data base consisting of actual data on 50 customers and 100 items. At least two such orders must precipitate negative credit approval conditions, and several omission backorder conditions must be simulated by adjusting on-hand balances to, or near, zero. The average processing time, using trained but inexperienced operators shall not exceed x seconds per line item over the elapsed test period. Ship-to instructions will . . . ."

Live operation. No matter how well planned and staged, demonstrations and acceptance tests are only simulations—minor league tryouts for the real thing. Absolute guarantee: no matter how well tested and carefully installed your system is, "bugs" and anomalies will crop up for weeks and possibly months afterward. Furthermore, fundamental design problems which should have been perfectly obvious earlier simply won't be noticed until the system is in regular productive use.

For example, take something as simple as assignment of duplicate account numbers. Perhaps the system is designed to assign new numbers from a list of unused ones. Did somebody remember to question what action to take if a new transaction comes through using an already existing number by mistake? Can the system distinguish this from a "change" and therefore refrain from replacing the old correct information with new equally correct but wrongly identified information? Idiotic question, you say. Anybody would have thought of this. Besides, any application package, no matter how skeletal, would have duplicate number checking built right in.

Right. But what happens if the number is a duplicate *and* the operator incorrectly identifies this transaction as a routine change rather than a new account? How does the system protect the replaced data in case it has to be recovered if an error is discovered later? How does the system routinely attempt to detect such an error? For example is there a "record count" maintained to which some external manual count of previous records plus additions minus deletions can be compared? Conversely, is any of the foregoing even relevant? Can it actually happen in your particular system? If it does, is it so unlikely and the consequences so trivial that checks and balances aren't warranted?

The point is that systems design is tricky and complicated, full of human judgments which can range from "good" to "bad" to "completely overlooked." And, even a perfectly proper design decision can be implemented clumsily or incorrectly. So, the system is absolutely guaranteed to have problems: some big, some small, some quick and obvious, some subtle and hidden for many days and weeks until a certain combination of events occurs.

The author is reminded of a financial accounting and reporting system which worked well for a year, went through a preliminary year-end close with no trouble and then "blew-up" in the final closing process. Specifications clearly stated that final adjusting entries could be processed against the partly adjusted, preliminarily closed files; but this feature had never been invoked or tested before. As it turned out, the only way to successfully circumvent the problem was to go back to the preclosed file and reprocess all adjusting and closing entries including the second-round adjustments. If that procedure hadn't worked, perhaps the board of directors would still be waiting for their fiscal 1977 financial statements, or more likely, the accounting department would have unlimbered the old eye shades and quill pens and burned more than a little "midnight oil," because there were over 3,000 accounts involved.

One never knows how well a data processing system will function until it is put to regular use. The final acceptance test is routine daily usage. The system, therefore, should not be "signed off" as fully acceptable until all applications are installed and working in a stable fashion. Some reasonable degree of contractual and financial leverage should be retained over the vendor until this final hurdle has been cleared. A holdback is recommended.

The vendor will argue vehemently against withholding final approval and the last dollar installment owed until a month or two or three past the installation of the concluding application. The author's somewhat jaded attitude remains constant on this issue: when the vendor has all he is going to get from you he may very well find better ways to spend his time than responding to your inquiries, change requests and trouble calls. He may argue that at this point payment could be arbitrarily withheld and perhaps used as a whip to force unreasonable concessions from him. Cash-flow may also be a problem for the supplier. However, the greater the specificity of the performance criteria built into the agreement, the less arbitrary you can be. And, as discussed later under the heading of remedies, there may be ways of softening the financial impact on the vendor by placing funds in escrow and by adding special bonuses if targets are met or exceeded.

Warranties

Given the opportunity, most vendors will guarantee nothing in writing. They are only too aware that computers sometimes exude a distinctly lemon fragrance, and that even the best planned software sometimes just doesn't "jell" in a given user environment. Sometimes troublesome computer components, problems with phone lines if they're involved, misunderstandings regarding software design and mistakes concerning selection and training of operating personnel, sudden unexpected turnover of key vendor or user personnel at crucial junctures in the project and a whole host of other not-so-rare occurrences can generate extensive cost overruns, even abject failure. Who should have to pay for these problems? If the fault is clearly yours, then maybe, just maybe, you.

But remember who induced you to buy the equipment or service, told you how easy it was going to be, calmed your every concern and assuaged all your doubts. Perhaps we can add a special note of realism to the vendor's sales recitation and to the conservatism of his planning by requiring him to *guarantee* the system: not just that delivered equipment is free from defects in material and workmanship for 30 days, but that the whole system *works,* that it does what it was purchased to do!

That is a very simple and equitable concept on the face of it, but, of course, it is very complicated to apply. The vendor can't wait for a year after installation, which might be two years after commencement of development work, to be paid. He can't be held perpetually at ransom by a client who orders him to take one more dance around the head of a pin or one more trip through the eye of a needle before considering bestowal of that final blessing that will at last unlock the royal vault and bring forth the long overdue and keenly merited payment for services rendered.

The answer, of course, is, first, a schedule of payments in step with demonstrated progress and performance, tied especially to such identifiable and quantifiable milestones as written specifications, demonstrations, acceptance tests and live operational tests. Second, guarantees of what the vendor is contractually obligated to do if any of these milestones are not met. And, third, some ongoing protection against difficulties encountered *after* all the tests and initial live performance criteria are met.

In the first category is contractual language such as, "The purchaser shall pay a deposit of 15% of the total purchase value of the equipment and services described at date of contract, said deposit to be refunded with no further obligation if seller fails to submit written specifications of the proposed system within x days of date of contract or if said specifications are not accepted by purchaser. . ."

In the second category is language like, "In the event the acceptance test fails to meet the specified levels of performance the seller is obligated to attempt to cure defects and arrange subsequent retesting no less frequently than every x days until such time as specified acceptance criteria are met. In the event y days have elapsed without said acceptance criteria having been met, then buyer's further obligations under the terms of this agreement are terminated. . . ."

Third-category language might run along these lines: "Seller further warrants that should defects subsequently arise which are not identifiably the fault of the buyer arising from accidental or willful neglect, damage or misuse of the system, the seller will undertake free of charge to cure such defects promptly and expeditiously within the reasonable constraints of. . . ."

No one can write your contract for you in advance without the specifics, but he can advise you not to settle for anything less than *some* kind of warranties for each of the three categories discussed in the foregoing—no matter *who* the vendor is. One thing very clear in dealing with vendors of small computers regardless of company size and reputation is that performance varies from time to time and place to place. Why risk the possibility, however remote, that yours may be the time and the place for a foul-up, uncharacteristic though it may be of the vendor elected?

Remedies

What if the vendor fails to live up to his warranted claims? What kinds of remedies should be built into the agreement to compensate the buyer for the failure? As a general principle, remedies should be chosen for their effect in goading the vendor to perform rather than as compensation for his failure to do so. The user will be far better served by a successful data processing implementation than by an administrative shambles, an arduous court fight and, perhaps at some later time, a few dollars of the vendor's money.

The best goad is conditioning something the vendor wants very much upon his meeting the goals appropriate to it. Therefore, the best sanction is withholding payment, wholly or in part, for equipment and services not delivered or not performing adequately. The vendor should never find himself in the position of being better off to "cut and run" than to put in the effort required to nail down the system and collect a final token payment. Settlement or write-off of the balance owed should never be a viable alternative for the vendor; the balance owed should always be far greater than the cost of completing the job. On the other hand, life is never that simple. Events can't always be perfectly synchronized with payment schedules, and some kinds of default could have ramifications far beyond the value of the unfulfilled portion of a contract. Some of the additional remedies you might want to consider are enumerated below.

Penalties. Although a very common feature of major contracts, penalties are not often applied to small business computer procurements. But why shouldn't they be, particularly if coupled with performance bonuses for meeting or exceeding objectives? For example, suppose a vendor says he can deliver a working system capable of processing 30 transactions per hour of a specified type over a sustained 8-hour workday, by October 1, for a total contract price of $28,750. Why not offer to pay $30,000, or a 4.3% bonus if he meets the commitment? After all, didn't we save a good deal more than 4.3% in choosing this vendor over, say, the XYZ Company, who wanted $35,000 for a comparable system? On the other hand, if delivery is delayed, or the time to reach a satisfactory production level protracted, there will be a growing chance of not making the full changeover as planned. If so, a great deal of expense and inconvenience will result. So, to go along with the performance bonus, how about a $50-per-day penalty for each calendar day beyond October 1 it takes to achieve the specified goal?

Credits. Certainly one should not be expected to pay lease, maintenance or ongoing service charges for deficient performance. The contract should specify relief in the form of credits against amounts otherwise owed in such cases. For instance, hardware maintenance charges should be suspended for any period in excess of a reasonable one, say one or two days, that a system is "down" and unavailable for use. If you are contracting for services on a monthly fee, it seems only reasonable that you should not pay for work not performed or performed in error through no fault of your own.

Most preprinted service bureau contracts limit liability in such cases to reprocessing of the work in question at the service bureau's expense. The problem in this case may be that information delivered late may be of no value whatever, and in some cases may produce consequences far more important than the cost of processing. For example, the negative cash-flow impact of mailing accounts receivable statements a month late or the implications of missing a payroll may easily justify credits for the whole month's processing and perhaps a good deal more as discussed below.

Damages. If you are going to fall short anywhere along the way in extracting contractual concessions from the vendor it will be under the heading of damages. Most vendors of products and services of *any* kind, computing included, abhor damages and will fight hard to avoid accepting responsibility for them. But all damages are not alike, and it may be possible to negotiate *some* form of compensation for damages into your contract.

Direct damages. Under this category are the costs of obtaining the contracted products for services from another source in the event that the vendor defaults. Continuing to operate the old system beyond its expected turnoff date, incurring overtime and temporary help expense, and turning the work over to another, possibly more expensive vendor and encountering additional conversion costs in the process are some of the direct damages a defaulting vendor might be logically expected to pay for. Getting him to agree to do so, however, will take some powerful persuasion.

Liquidated damages. Under this heading are penalty-type damages intended to strongly discourage inadequate performance and/or make the customer feel adequately compensated if the vendor does default. It will be a rare small business whose leverage or hypnotic bargaining skills can effect substantial liquidated damages provisions in a data processing contract. Nevertheless, it's worth a strong effort: it may be acceptable to a vendor who has been conservative enough to be absolutely certain of his performance claims, or it could set the stage for acceptance of some of the lesser remedies talked about earlier.

Consequential damages. The enormous power of computing works against the buyer in attempting to negotiate compensation for the indirect or consequential effects of a data processing failure. The potential consequences of late or incorrect information, loss of control, misallocation of resources, loss of customers, diminution of public trust and so on could be enormous, possibly tens or hundreds of times the price of data processing equipment or services. It is unrealistic to expect the vendor to shoulder unlimited exposure to any and all such risks. The vendor may be willing to listen regarding one or two specific areas of vulnerability against which he and you can take special precautions, perhaps at some extra cost. By and large, though, consequential damages will be excluded from most computer contracts.

Other Provisions

There are a number of specifics that may appear in a contract for data processing equipment and/or services concerning misuse and misconduct on both sides. For example, the vendor may impose very specific restrictions with respect to resale of, or divulging information to others about, licensed software. A license to use software usually does not entitle you to violate the supplier's trade secrets and proprietary rights or to misappropriate his property by selling or giving it to another party. Correspondingly, the vendor shouldn't have the right to divulge any trade secrets, customer lists or other proprietary information about *your* business to anyone without your express consent. All data related to the system should contractually remain your sole property.

One other "treaty" sometimes found in computer contracts has each party agreeing to refrain from recruiting each other's employees for some stated period of time unless expressly waived by the other party in a given circumstance. The reasoning behind this is obvious. Vendor and customer can become fairly intimate with one another during implementation of a data processing system. Out of proximity and familiarity may bloom an irresistible temptation to pirate key performers unless a prior agreement prohibits such unprofessional deeds.

One other provision you might wish to include is an arbitration clause whereby all disputes under the terms of contract, if not resolved by mutual consent, are submitted to binding third-party arbitration. Arrangements of this kind are attractive to buyer and seller alike because they stand to avoid lengthy, costly litigation. From the buyer's point of view, arbitration may provide the only *practical* means of action in the event of vendor default—litigation is too draconian a weapon to employ except in a hopeless situation, in which case it may be too late to be of any real benefit. The American Arbitration Association, 140 West 51 Street, New York, NY 10022, is an agency whose services are often employed for such purposes.

IN SUMMATION, YOUR HONOR...

The main object in contract negotiating is to build in specific incentives which encourage the vendor to make good on his claims. In the event of default, the contract should provide remedies which fix the problem and/or which compensate the buyer for the resulting trouble and expense. These should be realistic and easily invoked, compared to draconian penalties that look good on paper but pragmatically can be employed only by instituting a lawsuit, the outcome of which, of course, always remains uncertain. The best medicine is preventative, keeping ahead of the vendor financially, so that he is always eager to finish, to correct and to please in order to obtain his just reward.

Buyers can negotiate good contracts with almost every seller of computers, software and services, but only if they come to the table *prepared* with:

· Plenty of time and fortitude to see it through, no matter how frustrating and time-consuming.
· A list of demands that are logical, defensible and above all *specific*.

· The benefit of competent legal advice and assistance.
· A passionate insistence bordering on the fanatic that acceptance and payment be conditioned upon *performance*! Payment and performance can be finely graduated into various specification, demonstration, test and operating stages, but the two should be inextricably linked.

14
Implementation

Part of the decision to settle on a particular vendor had to do with his apparent grasp of the implementation process and his willingness to commit planning assistance and actual help in the doing. Undoubtedly contract and specification negotiations were also influenced by considerations of implementation and by the vendor's willingness to become involved. And doubtless, too, the vendor has his own version of a "pat" implementation plan into which dates and names of people and events have already been "plugged." So what else remains other than to let this preordained process take its course? Plenty! The rules about placing yourself totally into the hands and upon the tender mercies of vendors apply to implementation as well as to all other phases of a to-be-successful automation project. You need to take the lead, to set the pace, and to follow through relentlessly to see that everything gets done correctly and on time.

PLANNING

The importance of thinking ahead and setting those thoughts down into a coherent, more or less formal plan cannot be overemphasized. Failure to do so can cause serious blunders and, perhaps, a false start, recovery from which may be difficult or even impossible. Think of it this way: if despite announced intentions and feverish preparations the whole conversion process collapses into error and pandemonium, everyone's natural fears and skepticism are instantly realized. Incipient distrust of computers is reinforced. The last shred of hope and confidence may be lost. In short, if they ever were, the team now ceases to be "believers." All this, of course, is in addition to the dollar costs of a serious disruption or delay.

Certain applications systems may depend on historical data for comparisons, running averages for making projections, and existing balances and open items for proper accounting and reporting. One must plan carefully how to best pick up or develop such information and how to do it in a time-phased sequence that yields a reasonable chance of synchronizing with reality. Let's illustrate the point with a horrible example or two.

Suppose one of the main features of a to-be-installed inventory control system is "average costing"—each shipment is received at its actual cost, and that figure and the number of units involved are added to respective totals in each inventory record; then the first is divided by the second, and a new average cost is computed for purposes of evaluating inventory, cost of sales and profit computation. The question is, how to get it started.

Let's suppose the strategy is to go through an elaborate manual recapitulation of recent costed inventory receipts to come up with an accurate "going-in" average cost for each item. Then, after some selected "go" date, all new receipts, together with cost information, are entered through the computer, resulting in smooth and automatic updating of both on-hand balances and average cost information. Right? Wrong!

Items are physically received before vendor invoices arrive, or we experience initial problems matching up invoices with specific receipts. Stock is piling up on the loading dock waiting for cost information before being entered into inventory. The choice comes down to meeting customer needs while undermining the cost system, or saving the system and losing the business. So we naturally decide to put the stock into inventory, forget the cost figures and then later go through another manual recapitulation and cost catch-up to get the costing system working. Now we're facing another tricky cutoff problem, but it's worse this time because the system is already live and running, except for the costing feature, and we don't have the luxury of interrupting or delaying it while this conversion within a conversion takes place.

If the whole process had been carefully thought through in advance, we might have designed both the conversion and the application itself quite differently. For one thing, we might have given up on the idea of true average costs and used a standard costing system with separate variance accounting for adjustment of standard to actual. Or, we might have set up the program to assign any uncosted new receipts to a suspense category which, if still uncosted at time of sale, would be assigned the current average cost. Actual costs would then adjust averages only on unsold balances; the remainder would be posted to an adjustment account.

Another, much more common illustration has to do with picking up historical information, say, in a sales analysis application. Let's suppose we want to develop year-to-date totals of sales by product and by customer. If the system is up and running at the commencement of a new year, then the accumulation of product sales for each customer, assuming that's what we want, is a cinch. With the proper storage space allocated, as each order is processed the transactions are appropriately posted to magnetic tape or disk records for subsequent analysis. The posting is a totally automatic by-product of sales order processing.

But suppose conversion to the new order-processing system is delayed by six months. What happens to the running accumulation of sales data? There isn't any. The only way to create it at that point is to go back through a 6-month accumulation of orders and reprocess them through a program especially prepared for the purpose, which updates sales analysis figures. That would be an enormous task. Most companies would simply give up on the year-to-date detailed analysis, recognizing that the reported figures will remain deficient throughout the remainder of the year and, worse, will confound year-to-year comparisons throughout the next full year's operation.

A better answer might have been to contract with a service bureau to perform sales analysis, perhaps coupled with receivables, for a year or more prior to the conversion, with a clearly understood prior arrangement to deliver the accumulated detail data in processible form on a tape or disk at the time of actual conversion, regardless of when it finally occurs. The exact media, format and cost of such an exchange would obviously have to be defined in advance so as not to be hostage to the service bureau when the appointed moment arrives.

Planning is the key. Not only must the grand strategy of conversion and implementation be planned, but each component must be carefully worked out so that the whole process fits within the available time and resources and that everyone upon whom the project depends knows what he or she has to do and by what date.

There is no practical way of doing this without painstaking thought translated into written documentation. The document is as important as the thought, because the details must be communicated on a continuing basis to all the participants. The Gantt chart is a well-established component of such plans. A sample is shown here as Table 14-1. The chart is a means of quick visual reference to what is supposed to happen. Each activity on the chart must be fully explained, usually in a narrative section of the plan.

Sometimes major activities appear on the "master" chart as one line but are broken down into subcomponents on more detailed subsidiary charts. There is no one formula best for every situation, but it is hard to imagine any implementation project able to go forward smoothly without start, duration and completion times specified for each activity in an easily understood graphic form like the one illustrated.

Equally important is posting progress against each planned activity as the project unfolds so as to be aware of which ones are falling behind, and what impact these are likely to have on other related functions and upon the projected completion date of the project as a

Table 14-1. Example of a Gantt Chart Depicting a Portion of an Implementation Schedule.

Activity	1	2	3	4	5	week number 6	7	8	9	10	11	12......
Develop functional specifications		X---------------------------------X										
Approve specifications						X----------X						
Finalize forms								X----------X				
Order forms									X			
Develop external control procedures							X------------------------X				
Review with auditors										X-------......		
Carry out programming								X---------------------------			
Demonstrate A/R											X--.....	
Train operators for Phase I											....	
Review inventory											....	
Test A/R											....	

whole. Many people simply post actual start, progress and completion data to the same Gantt or similar type charts in close proximity to the originally planned data. An example might look like Table 14-2.

Any one of the activities depicted in the example could, and should, be further broken down into distinct segments and, although not shown in the table, names of responsible individuals attached. For example, if an accounts receivable application is to be tested, a given number of sample customer accounts must be selected or created, sample transactions prepared, an operator trained, a specific time reserved on an available machine on which to run the test, a series of deliberate mistakes—both data and operator errors—planned to ascertain how the system reacts to them, and so on. Each of these subactivities has a necessary begin- and end-date and must be assigned to a specific individual to accomplish.

As is almost always the case in dealing with computers, the more painstaking and detailed a job one does with this documentation, the

Table 14-2. Actual Progress Data Posted on Implementation Schedule.

Activity	1	2	3	4	5	6	7	8	9	10	11	12......
							week number					
Develop functional specifications	X	X———————				X	X					
Approve specifications						X———X	X-----X					
Finalize forms							X—————X	X------X				
Order forms									X	X		
Develop external control procedures						X--------			X———	X		
Review with auditors										X-----		
Carry out programming						X--------			X———	......		
Demonstrate A/R											X--	
Train operators for Phase I											...	
Review inventory											...	
Test A/R											...	

better. Also, a weekly or biweekly meeting among all the key people involved, user and vendor alike, is a must. At this meeting the plan is brought up to date based on actual progress (or lack thereof), future plans are altered based on the reality of the situation, problems are discussed and solutions decided upon.

It is advisable to create a problem-solving versus a confrontational atmosphere in progress-review meetings. The tone should be honest, open and businesslike, perhaps stern to the extent that participants know failure is not condoned, yet not to the extent that problems and slippages are concealed to avoid unpleasantness. A tongue-lashing may be well deserved, but a more constructive approach might be to say, "Look, I'm not at all happy about not having the x phase finished this week as planned. Now let's see what can be done to minimize the impact on the rest of the schedule. And, I'd like some suggestions on how we can prevent something like this from sneaking by us in the future."

Someone should be assigned the job of taking notes at these meetings, updating the charts and distributing copies of the minutes and updated charts to all concerned. This goes a long way toward preventing future confusion over what really *was* decided at the last meeting.

SPECIFIC MILESTONES

The sum total of your implementation project is made up of a myriad of individual activities, but there are some key, cardinal events deserving of special attention and the title of important milestones.

Specifications

Up to now, we've said a good deal about the nature and importance of written specifications, so it will not be necessary to retrace all that ground. It is relevant, however, to place submission and approval of specifications as *the* key milestone in the opening phase of implementation. Virtually nothing else except ordering equipment and physically preparing the site for it can go forward until specifications are approved. Programmers can do nothing until the design is settled, forms can't be finalized and ordered, operators can't be trained, procedures external to the computer developed and so on.

Whoever is responsible for drawing up the detailed design of the system is going to need time and cooperation. Cooperation means lengthy interviews with key people, sometimes repeated ad nauseam, to go over requirements and evolving design details until the pieces all fit. These "nit-picking" design sessions can be exceedingly frustrating and boring for managers, but there really isn't any alternative. The process can be likened to designing an airplane, all or the vast bulk of which is better done on the ground before flight, not during.

Carrying the analogy a bit further, there are numerous "degrees of freedom" inherent in the finished product as to where it can be flown, with what cargo, on what schedule and so on, if it has been properly designed and constructed. And numerous enhancements and refinements in the basic design will evolve through time, experience and with continued use, many of which can be added "in the air" or "between hops" on the ground. But don't expect to fly with two left wings and "work out some of the details later." Basically, your whole system has to function, as a unit, safely and soundly from the moment of lift-off, because you and your entire business are going to be on-board passengers. Overlooked design details can cause unstable or uncontrollable operation leading to sudden, unplanned contact with ground and surrounding objects.

It pays to put a great deal into design at the drawing-board stage, rather than having to face the same problems later when changes are not as easy to make as applying an eraser to pencil marks. One of the areas that users consistently get into trouble over in this respect is classification and categorization. Things like the financial chart of accounts, part numbering, customer coding, commodity classification, operations coding and many others have profound impact on how well the system will work, how adaptable it is to further expansion, and on flexibility to meet future conditions without serious disruption, redesign and redevelopment.

For example, adopting a comprehensive, open-ended chart of accounts for fiscal reporting purposes is a clear prerequisite to computerizing general accounting. The establishment of division, department, cost center and other breakdowns is important, and doing it correctly, with the proper structure, number of digits in each classification and adequate reclassification and cross-referencing capability, is essential. Have you thought about whether a department or cost center is ever going to be transferred to another division? Okay. What happens to historical, comparative data: month to date, year to date, same period last year, and so on? Does it stay with the original division or transfer to the new classification as well? If so, how? And how is this going to affect established budget, ratio, allocation and other formulations? Couldn't you, your accountant or bookkeeper and a computer systems analyst spend many hours thrashing out this issue?

It's far better to invest the effort now than to face the possibility some time in the future of not being able to make an important restructuring move or meet a new government reporting requirement because "the computer can't handle it."

The rules on specifications are simple:

- Allow plenty of time for their development
- Budget personal and staff time for active involvement
- Get specifications in writing and in full detail
- Review them exhaustively, imagining every conceivable exception, error and future change while doing so
- Sign every page along with the vendor, to indicate approval and to put the design "on ice"

Demonstrations

Demonstrations are useful, but hardly conclusive. They are a good opportunity to spot gross misunderstandings fairly early in the implementation process, and they give a clear signal, as any milestone should, as to whether the project is or is not on schedule. After all, though a demonstration is always artificial to some extent, if only because some of the supporting systems and data bases don't yet exist, if the vendor can't demonstrate it *at all,* artificially or otherwise, that's a pretty good indication that the project is in some kind of trouble.

The demonstration is also a good point at which to ask a lot of questions, particularly of the "what-if-this-happens" variety, to seek out flaws in the design, failures in human communications between specification writers and approvers on the one hand and the actual implementors on the other, and to uncover those exceptions that were overlooked in the earlier design discussions.

But, even if the demonstration comes off smoothly and flawlessly, there's still plenty of opportunity for hair-raising misadventure ahead, so don't let down your guard.

Tests

Tests differ from demonstrations in that they are supposed to be legitimate, scientific experiments to see how well some facet or facets or the system perform under simulated live conditions. Programmers do a great deal of testing at the microscopic level in developing parts of their programs. They are also supposed to do broader, overall function and system testing; but most programmers do not regard exhaustive, carefully prepared tests as much more exciting and personally rewarding than preparing documentation—which is to say, not at all.

Part of the plan may include individual subfunction and subsystem testing in a more or less structured, laboratory format, or all the formality may be saved up for the ultimate test, the *acceptance test*. However, even if the preliminary tests aren't formal clipboard and stopwatch affairs, they are going to need data, sample transactions, perhaps totals to balance to, perhaps an operator and a machine, and a careful examination of the results by someone who knows what they should look like. All of the foregoing are activites that are a part of the overall implementation plan, and provisions should be made for them within it.

Acceptance Testing

Perhaps enough has already been said about the acceptance test in Chapter 13, but it is among the key implementation milestones: probably the most important in terms of financial commitment and as a final go/no-go indicator. As such, a good amount of effort and time should be budgeted, not the least of which will be devoted to developing sample data and test-case transactions.

It is entirely possible at this stage that data conversion has already progressed to the degree that much of the required *static* information is already captured on disk or tape in usable condition. Static information would include such things as codes, account numbers, names, locations, terms, previous period historical data and so forth. Usually, current financial and operating data, such as account balances, open items, on-hand inventory balances and the like will not be introduced until the very moment the system is to go "live," in place of or parallel to the existing system.

Creating a complete test data base, therefore, may be as simple as selecting a portion of the already converted static files, copying to a separate medium, and adding current balances to the copied files either by inventing them or by picking up actual live data in much the same way as it will be done at the time of the real conversion.

Transactions for the test can be invented or "borrowed" from activity being carried on currently. Borrowing transactions from the present production stream may save a great deal of work but may require careful screening to eliminate references to data records that are not going to be a part of the test data base. Also, the sample selected will most assuredly not contain every exception and error condition you desire to test. Accordingly, some modifications and insertions will have to be included.

The test itself should cover three aspects of each application:

1. Feature and function. Does the system perform each specified function exactly as specified?
2. Control. Are all affected records correctly posted, in balance and in agreement with one another? Are errors of all types properly recognized and appropriately handled? Is the system safeguarded from unauthorized access and from deliberate destruction?
3. Throughput. Does the system process the specified quantity of work in a given space of time under a reasonably realistic simulation of real-life operation?

Allowances can be included for such things as the operator's lack of familiarity with the system, but fundamentally the application or applications on the test block should run acceptably and as advertised, or else the test grade is "fail." A fair amount of time should be budgeted in the implementation plan for "fix-up" and retesting of applications that do not score a passing grade the first time around.

Data Conversion

Another important activity on the implementation chart is data conversion, and its completion is a key milestone. Conversion here means both conversion of existing data to machine-processible form and creation of additional data not now a part of the existing system but necessary to make the new one function.

An example might be creation of a payroll-personnel file. Static pay data including employee number, name, social security number, department, shift, pay rate and past period earnings and deductions might be picked up from the currently active payroll system. If it happens to be on a computer, perhaps in a service bureau, the information might already be in a usable format, or easily convertible to a usable state. Personnel information might exist mainly in original employment application forms, so a second computer file might be created by keying in information from employment records under control of a one-time data-entry program written expressly for that purpose. A third category of information involving, say, details on education and occupational training may not be available in any existing company record. Gathering this data might require circulating a questionnaire to all employees and then key-entering the results to a third file under control of still another single-use program.

A second major step might be electronically merging the three data files just described into an appropriately formatted payroll-personnel master file, once again using a data-conversion program written just for the purpose. Finally, at the moment of actual activation of the payroll-personnel system, the current period earnings and deduction information as of the last pay period might be entered and posted directly to the new, soon-to-be-complete data base.

It should be obvious from this example that a good deal of planning and preparation would have to go into the data-conversion process so that data are captured, proofread, balanced and available for processing at the precise time required.

Special data-conversion programs are often needed. They must be designed, programmed and tested. Information from manual records often requires purification and editing. Records may need modification prior to computer entry such as updating with new account numbers, category codes, uniform standard abbreviations and the like. In some special cases it may be feasible to obtain prepared data from an outside source which would otherwise be difficult or even impossible to develop internally. Standard item nomenclature files in the automotive field, universal procedure and diagnostic codes in health care, drug interaction files for pharmacists, census tract data, mailing lists, and a wide variety of econometric, fiscal and stock-price data are available for a price, typically on magnetic tape, for one-time use or on a periodically updated basis for continuous reference.

Live Parallel

One of the best and lowest risk methods for ascertaining whether a data processing system meets specifications and is ready for use is to run it "live parallel," which means to operate it side by side with the current system using the exact same data, duplicating the same functions and then compare results. If there are hidden flaws in the new system, or if it is extraordinarily clumsy to operate or control, these facts should become apparent quickly when operating in parallel with the present method. If the defects discovered are serious enough to require shutting down the system for further design and repair, little harm has been done to the regular flow of work which continues to handle business in the regular fashion.

Live parallel operation is not, however, without its problems. First, it literally doubles the amount of work to be done, demanding that all transactions and changes be processed twice: old way and new way. Further, the new way is unfamiliar, no matter how good an orientation and training job has been done. This means that the new system will never be more halting, error-prone and confusing than at the precise moment when first introduced in a parallel mode. And it is at this same moment when the maximum possible strain is imposed on clerical and operating personnel, who are asked to master the new system, process a full work load through it and, all the while, keep full pace with the old one. It's not an easy task; in some cases it may even turn out to be impossible. It may also be that the systems are inherently nonparallel and *cannot* be compared point for point. Obviously, if the new system is performing functions that don't exist in the old, such as computing optimum purchase quantity and timing for inventory replenishment, one can't look at what the buyer did and what the system would have suggested he do and "zero-balance" the two. It's a matter of judgment whether the computer decisions are as good as, inferior to or better than those of its human counterpart. Chances are the human counterpart won't be overly enthusiastic on this point, and only a long period of use will yield any indication of the real superiority, if any, of the new feature.

Also, some systems can't be run in parallel. A production shop can't be scheduled two ways, for example. Either machine center work loads are scheduled the old way or the new, supposedly more efficient way. You can't run the factory two ways at the same time. Furthermore, feedback of actual production data into the new scheduling system may be irrelevant if it comes from a plant being run by the old method. The best one can hope to do under such conditions is to *simulate* a parallel operation on paper, creating assumed interactions with a mythical system which is diverging from present reality with each passing moment. Then it's once again a matter of judgment whether the new method has proven itself sound and superior, unless the simulation is carried out to unusual lengths covering many weeks or months of assumed operation.

Nevertheless, live parallel runs are useful, especially for straightforward clerical and accounting functions where comparability of results can be ascertained. Now then, how much is enough? Is it enough to run Friday's regular work over again on the new system during the weekend, and, if the two are in balance with one another, change over to full running staus on Monday?

Probably not, for two reasons. One, a single day's work is too limited a sample of the various conditions the new system is likely to meet in full-time operation. Second, business systems tend to run on a cyclical basis, with daily, weekly, monthly, quarterly, yearly and sometimes even longer cutoff points at which certain data are summarized, categorized by period, dropped or moved forward, and new projections made, reports created and so on. Operating the new system for a year or more in parallel with the old to experience and test each of these cycle points would be carrying prudence a bit too far. But it may not be unreasonable to do so for several days, crossing a month-end closing and, additionally, very carefully simulating quarter-end and year-end activity purely on a test basis. A good rule is to run parallel as long as there is any remaining doubt about the new system and/or as long as you can stand the economic and human strain of doing so.

One common strategy is to plan one month of full parallel, followed by a second if only minor troubles arise, and then go directly into full live operation at the conclusion of the paralleling if it has proved successful.

On the other hand, if serious problems are unearthed during the parallel run which cannot be quickly and easily remedied, then the whole process must be "frozen" until changes are made, new tests performed, and the parallel process reinstituted. The gap could be days, weeks or months, depending on the nature of the problem. However, many a hapless computer "disaster" victim now wishes he'd run his system in parallel for a month or two before installing and paying for it, no matter how inconvenient and expensive it might have seemed at the time.

Live Operation

Live operation is the milestone most eagerly awaited and of greatest drama, at which point the new system casts off under its own power without further support from the old one. Almost everything that has been done with respect to the computerization project has been pointed toward and is a mere prelude to this single event. It is to be hoped that all the demonstration, testing and parallel operations have melded smoothly into a continuous progression of stronger and stronger evidence of success, developing sufficient confidence to discontinue the old system altogether and operate solely on the basis of the new.

When is the new system truly "live"? When is implementation "over"? First of all, initiation of live operation is usually a sequence of events, not an all-at-once phenomenon. Each application, or group of related applications, has probably been activated by itself in accordance with a schedule spanning many months. It is illogical in most, but not all, cases to try to "bring up" all application systems at once. Often it's wiser to gain experience one subsystem at a time, also using those implemented earlier to help build the data base and operational framework for succeeding ones. It may well be, also, that certain future applications are still in the design or even the wishful thinking stage. So from that point of view, the job isn't "done," completely, for a long time.

And from the point of view of software maintentance, ongoing discovery and correction of minor errors, further evolution and adjustment of the system and preparation to meet changing business conditions, the job is *never* done. So what is live operation? When is the system successful? When does the vendor get the last penny of his money?

We discussed this question rather thoroughly under the heading of contract negotiations in Chapter 13, concluding that several weeks of operating experience with each application might be required to certify each as fully functional. One thing is certain: the commencement of live operation is no time to relax one's guard. Careful inspection, verifying and balancing of output must continue, and, in fact, must do so for the entire life of the system, but special measures and extraordinary care must be taken during this inaugural period. Furthermore, the standard weekly or biweekly progress-reporting meetings with the vendor should continue during this time to help ferret out difficulties and solve problems as they arise. At these meetings, people in charge of operating the system should be encouraged to speak up about questions and difficulties, giving developers an opportunity to make corrections or straighten out misunderstandings.

RESPONSIBILITIES

The vendor's responsibilities within the overall implementation project will, of course, vary depending on what you have contracted with him to do. Generally speaking, however, the vendor is held responsible for: delivering the various agreed-upon products and services per specifications and proving their soundness, orienting top managers and supervisors and training user personnel directly involved with system operation and use in all the disciplines involved, providing technical support and consultation throughout the project and, finally, for maintaining hardware and software in operable condition on an ongoing basis.

The user's responsibilities are equally easy to list but are not always easy to meet: provide a suitable physical environment for people and equipment, including proper space, power, heating and air conditioning, access and security; provide full, clear and unambiguous guidance in the development and review of systems specifications; and provide full cooperation at all levels in the planning, implementation and operation of the system.

It is on the last term of agreement, cooperation, that many users fail to live up to their commitments and responsibilities. Sometimes, but not often, the problem is the chief executive who just won't take the time to make sure everyone in the organization is toeing the mark or who lacks the time and interest to review specifications and schedules in detail to insure that work is progressing rapidly enough and in the proper direction. The cure is simple in this case: either do the job or appoint someone else with the full responsibility and authority to do it with two further provisos: that the delegated coordinator possess the requisite skill, knowledge of the business, drive and decisiveness to be successful and, second, that having abdicated, you stay out of it. You have a right to demand periodic progress reports and to carry on private critiques with your coordinator: you do not benefit from crossing him or her up in public meetings, issuing conflicting orders, reversing decisions and sowing confusion and distrust among the ranks. If your management surrogate needs that kind of supervision, then you've made the wrong choice.

A much more common problem not having directly to do with top management but often influenced thereby is the failure to obtain cooperation at lower levels in the organization. There is no system dead or alive that can't be defeated by its users—the people who prepare the forms, press the keys, read the reports, handle the documents, post the external controls, answer inquiries, coordinate their work and that of others with the computer and, in general, have to live and breath in the computerized environment.

Furthermore, there is almost no organization that doesn't start down the road to automation with a heavy load of hostility and fear—usually sufficient, if left unchecked, to scuttle the project for certain. The reasons are not hard to find. Automation is going to upset the work/social/security balance in the office. People were formerly comfortable in their "niche," knew their job, their place in the organization, their "status" with respect to fellow workers and felt reasonably certain they could hang on to what they have, if not actually better themselves, without much additional effort. These people now suddenly find themselves dealt unfamiliar cards from a strange deck. New forms, new procedures, strange and intimidating devices, new job descriptions, new reporting relationships and a new "pecking order" is in the offing. Can you blame people for feeling resistance and fear, for wishing things could be left alone in the old comfortable and secure way? Is it surprising that paranoia creeps into their thought processes: "What is this going to do to me? What if I can't learn how to run this thing? Isn't it really a plot to show up my ignorance, highlight my deficiencies, *get rid of me?*"

Under these conditions, people react in a variety of negative ways. Some simply retreat in a kind of fatalistic, fear-induced paralysis.

Others become professional skeptics, pointing out all the things that can go wrong instead of pitching in to see that they don't. Others try to build a mystical and artistic barrier between themselves and the computer by contending that "computers can do simple tasks but not *my* job! I use subtle judgment based on history and intimate knowledge of. . . . You have to be sensitive to mood, to fast-breaking events, even to the humidity and barometric pressure to make the kinds of decisions I do."

And, of course, unwittingly or otherwise, some people become saboteurs, edging the project into a "can't-win" situation by refusing to reveal all the details of a procedure, by failing to deflect bad data on its way to the computer, by stalling, equivocating, failing to cooperate and refusing to put forth their best efforts at points in conversion and early operation when all-out support is crucially needed.

Putting these fears to rest, creating positive, optimistic attitudes and gaining full support of the data processing adventure is *your* job. Only the top decision maker can drive home the following three points convincingly:

1. We really need this proposed system. It will do great things for the business, and without it we'll sooner or later "go down the tubes."
2. I really mean for it to work. All kidding aside and time, energy, money, and personal feelings notwithstanding, I'm determined to make this thing a success. There are no options. Resistance is futile.
3. Nobody here is going to get hurt. There may be a few changes, some new opportunities to learn exciting new skills, along with some discomfort. But basically everyone's past loyalty will be rewarded and no one need fear being left out in the cold.

If the decision maker can make these pronouncements convincingly in the beginning and then lend unwavering support as the project progresses, the battle is nearly won. If, however, resistance does surface and proves insusceptible to further exhortation and blandishment, then the offender ought to be transferred out of the area or out of the company altogether before the damage becomes irreparable.

It is not altogether unprecedented for a chief executive to harbor secret thoughts about his staff at variance with the earnest pledges enunciated above. In other words, he may really intend the computerizing to make possible the removal of one or several substandard employees. There are two distinct dangers in taking this approach: First, the assurances won't be believed, namely because they are false and the employees sense that to be the case.

Second, employees who are on the "hit list" but are being played along until after the conversion is complete are very likely to quit right in the middle of the most pressing phases of implementation, when their loss is least affordable. During tests, parallels and early live operation, people are going to be called upon to give their all, to work harder and longer than they have in years, and to do so under the most trying circumstances—errors, pressure, confusion, double work. It is precisely the disaffected, underappreciated worker (who feels the same way about you as you do about him) who will "throw in the towel," reasoning quite logically that he doesn't have much of a future in this company anyway, so why put up with all this extra work and pressure? This likelihood militates in favor of making overdue staff changes first, up front, before automating and leads naturally into the next topic.

DON'T AUTOMATE A MESS

Many business people regard computerization as a panacea to cure all manner of procedural, organizational and personnel problems. The facts are simple: if you try to automate a mess, you will get an automated mess. As a corollary it can be stated that nothing makes mistakes faster than a computer wrongly programmed, improperly operated or fed invalid data. Nothing. Think of it. Even the smallest, least expensive machines now execute tens or hundreds of thousands of program steps per second. Most spew out reports measured in dozens or hundreds of lines per minute. That represents a staggering potential for making millions of bad decisions and printing out thousands of wrong numbers every day, and at no small expense.

If the business problems confronted by computerization run very deep into areas of management incompetence, poor organization, poor morale, low-quality staff, inadequate training, low pay and flimsy benefits, understaffing, carelessness and so on, then the first order of business has to be "cleaning up the act" as it is, rather than bringing in automation to further confuse the picture. Computer systems work best on a solid foundation of loyal, disciplined, well-organized and competent staff. Without these ingredients, there is very little support on which to build a dependable system. The risks are unacceptably high.

The best prescription under such circumstances is: clean house, rebuild and then reconsider automation. You may not even need it, but if you do, you'll have something solid and worthwhile to build on. Part of the study undertaken of the present system which led to developing systems requirements and an RFP focused on making improvements to it now, in the short run, prior to further consideration of automating. The same thing applies to organization and staff. In parallel with the systems study should be a careful analysis of current job assignments, reporting structure and employee performance. Much has been written on the subject of organizational analysis, performance appraisal, management by objectives and other tools and techniques for better managing an organization. Consulting firms, universities and other institutions offer literature, training courses and direct assistance regarding the "human resources" side of business. In the face of this body of knowledge there is really no excuse for putting up with serious deficiencies without at least an attempt at solving them.

Much of what a painstaking analysis of your organization and staff will reveal, you already know. Perhaps you have hesitated to take action for humanitarian reasons or because you lacked outside confirmation. What you do is entirely your concern, but consider that computerization merely amplifies the work of the organization in the way a power saw amplifies the capabilities of a carpenter. If the carpenter doesn't know what to do, or knows what but not how, the power saw will simply help him spoil a lot more lumber than he could by himself.

Finally, if there are fundamental weaknesses in the way an organization is structured or staffed, introducing a radical change like automation will bring out the very worst in it. Many businesses, like nonswimmers, will drown in heavy waves. And nothing makes waves like a computer. "Beefing up" the areas to be automated by means of judicious staff changes, extra management attention, deliberate overstaffing and use of temporary help may very well be justified.

FOLLOW-THROUGH

Having successfully installed an automated system is only step one. Beyond this minor miracle is a long road ahead, strewn liberally with potholes and boulders. Many things can still go wrong and certainly will, without continuous attention and care.

The Break-in Period

You will probably hear about outrageous problems that crop up during the infancy of your computerized system. Many of them will have a sky-is-falling tone requiring the utmost in self-control to refrain from leaping out of the chair to challenge the computer supplier to a duel, throttle the programming staff, head for the nearest psychiatrist, chaplain, or tavern, or even arrange to meet the former at the latter. Some of the common hardware and system-related failures that plague computer installations, along with suggested remedies, are discussed in the next chapter. Rest assured, they will occur in their most frightening and frustrating form; more frequently at first but, let us hope, less so as time goes by.

The consequences of such failures can usually be overcome by calm, patient reasoning and hard work. Suppose, for example, all or a large part of the inventory file has been wiped out through an obscure program error triggered by a rare combination of circumstances. The regular file backup procedure was not run either last night or the night before, because the second disk drive was "down" and awaiting replacement parts being flown in from the vendor's plant in Nepal. And, to top it off, someone used the disk pack containing the backup information from three nights ago for another purpose because, under normal circumstances, that is a perfectly normal and acceptable thing to do.

Farfetched? Something just like this is almost certain to happen to every computer user now and again. What to do? Don't panic. Get the best heads together: the data processing supervisor, the vendor's serviceman, a programmer/analyst and affected department heads and work out a plan. Is there an overlooked tape or disk containing the information? A recent printout containing most of what's needed? Or must the records be reconstructed from a combination of static data from a listing plus current balances from a hastily in-sititued physical inventory count? Do the input programs exist to perform the reconstruction in the prescribed manner? If not, how long will it take to develop them? Can manufacturing and/or distrib-ution continue on an interim, makeshift basis in the absence of the inventory file? How will transactions "catch up" with the system when it is finally reactivated? Simply reprocessing all the makeshift paperwork on an after-the-fact basis may not work without modifi-cation, because actions of the computerized system are dependent on the exact timing and sequence of transactions. The logic of the pro-gram will likely not duplicate the actions and logic employed by peo-ple performing the task manually. Is there a "manual override" pro-vision with which to overcome this problem?

There is no way to anticipate all the rich varieties of crisis situa-tions that may arise in a given installation. Prudent safeguards against destruction of data, adequate backup, sound procedures and programs, good documentation, good people and good luck are all valuable factors in preventing or minimizing trouble. But once it oc-curs, calm, innovative problem solving is the order of the day. It may be well to save the table pounding, recriminations and retribu-tions for later, after the crisis has passed.

Keeping Up Momentum

Even in the best of circumstances, with a relatively smooth conver-sion and break-in, lacking major crises and disruptions, there are still likely to be irritations, discrepancies and misunderstandings sur-rounding the new system during its early stages and for a long time thereafter. Left unchecked, the accumulation of minor irritants can have a corrosive effect on people's attitudes, turning initial enthu-siasm into indifference and even hostility as time goes by.

There is no substitute for communicating with the people who use the system and upon whom its continued success depends. Discus-sion meetings, training sessions, feedback forums or some other ap-propriate means ought to be employed to draw out reactions and problems on a more or less regular basis. In small organizations this can be very informal, but it ought to be fairly regular and may re-quire coaxing and bantering to get some people to respond. The last thing you need is employees nursing secret grudges against the system. Airing the difficulty and explaining the reasons for it are often enough to satisfy a complaint. No system is perfect; furthermore, conditions do change. Keeping an ear to the ground for rumblings of trouble will detect legitimate needs for improvements and alterations. How does one go about effecting such changes?

Program Maintenance

The case has already been made that both correcting errors and adjusting the sytem to changing business conditions is inevitable and ongoing. Does this imply having a full-time programmer on staff or teaching one or more of the senior operators or supervisors how to program? Possibly.

The three main requisites for system maintenance are:

1. Deciding what to do
2. Obtaining the services of somebody qualified to do it
3. Having a system well enough constructed, documented and understood so that maintenance is possible

On the last point, the author is reminded of a visit to a huge insurance company's data processing installation which occupied literally acres of floor space and contained dozens of large-scale computers lined up in long rows like platoons of soldiers on parade. Off in one corner of this super-large, super-modern facility was an antique punched-card computer, the first of its kind, and many, many years out of date. It looked, and was, totally out of place. When asked, the general manager of this "leading-edge" department explained that the tired old machine couldn't be dispensed with because it was needed for one very complicated actuarial calculation each month, the programmer of which was long gone, the documentation for which was indecipherable and the language in which it was written a lost art. The manager lived in terror against the day that someone would come along with modification to the actuarial formula and expect him to effect changes in the program.

With respect to what is to be done, that decision usually results from an assessment of how expensive and time-consuming a particular change will be versus where it sits on the priority list in terms of potential benefits and/or urgency. An extensive dialog between management and the person or persons charged with the responsibility for program maintenance would seem to be in order. Yet, in the final analysis, management must decide which changes to make, in what sequence, and must establish a schedule and budget for their accomplishment. Don't be at all surprised if the total cost of maintaining and enhancing programs over a period of a few years equals or exceeds their original development cost.

To find qualified help, many small businesses rely on the original developer to maintain software, while a similarly large proportion find in-house resources to get this job done. A few use hit-or-miss arrangements with other outsiders. If the original developer offers ongoing maintenance at reasonable rates, responds when called upon and does a good, professional job of effecting changes and making the necessary corollary changes to system documentation, then that is usually the preferable choice.

If someone inside the organization has the time, native ability and develops enough experience to function effectively in the role of maintenance programmer, then an apparently low-cost alternative exists. The qualifier "apparently" reflects the possibility that this person's other regular work could suffer during periods of heavy systems involvement, representing a hidden cost. If the would-be programmer is a high ranking executive, the hidden cost could be considerable.

The hit-or-miss approach, if it hits, can be very effective. Finding just the right moonlighter, who is competent but more importantly steady and available, can be a godsend. Using the same one over a long period of time eliminates learning and familiarization time, and saves money by providing the equivalent of a readily available fully trained staff member without the corresponding employment expense. The problem with this approach is finding such a resource in the first place and then controlling it. Being "captive" to an outside technician can be an uncomfortable position. Depending on a vendor or software house is disquieting enough, but a single individual is an uncertain quantity indeed. Free-lance programmers can change professions, move to Vermont, become sick or disabled, get married, divorced or join a commune.

The optimum plan has fallback positions such that if source A fails, source B, who is reasonably familiar with the system can take over and, if B is unavailable, C can be called upon in a pinch. One thing is certain: a good deal of attention must be given to this crucial determinant of the long-run success of the installation. Will your system be a dynamic vehicle for growth, or will it be an airless tomb? Only your maintenance programmer knows for sure.

Progress Reviews

Within a few weeks after the system is certified to be installed and running, it is a good idea to perform a review of its effectiveness. A study involving interviews with and observations of users, analysis of final development and running costs of the system and a hard, analytic look at displaced costs and other anticipated benefits is in order. So what? The deed is done. If we miscalculated, we're certainly not going to take the whole thing out and start all over.

Probably not. However, if there are shortfalls in the realization of benefits or overruns in effort and costs, two good reasons exist for exposing and examining them:

1. Learning from the mistakes so as not to repeat the same ones in the future.
2. Modifiying the approach, sometimes only slightly, to remedy the shortcomings after they become apparent. The systems world is replete with examples of failed methods that suddenly blossomed into successes with a switch from cards to envelopes, tags to labels, repositioning data on a report, adding a tear-off stub to a document, or simply retraining operators and users.

Most problems are amenable to one solution or another, but only if the problem solver has gone to the trouble of finding out what exactly is wrong. To discover that the anticipated reduction of one person in the production-expediting department has not been effected because of a continuing high level of activity in that area isn't sufficient. Why hasn't the system helped reduce the volume of expediting? What are the sources of the current cases? What can be done about it? The answer may be: nothing, that the reduction was based on naive assumptions, or that some element of added control over work-in-process, scrap, the tool room or some other aspect would cause a dramatic breakthrough in bringing about the hoped-for savings.

Sometimes the solution to a problem is laughably simple when viewed in the right way. The author recalls a vexing difficulty concerning a computerized payroll system called upon to incorporate expense reimbursement for a certain category of employees. The problem was how to identify the transaction and control the system such that it added to net pay without being taxed and without affecting salary records. The answer was ridiculously simple: enter reimbursable expenses as negative deductions. Not only did a minus deduction add to net pay without affecting tax liability and payroll totals, but it neatly accounted for itself as a separate entity on the deduction register, to which expense reports could be balanced.

Progress or systems reviews are emphatically in the plural. That is, one is not enough, because the target is continually moving. The analysis of needs, problems, costs and savings should be renewed on a periodic basis; probably quarterly in some businesses, annually or semiannually in others, depending on the velocity of change. This is the best insurance you can buy that your system will attain the cost-effectiveness you originally projected and keep it over its entire life span.

SUMMARY

Successful implementations don't just happen; they're planned in meticulous detail, and progress is checked each step of the way. The plan must spell out specific milestones: events that can be recognized unequivocally as having been achieved or not, to which specific dates and names of responsible individuals are attached.

Of the important milestones, detailed system specifications, their review and acceptance, and the formal acceptance testing of the delivered system are probably the most essential and most deserving of intense concentration. Running a new system in parallel with the old is almost always advisable. Problems will surface here that would be far more damaging after the changeover.

The system is never "done." Problems, errors, improvements and changing business requirements are never-ending; therefore, ongoing software maintenance is extremely important, and dependable arrangements for it must be included in the project. Ongoing periodic review of the health and welfare of the entire data processing operation is strongly recommended.

People problems almost always dwarf technical difficulties in automation. Sound organization and competent staff are a prerequisite for success. Further, motivation needs constant attention: handle attitudinal problems by promoting free expression of grievances, displaying unwavering support and staying calm in the face of crises.

15
Continuing Considerations

Computers, like most people, usually don't continue to perform well if unmanaged. There are a number of steps the executive responsible for the system must take in the "preventative medicine" realm to keep it healthy, and a few things he or she should know about what to do when the beast is ill—before, during and after the doctor comes.

ONGOING CONCERNS

Audit and Control

Certainly, no system should be operated—automated, manual or otherwise—without foolproof accounting controls, periodic audit and periodic review of performance from an audit and control point of view. Presumably the user's auditors satisfied themselves that the procedural controls to prevent serious error and fraud were sound at the outset, at least *in theory*. Furthermore, provisions were probably incorporated in the system to facilitate the audit of accounting records, such as reference codes and batch numbers to simplify tracing transactions, production of A/R confirmation statements and so on.

But, who has tested the system lately to see if the control provisions still work properly, if indeed they ever did? If your auditors are reluctant to undertake testing the accounting controls in a computerized system, perhaps due to inexperience, they should be encouraged to employ the outside services of others who are better able to review the soundness of the system.

Remember, a very clever employee with access to the computer and strong motivation—perhaps a poor win-loss record at the track—may even *alter* the system in some obscure way that defeats the controls put in place originally. This possibility needs to be guarded against with surprise audits, periodic rotation of personnel, changing passwords, and testing of working programs to see if the control features still function properly. On an informal basis, the chief executive should demand occasional printouts of certain master files and transaction files on the spot, and review them personally. An hour or two of browsing through vendor or payroll history files or physically balancing transaction records against disbursement totals could be very useful in deterring any possible abuse.

Security and Backup

An important pillar in the original implementation plan undoubtedly was keeping the system "covered" against various natural and man-made threats and contingencies. Provisions to store copies of magnetic files and printed reports off-premises and/or in a fire-resistant vault, use of physical barriers like a locked room and electronic barriers like coded passwords to control access to the system, extra precautions in the case of remote telephone access, arrangements to use another set of equipment if the primary one becomes unavailable for a long period and training of backup personnel were all probably part of the picture.

Yet, no matter how carefully these security arrangements were made in the first place, they must be examined every few months to be sure they're still in place and still appropriate. Use of a password scheme over a long period of time or after experiencing turnover of some of the people acquainted with it may require revising it and issuing new access codes. File backup and storage procedures may become lax over time. Are they still being rigidly observed? What about extra copies of crucial data files and reports? Has a natural deterioration in housekeeping permitted some of these to lie around on desks and other exposed areas where outsiders could conceivably gain access to them?

It doesn't hurt to review fallback provisions periodically. Does the vendor still maintain a readily available computer for programming, testing and customer backup in his local branch, or has it been recently moved to Cincinnati? Are the backup programmers and operators still "up to snuff"? Are they still even on the payroll?

In general, it's a good idea to have people, equipment and facilities lined up to take over some or all of the data processing work in an emergency. Some companies are now making a business out of providing these facilities on a subscription basis to large computer users, but to the author's knowledge none cater to the minicomputer and small business market. Perhaps the day will come when such services will be extended to the smaller users, although the dizzying profusion of different, incompatible small systems in use makes this less than likely. Meanwhile, users must make their own, unique arrangements.

The price of security is eternal vigilance. The user must keep asking himself "what-if" questions about every conceivable mishap, guard against them, and then perform "white glove" inspections to test their efficacy.

Reliability

One of the most frequent sources of ongoing frustration among computer users is poor reliability. It sometimes happens in fits and starts, sometimes rather regularly and always at awkward times when it can be least afforded—but computer systems do go down.

Hardware problems. Repeated hardware failure in the same system sometimes the same component, is not the rule in the small computer field, but it certainly isn't rare or unheard of. Often the manufacturer recognizes design errors or material defects long after systems have been delivered, after accumulating evidence that a part of the system is failing statistically more frequently than it should. But sometimes it takes a long time for this accumulation and feedback of information to occur, and even longer to come up with a solution to the problem.

The worst kind of hardware problem is the "intermittent" failure, the one that occurs at random, for no apparent reason, and never seems to repeat itself when the service man is in the room. There are software and hardware maintenance aids on most modern small computers to record and track down such errors, but nevertheless the illusive intermittent hardware "bug" is still a plague on many machines. Very often it takes creativity, imagination and long experience on the part of the service representative to track down such problems, and very often the person on a particular account is too new to possess those characteristics.

The quality of service personnel, their training and also their availability, and the availability of spare parts are major determinants of the effectiveness of preventative and remedial maintenance of equipment, which in turn translates into reliability. Statistically, a minicomputer system ought to be available at least 95% of the time it is scheduled for use. Many installed systems have attained availability records of 98% or 99% over protracted time periods. A system falling noticeably short of the 95% level needs management attention.

Solving hardware problems. The first difficulty in solving a problem is knowing you have one. The second is convincing the vendor's service organization. Putting on enough pressure to get the problem fixed is the third. Let's examine each of these.

Actually, the first and second are solvable together by keeping an accurate log of system operation. Every single day in the life of your system, be it outside service or in-house hardware, must be chronicled in the log. At the very least, each daily log should contain the following:

- Date
- Time the system was first started up for the day's activities
- Time it was shut down for the night
- Nature of any difficulties encountered, including time and duration
- Time a call for service was initiated
- Time the service representative arrived, his description of what the problem was, what he did to correct it, his signature and time of departure
- Notation if any further difficulty was experienced after the system was turned back over for your use

Many users also keep a production log of what jobs were on the system at various times of the day and what machine resources, terminals and operators were involved. In the case of the more advanced systems with elaborate system software, this information is recorded automatically by the computer itself, stored and made available for cost-allocation, efficiency-reporting and production-scheduling purposes.

Getting problems to the attention of the right people and motivating them to act upon them depends heavily on the operating and service log, the leverage written into the contract and on the user's ability to raise a rumpus. It's hard to choose the most important of these three attributes, but without a log it's your word against theirs. With a log you have something very concrete upon which to negotiate better service coverage, base a complaint to higher authority or, if necessary, support arbitration or legal action. By all means, keep a log.

Sometimes the vendor's service department will cast suspicion for recurring hardware problems on misuse or environmental difficulties. If operators are a causative factor, allowing the vendor or an outside consultant to keep watch for a day or two can conceivably resolve the issue. The environmental question is an easy one. Continuous recording instruments are available for purchase or loan that create a permanent record of temperature, humidity and power fluctuations. If the strip charts from the recorders indicate an "out-of-spec" condition, it can usually be fixed. If no difficulties show up on the charts, the ball is back in the vendor's court.

Software reliability. System instability and downtime can just as easily stem from software problems as from mechanical or electrical ones. It's hard to imagine that a program thoroughly tested and in productive use can still contain "bugs"—but it certainly can. Certain unique and rare combinations of conditions involving split-second timing can set off an error that is (1) illogical on the face of it and (2) almost impossible to reproduce. Occasionally a user is forced to live with a strange and infrequently recurring error condition because absolutely no one can find the source. More often, though, careful detective work in concert with the vendor's field and home office experts can track it down, especially if evidence of similar problems is beginning to accumulate from other user organizations.

Having a written record of problems, strong leverage with the vendor and a loud voice is as helpful with regard to software problems as it is with those related to hardware. The picture is vastly complicated if several different vendors are involved, however. The ultimate patience-straining situation would concern a remote terminal procedure yielding inconsistent results in which the list of suspects reads like an Agatha Christie mystery: the operator, the terminal, the modem, the phone line, the modem at the computer center end, the systems software, the application program, the machine, or a peculiar combination of any or all of the above.

Having fairly free and open access to experts in hardware, software and communications can be a big help. Often, problems can be diagnosed by discussing them with appropriate experts over the phone. Some systems permit experts to access the hardware and software directly via telecommunications, using remote terminals and special diagnostic software to detect and even repair problems remotely. Whatever the case, the user should have a series of prepared fallback positions for resolving such problems, escalating from stage to stage if each prior one fails to evince a solution, culminating, perhaps, in arousing the system's designer at home at 3:00 a.m. on a Sunday morning when necessary.

However, don't expect the home office expert, bleary-eyed and dazed from lack of sleep and a long, unexpected and unwelcome airplane flight, to make much progress without documentation. File layouts, input and output formats, flowcharts, program listings and descriptions, reference documents and operator instructions will be required, plus operating logs and actual samples of the problem: printouts of the incorrect documents and files, contents of main memory and any other obtainable evidence of the status of the system when the problem occurred.

Performance and Cost

There is a tendency for systems to change over time in a negative direction with respect to productivity. Changes frequently add extra processing burdens because they simply require more work than the original. Very often, changes, even of a positive nature with respect to throughput, are not very adeptly implemented and may therefore have an adverse effect. Sometimes files grow to an unmanageable size, overburdened with inactive data. Whatever the reason, the productivity of a system is subject to decay and ought to be reexamined periodically. If performance has fallen off materially, perhaps steps should be taken to revise and simplify programs, upgrade the hardware or, if there is no other alternative, eliminate some of the work load or extend the operating schedule.

The latter is not only an inconvenience, but can translate directly into higher costs. So does expanding the capacity of the computer system, but very often expansion costs are less than commensurate with the resulting performance improvement. To make this clearer, suppose a single terminal computer system has reached the point of severe strain. For argument's sake, suppose a second shift either is already in place or is inappropriate for certain key applications because they are tied to customer or plant activities that occur only during normal daytime business hours. Let's also suppose that the hardware portion of the system, exclusive of applications programs, cost $30,000.

What to do? If the particular brand and model can support multiple terminals and two or more concurrent processes (multiprogramming), and most systems in the $30,000-price class do, then the answer may be as simple as that: add a second terminal, another 8K or 16K characters of main memory to support the extra terminal if required, and hire another operator.

It would not be unusual for this kind of upgrading of capacity to cost as little as $2,000 for the additional memory and $2,000–4,000 for the extra workstation; let's assume a total of $6,000 in this case. Therefore, for a 20% increment in hardware cost, it may be possible to ostensibly double its capacity. In actual fact the throughput capacity would probably not double because:

· Additional systems software overhead could be incurred to manage the second workstation, reducing the realizable gain significantly.
· Other components of the system such as the printer, auxiliary storage or the processor, may now become limiting factors, putting a "ceiling" on how much is gained by adding the new terminal.
· Work scheduling may be such that full advantage of the second workstation can only be realized during certain portions of the day.

All of these limitations notwithstanding, it would be unusual not to achieve a gain of 40–50% in capability in the hypothetical situation described. Thus, paying an extra 20% for 40% more capacity would seem to be a logical move.

Unfortunately the opportunity to solve production bottlenecks in a computer system isn't always as simple and clear-cut as portrayed in the example. Problems may involve conflicts for machine resources, file-accessing conflicts and/or inefficiencies, inherent limitations in device speeds, hardware and software architecture and difficulties in scheduling work optimally.

With respect to scheduling, it's not unusual for a high-speed printer to stand idle for hours while data is being entered, updated, sorted or otherwise prepared for a report and then run on into the night at full speed to "catch up." Many scheduling inefficiencies are inherent in the nature of the work and therefore unavoidable; others can be reduced with planning and foresight. Having a production log showing what jobs were on the system throughout each work period, when they commenced and ended and some indication of the number of records or transactions processed in each case will prove helpful in resolving conflicts and planning future production.

Keeping tabs on data processing costs will also prove helpful in planning and controlling operation and orderly growth of the system as a whole through time. The data processing function should be budgeted and measured like any other cost center in the organization, including all its direct and indirect equipment, labor, supply and overhead expenses. Comparing the total with previous periods and, especially, as a ratio to transaction volume, sales dollars or some other relevant work-load indicator, can reveal changing trends in the efficiency of the operation. Clues as to what to do about reduced efficiency will be suggested by close examination of operating logs to see where bottlenecks are occurring. Solutions may include rewriting particular programs to "tighten them up," reorganizing files, upgrading hardware capacity, improving job scheduling, retraining or replacing operators or even revising procedures external to the computer to speed up availability or improve the quality of source information.

One problem observed in computerized firms of all sizes, especially prevalent in the bigger ones but not infrequent in small ones too, is "creeping reportitis." Over a period of time a buildup of special computer reports, analyses, audit trails, and reference listings can occur. Because it happens slowly, and because there always seems to be good justification for each individual instance at the time it arises, the accumulation is hard to control; yet in total it may represent an enormous waste of computer, handling, reading and filing time. The best way to contain the problem is not to allow it to happen, imposing a very hard-nosed attitude toward any proposed new report or enhancement. If the decision maker is unable to maintain such an unyielding posture, it's a good idea to review all documents, an application at a time, at least once a year—challenging each one to see if it can be eliminated altogether or combined with another. Converting data to microfilm or microfiche may be a way of easing the printing and storage burden in some cases and can, by virtue of its ready availability, reduce the demand for other reports and reference material. Nevertheless, producing useless microfilm is no less foolish than unneeded conventional forms; it's just more convenient.

COMMON PROBLEMS

The following sections describe some common difficulties encountered by many small businesses in the ongoing operation of their automated systems. The list is by no means exhaustive, nor are the suggested remedies the final word in every case, but the recitation may at least serve as a starting point in developing a solution. In any case, the afflicted reader may feel a little better knowing that others have experienced similar problems.

Electrical Power Problems

Losing electrical power altogether makes computing rather difficult because the machines generally don't come with a crank, solar cells or penlight batteries. Obviously, if the power goes out, so does the computing system, unless you are equipped with something called a "UPS," which stands for Uninterruptible Power Supply. A UPS is quite expensive; one big enough to supply a small computer and surrounding office and plant facilities (there's no point in having just the computer running without the business functions it supports) costs as much or more than the computer.

On the other hand, in most industrialized areas, power failures are rare and brief. The real problem is transient variations in voltage, sometimes resulting from inadequate power company service but more often, from sharing service with start-stop electrical devices in the immediate vicinity of the computer—usually elevators, large electric motors and other heavy electrical equipment in the same building.

The symptoms are erratic, unstable operation of the equipment, repeated damage to certain computer components and, sometimes, hard-to-trace errors. A strip-recorder attached to the power line serving the computer equipment will generally verify the problem.

The cure is "cleaner" power obtained by (1) operating the computer on its own line directly to the power distribution point in the building, (2) attaching a separate external "ground" for the equipment, (3) the power company's improving the capacity and quality of the power it delivers to the building and (4) installing an isolation transformer which compensates only for momentary fluctuations in power without the far more expensive UPS-type function mentioned above.

Another, rather silly-sounding problem that can produce symptoms similar to those stemming from impure power is static electricity. Many offices operate in an atmosphere of very low humidity, especially in winter, and compound the problem with carpeting. The combination sets off sparks which don't look like much but can throw delicate computer circuits into a "tizzy." Humidification to normal office comfort standards, tile floors or use of specially treated static-free carpeting, and adequate independent grounding of terminals and other components usually solves the difficulty.

Poor Maintenance

If the mechanical and electrical performance of the system is poor, the service department response to trouble calls exceedingly slow, and if the time taken to repair failures is exceedingly long, then the customer needs to take matters strongly in hand. Complaints, threats, or refusal to pay bills, may be employed with varying degrees of success. Generally speaking, if the customer is aggressive enough, the problem is usually rectified. If not, the user can sometimes find another source for maintenance in the form of an independent computer service company that works on terms and prices similar to the manufacturer's service department. Raytheon Computer Maintenance Services and Sorbus, Incorporated come immediately to mind as two nationwide organizations that perform independent computer maintenance for a wide variety of different types of equipment.

A do-it-yourself approach to maintenance is not impossible, especially with the newer, small microprocessor systems, but is generally confined to "swapping" failed components with spares or "loaners" while the original is being repaired at the factory or service depot. Mechanical components like printers and disk drives are the most difficult to handle on this basis, because spares are expensive and not always readily available. Subtle interaction between the equipment and its systems software is often at the root of the problem, so the user may find himself adrift without the support of a strong technical maintenance and support organization. Ideally, the user should be able to take care of the simple problems at reduced cost, backed by a local depot for spares with further technical support available from the manufacturer as needed. For the moment, generally speaking, workable options along these lines are rare. Most users will continue to find comfort and security in standard contract maintenance either from the manufacturer or a third-party service organization.

Inadequate Software Maintenance

The crucial importance of proper ongoing support of application programs has already been stressed (systems software is important, too, but usually falls under the heading and within the responsibility of manufacturer-supplied maintenance). The question at this point is what to do if the original well-intentioned measures fail to provide adequate results; that is, programs and their associated training and reference documents are not being kept up to date, needed changes are not being accomplished and/or desired changes frequently set off a chain of untoward consequences that make the user wish things had been left alone in their earlier clumsy but workable state.

Beyond limited managerial, contractual and moral sanctions, the user is at the mercy of his software support supplier. If he has written a decent contract and can get both possession of and the right to use original source programs, then the remedy is simply to turn the responsibility over to another source inside or outside the company. If the user does *not* have access to adequately documented source programs, this approach is doomed to a very difficult, expensive and uncertain course, not to be lightly undertaken.

Unhappily, there aren't any simple, universal remedies for the problem. The best medicine is preventative. The user who finds himself in an untenable position with respect to program maintenance may have to start over with a new implementation, on a sounder, more professional basis.

OBSOLESCENCE

A number of factors work against the longevity of a computerized system.

- The equipment itself may cease to perform adequately over the years as components degrade because of wear and age, spare parts become less available, and the skill and familiarity of service personnel decline.
- The basic architectural framework of the "system" in its entirety, the whole original approach, may cease to be serviceable. A case in point is what is happening to most batch processing systems today as interactive ones gain ascendancy.
- Complexity and volume may rise to a point no longer supportable within the limits of the system.
- Improved technology most certainly will render the equipment in use today hopelessly obsolete, clumsy, expensive to maintain, and inflexible by comparison.

So, at some point, the new system purchased today will be the old system in need of replacement. The trick, of course, is to postpone that inevitability as long as possible, within the limits of good sense.

Preparing for Replacement

Using a so-called higher-level programming language, observing accepted documentation standards and, above all, keeping documentation up to date with all changes as time goes on is the best preparation possible for the ultimate conversion of the new system to its successor. Along with this should go notes on strengths and weaknesses of the system, techniques tried but subsequently abandoned as unworkable and a list of proposed enhancements which have not been implemented for one reason or another.

Continuous operating statistics in the form of periodically posted charts and graphs depicting the work load, including such things as number of each type of active records, numbers of transactions processed, number of lines printed on various output documents, and running time and operator hours spent on each function will be useful in the day-to-day management of the installation and in planning for the extension of its capacity. Projections of future peak processing and file capacity needs will be easier to arrive at and more accurate based on this documented historical perspective. Seasonal patterns and long-term trends will stand out clearly.

Finally, all or most of the data needed by a future system will already exist in computer-readable form on magnetic tapes or disks, needing only to be mounted, read at high speed, and be programmatically reformatted for the new data base design. What a far cry from the toil and tribulations involved in the creation of its predecessor! By comparison to what the reader is going through, or about to, the *next* system will be "duck soup."

Postponing the Inevitable

Premature demise of the system is to be avoided at all costs. Why? Because for one thing the acquisition and start-up expenses incurred in its creation need to be amortized over a reasonable period of time, at least as long as the one chosen for justification and budgetary purposes. Second, the management time and effort expended on still another data processing procurement, though possibly less than in the present case, will still be considerable. Future options may be even more profuse and difficult to choose from than now. Third, another major systems change will bring with it the same kind, if not degree, of disruption, uncertainty, reorganization and relearning as at present. There is little justification for exposing the organization to such trauma sooner or oftener than absolutely necessary.

Certainly, the existence in the marketplace of a cheaper, faster, shinier computer is insufficient reason to cast the old one over the side so long as it is serviceable, cost-effective, dependable and capable of providing a type and level of service that does not seriously impair the company's competitive or community standing or its overall efficiency.

In other words, if it works, keep it. There's no disgrace in using last year's model, or even one from the last decade, as long as it remains serviceable. The question then becomes how to keep it serviceable.

Extending System Life

Beyond the obvious—upgrading the capacity of the hardware and expanding application programs—there are other steps a user can take to extend the viable life span of a data processing system. One is not to stubbornly insist that "everything" be put on or remain on the computer. A careful examination of how the system is spending its time may reveal that some functions, perhaps entire applications, are not worth the effort.

Some functions require a degree of precision, amount of processing time and/or volume of input out of proportion to their value. Some, but not all, motor freight companies have found automatic rating of freight bills to fall into this category. Some insurance agents and brokers have found automatic policy quoting not worth the effort to maintain the pricing files. Some manufacturers have given up plant scheduling by computer, preferring to handle that part of the application manually. Certain clinics and medical practices have found the accounting aspects of computerization extremely effective, while deciding against the use of a computer to schedule appointments.

The list could go on. The point is that manual or semiautomated procedures in support of a computerized system may make sense from the very outset or as extenders of the computer later. Many of these "frills" and even some very basic or essential functions look good on paper but prove of less value than their cost in actual practice, or when volume and complexity reach a given level. Any application which requires a great deal of file maintenance or complex processing for a result which can be achieved manually without much trouble or expense is a candidate for exclusion. For example, a very complicated piecework payroll involving thousands of individual item or job tickets may be more practical to preprocess manually; that is, count and extend the tickets clerically, total and price on an adding machine or calculator, then enter gross pay amount into the computerized payroll system and let the computer take it from there.

Another extender of system life is buying another one. Not all applications lend themselves to fractionating, but some definitely do: a division, subsidiary, a particular product line, a customer group, a designated warehouse or plant or some other convenient segment of the business may be separated from the mainstream and placed on a second computer using duplicate software and procedures. Sometimes the second machine is available at a substantial saving because it is now a used or superseded model; but, because the buyer knows exactly what he wants, such equipment can be purchased confidently and advantageously.

Distributed Processing

In the previous example, if a second machine were purchased for plant B and moved physically to that location, say, in another city miles away, we could truly categorize this approach as Distributed Data Processing (DDP), one of the current leading-edge watchwords in the data processing industry. Someone might quibble that since the systems were not interconnected to one another, the term doesn't apply. Whatever your favorite definition of DDP, this author believes that splitting off a segment of the overall data processing job and putting it in the hands of another operating unit of the business on equipment under that unit's control *is* distributed data processing. Interconnecting the constituent pieces of equipment via telecommunications merely facilitates *integration* of the results. In the final analysis, integration of these separate systems is going to take place to whatever extent is required anyway, if only in a manually posted financial consolidation report.

However, the previous distinction does bring up an interesting point in system life extension. There are integrated forms of DDP that can be added to an existing system that have the potential for extending its usefulness short of simply duplicating it. Some of the functions *within* a centrally processed application can be moved out to interconnected small processors or "intelligent" terminals, thus relieving the central computer of some of its processing burden and often improving system responsiveness and availability of information at the remote end.

The classic example of this form of DDP is branch order processing using intelligent terminals. In the typical case, the terminals capture and store order information, produce picking and shipping documents and then periodically forward preprocessed and summarized information to a central computer which handles invoicing, receivables, general accounting and, perhaps, inventory replenishment. Since the remote operators are not on-line to the home office computer but to their own terminals most of the time, the capacity of the central system is extended significantly and with that, presumably, its useful life span.

Anticipation of possible future extension might very well suggest to today's buyer that he make sure the approach and the equipment selected has the potential for expansion along one or more of the lines discussed.

SUMMARY

Computers are like children that grow and grow but never leave home: the responsibility for their care, feeding and direction is unending. Problems change through time, sometimes becoming fewer and larger, sometimes diminishing, but never becoming safe to neglect.

The user needs to personally review the performance of a data processing system periodically in all its aspects: audit, control, security, backup, reliability, cost, productivity and currency in terms of developing needs.

Many users find themselves plagued with hardware reliability and service problems and with difficulties in maintaining software programs. Some possible approaches toward solutions have been discussed.

All systems live out their useful lives and must eventually be put mercifully to sleep with a quick, clean and painless severance of their main power cable. What happens after this is a function of how well the software, data and documentation have been kept up, but it is almost sure to be a more organized, less traumatic change than the previous one.

Extending the life of the present system often makes good sense. This may mean keeping off or removing applications that consume excessive resources in relation to their value, employing manual or semiautomated supporting systems, "cloning" the computer by acquiring a duplicate or venturing into various forms of distributed data processing.

Like everything else connected with data processing, extension and eventual replacement of the system must be carefully planned and managed if only because of the long lead times involved.

16
Epilogue

The reader is to be congratulated for having survived the endurance test thus far. The journey may have been like crossing a swamp amidst a heavy fog. The going has probably been heavy at times, the terrain unfamiliar and only dimly perceived en route and perhaps even less clearly remembered now. It may be well to go back over the territory, reemphasizing the really important landmarks and adding some projections of what lies ahead.

THE SMALL COMPUTER COMES OF AGE

Absolutely incredible are the only words to describe what has happened to the electronic computer over its 35-year history, with steady progress in basic design and software architecture, but most of all the transistor, its more complex progeny, the integrated circuit and, now, solid-state integration carried to unimaginable levels of microscopic aggregation and precision. Entire computers in the form of all the central arithmetic and logical circuitry, more than 8,500 individual circuit elements in all, are contained on a single silicon chip one-tenth of an inch square. There are 64,000 memory bit positions on a similar sized, single photoengraved chip and one million positions of slower "bubble" memory in a complex semiconductor "sandwich" only a few centimeters larger. Whole computers, with CRT-display, keyboard, processor, memory and magnetic tape or disk auxiliary storage the size of an office typewriter, cost less than a 3-week winter vacation for two on a warm island. Earthbound and satellite data communciations networks into which almost all of today's terminals and computers can be linked easily and inexpensively span the globe. Thousands of software packages covering hundreds of different application and industry specialites are available for prices ranging from as low as $20.00 to many times the entire cost of an average minicomputer. More than two thousand data service companies (service bureaus) in the United States alone offer batch, on-line and even in-house hardware systems of their own in a vast profusion of types, kinds and costs.

All this comprises the data processing industry as it is now and as it squarely confronts the small business and small self-standing unit of a larger business for the first time. The reasons for this massive confrontation and for its suddenness are economic. The computer is suddenly so cheap that no business can afford not to at least consider having one, or the equivalent in computer services. The risk is possible loss of competitive position, and loss of opportunity to contain costs and manage and control the business as well as more advanced computerized competitors, who incidentally no longer have to be members of the Fortune 500 to enjoy that advantage. As 1979 drew to a close, small business computer shipments in the U.S. were approaching 5,000 per month and growing faster than any other segment of the computer marketplace.

Furthermore, small business people are putting many of these systems to good use, not because they were especially well trained and prepared to do so—quite the opposite is generally true—but because business ingenuity has found ways of making these systems easier to use. Twenty years ago it took an army of highly trained specialists to install, program and operate a computer with one-fiftieth the power of today's average minicomputer. Yet thanks to good engineering, excellent systems software design, availability of quality applications software packages and hundreds of new companies dedicated to creating and supporting the various elements in this picture, today's small business computer is typically installed and maintained without the services of a single professional computer specialist within the using firm—not one! Many of these installations are unquestionably successful, returning many times their cost in better customer service, control and management of financial, productive and human resources. Many of them grow in size and scope apace with the using business in a steady, unspectacular and untraumatic fashion.

And why shouldn't this be the case? Haven't we demonstrated that computers are basically electronic simpletons capable only of counting from zero to one, with absolutely no "intelligence" as we understand the term, incapable of making even the simplest judgment? Yes, this is all true, but perhaps because computers are such simpletons, able to follow only the most detailed and routinized instructions, we get into so much trouble with them.

GETTING THERE ISN'T EASY

Because computers can't exercise judgment and can't "learn," the tasks they are applied to must be laid out for them in advance in the most tedious imaginable detail in the form of a program, which itself is in the only language a computer "understands," namely strings of ones and zeros. Now, how does a complicated, highly organized, judgmental and often variable business process get translated into a row of ones and zeros? There's the rub! There's the real miracle and where most of the past, present and future problems lie.

Systems analysis, development of specifications, actual programming, program testing, documentation and ongoing support and maintenance of programs are the key areas in data processing. These are the main determinants of success or failure of automation, although "people problems" among those who feed or consume computer data are a close second. Actually, an adequate software set goes a long way toward minimizing resistance outside the computer, but sound management and organization is required to contain the problem altogether.

Despite their high potential for disappointment, devilment and devastation, computers are still being purchased like no other major and complex piece of capital equipment: cavalierly, without economic justification, without meaningful competition, without contractual protection and, most of all, without adequate knowledge and preparation on the part of the buyer.

Buyers should take their time, do an exhaustive analysis of their existing business procedures, analyze costs and deficiencies, develop the conceptual design of the new system themselves and then set out to procure a solution on an organized, self-determined basis. Not only should multiple suppliers be considered but multiple approaches as well: service bureaus, time-sharing vendors, hardware companies, software houses, turnkey systems integrators. A plentitude of factors need to go into the decision mix including not just price and claimed features, but expandability, operating ease, training and installation support, ongoing hardware and software maintenance and a whole host of others. Each of these dimensions needs to be separately and objectively evaluated for each of the likely choices and somehow combined into a single decision framework, leading to a balanced selection of the winner.

The best known method for reaching the kind of decision recommended is a formal RFP (Request For Proposal), in which the user specifies on what basis vendors are to bid and what information is to be supplied. In that way each contender is measured on the same scale, the measurement being best expressed as a numeric score which can then be weighted according to importance of the factor and then arithmetically combined into an overall score. It is as feasible to rate subjective and intangible factors on this basis as it is the more concrete ones; it is just a matter of setting up the proper scale of measurement and defining what the points along it are to mean.

MINIMIZING RISK

Regardless of how careful (and arduous) the decision process, the buyer stands to win or lose on the strength of his skill as a negotiator of contracts and a coordinator of implementation. Vendors will proffer standard agreements which protect them from any and all peril and happenstance, and offer virtually no protection whatever for the buyer. Suggested payment schedules will tend to put the buyer at a further disadvantage, since he will have to pay for most products and services before he can test or use them.

The cure is obviously a modified agreement which does provide balanced protection and reasonable financial leverage in dealing with the supplier(s), but whose purpose is to rivet attention on getting the job done rather than to provide a foundation for litigation. Realistically usable sanctions such as withholding of payment or formal arbitration are far more effective than drastic penalties that can only be invoked through a long and costly court fight. Finding the proper, balanced negotiating stance in each situation is not easy; it takes time and preparation; and should not be relegated to the status of a last-minute add-on to the procurement process.

The other major determinants of the success of an automation project come from within: the skills and attitudes of personnel and the way in which they are organized and led through the process. The organization needs to be assessed the way a professional golfer examines the texture and slope of the putting green, cautiously, a blade of grass at a time, so as to impart just the right momentum, spin and direction to his shot, hoping to reach the cup on one, or at most, the second try.

The way in which the responsible executive "plays" the kinks and slants that characterize the human side of automation will be crucial in neutralizing resistance and enlisting essential cooperation among the staff. The important objectives here are first to build a solid foundation of competent, well-organized people, and then to assure them that their "security," in the broadest sense of that word, is not going to be threatened.

Still, the implementation of a data processing system will not move along under reasonable control unless it has been planned in meticulous detail, is monitored against the plan almost continuously and is subjected to frequent midcourse correction as hard reality intrudes upon the poetic symmetry of the plan. Nevertheless, the plan is important as a communications and coordinating medium; the several different people and organizations upon whom the project depends must be kept aware of what is happening and what is next expected from each.

SUCCESS IS A PROCESS, NOT AN EVENT

There is no successful conclusion in sight for the typical computer implementation but rather an unending evolution of functionality and finesse. Most conversions occur over a protracted time period to begin with, because development and installation of numerous applications is too big a job to accomplish all at once. A phased, step-by-step implementation usually works best. But no applicational system even after installation ever stands completely still. Business conditions are changing, customer demands and industry practices are evolving, and the user's appetite for and skill in using data processing as a tool are developing as time goes on.

At the very minimum this implies an ongoing software maintenance resource available to alter and fine-tune the system to meet changing requirements. In some cases it may mean employing an in-house systems analysis/programming staff, or an ongoing contract with a software house, for continued development. It very likely will involve upgrading and expanding hardware (or outside services) to handle increasing volume and/or broader application of the system.

And, eventually, out there somewhere is a probable point of diminishing utility at which it is better to replace the system rather than to modify or expand it further. Part of the success process is to recognize that point and plan an orderly transition around it.

THINGS WILL GET EASIER

The reader can take heart in the fact that computers are still getting cheaper and better and that software is definitely becoming more generalized and easier to use. Does this mean one should wait? Definitely not, if the benefits of automation are substantial; and if they're not substantial, there's no reason to automate now *or* later. The year-to-year marginal improvement in equipment, software and services in the data processing industry has ranged from 15–25% depending on who's making the estimate and on what factors. There certainly is no question about the equipment itself improving and continuing to improve, at least 15% per year in price/performance.

Nevertheless, the buyer can't look for startling, overall cost decreases until something strikes at the heart of the really critical and expensive part of every automated system: the one-on-one people component. Until the selling, analyzing, customizing, training, helping and supporting functions, which are all people-intensive and nonrepetitious, are vastly improved and "packaged," the costs of automating will remain high.

Fortunately, a strong mass-marketing and packaged support impulse is beginning to be felt in the small business computing sector. New, well financed and organized competitors are joining the fray with both eyes fixed squarely on this problem. Older vendors are refining their approaches to take the "sting" out of customizing and supporting user applications. More and more truly general-purpose applications packages are making an appearance, and many of these are adjustable to varying needs by the user himself, by means of a "friendly," well-engineered dialog with the system while seated at a CRT workstation.

Hobby computers with $20 do-it-yourself software are definitely *not* yet ready for across-the-board business use. They depend too much for success on the ability of the small businessman himself to do ingenious, painstaking tinkering. Iron-bound packages that give the buyer any vehicle he wants as long as it's a "black Ford" with no options aren't the answer either. The user shouldn't be asked to adapt his business to the limitations of a computer system; quite the reverse should be the case. The variability of the system should be almost limitless, yet easily achieved and supportable in the long pull in a dependable and affordable manner.

Many very intelligent, hard-working people are addressing the task we have here defined, perhaps because they possess the same entrepreneurial instincts that keep the reader learning and reaching ahead for more and better things, and because they see the numbers: the numbers that tell the story about the two million of you out there, ready in varying degrees to part with your money and entrust your future to the vendor who can demonstrate his readiness to answer your needs. That, in the final analysis, is what keeps this business going and growing and makes it exciting and rewarding for all of us who participate—vendor, user, consultant and critic alike.

Index

Index